MAUI
HANDBOOK

IS THIS BOOK OUT OF DATE?

In today's world, things change so rapidly that it's impossible for one person to keep up with everything happening in any one place. This is particularly true in Hawaii, where situations are always in flux. Travel books are like automobiles: they require fine tuning and frequent overhauls to keep in shape. Help us keep this book in shape! We require input from our readers so that we can continue to provide the best, most current information available. Please write to let us know about any inaccuracies, new information, or misleading suggestions. Although we try to make our maps as accurate as possible, errors do occur. If you have any suggestions for improvement or places that should be included, please let us know about it.

We especially appreciate letters from female travelers, visiting expatriates, local residents, and hikers and outdoor enthusiasts. We also like hearing from experts in the field as well as from local hotel owners and individuals wishing to accommodate visitors from abroad.

As you travel through the islands, keep notes in the margins of this book. Notes written on the spot are always more accurate than those put down on paper later. Send us your copy after your trip, and we'll send you a fresh one as a replacement. If you take a photograph during your trip which you feel might be included in a future edition, please send it to us. Send only good slide duplicates or glossy black-and-white prints. Drawings and other artwork are also appreciated. If we use your photo or drawing, you'll be mentioned in the credits and receive a free copy of the book. Keep in mind, however, that the publisher cannot return any materials unless you inlcude a self-addressed, stamped envelope. Moon Publications will own the rights on all material submitted. Address your letters to:

J.D. Bisignani
Moon Publications
Box 1696
Chico CA 95927

FREE MOON BOOK FOR CONTRIBUTORS!

For all those who send us substantial information, we will send a free copy of the next edition of *Maui Handbook* or any other Moon Publications guide they wish. We reserve the right, however, to determine what is "substantial". Thank you for your help.

MAUI
HANDBOOK

J.D. BISIGNANI

PUBLICATIONS

Please send all comments, corrections, additions, amendments and critiques to:

J.D. BISIGNANI
MOON PUBLICATIONS
P.O. Box 1696
Chico, CA 95927, USA

MAUI HANDBOOK

Published by
Moon Publications
P.O. Box 1696
Chico, California 95927, USA
tel. (916) 345-5473/5413

Printed by
Colorcraft Ltd., Hong Kong

All Rights Reserved 1986 J.D. Bisignani

Library of Congress Cataloging in Publication Data

Bisignani, J. D., 1947—
Maui Handbook

Bibliography: p. 219
Includes index.
1. Maui (Hawaii)—Description and travel—Guide-books.
I Title
DU628.M3B57 1986   919.69′21044   86-8355
ISBN 0-918373-02-6

Cover painted by Susan Strangio from an original photograph by J.D. Bisignani.

*To Sylvester T.,
the best long-distance man
there ever was*

ACKNOWLEDGEMENTS

This is one time that mere words can not express my heartfelt gratitude to the following people whose efforts and contributions made *Maui Handbook* possible; I owe them so much more. Bill Dalton, the "full moon" himself, who published this work. Deke Castleman, Moon Publication's *all world* editor, who took my manuscript and extracted gems from raw stone, while mercilessly whipping it into Moon format and managing to stroke my writer's ego at the same time. Dave Hurst, Moon's production manager, whose easy-does-it style makes order from chaos taking all the nuts, bolts, bits and pieces and *actually* making them into a book. Louise Foote, who drew all the maps in *Maui Handbook* with minimum direction from me and maximum care from her, and whose skilled hand also contributed many of the illustrations. Louise Shannon, Moon's typesetter, who works like an elf in the night leaving her handiwork for us to find in the morning. Asha for her "crisis intervention" when I just *had* to add or delete items in my manuscript. Donna "Classy" Galassi, who adds a touch up front as Moon's sales manager. Randy Smith and Gary Manning, the computer wizards, who calmly answered my hysterical pleas for help when I mixed my RAM with my ROM and chewed up all my bytes. My illustrators Diana Lasich, Sue Strangio, Mary Ann Abel and my contributing photographer Gary Quiring whose remarkable talents turned *Maui Handbook* from a "plain Jane" into a beauty. These fine people are profiled in the backmatter of this book. California State University at Chico professors Bob Vivian, Ed Myles and Ellen Walker provided me with interns from their respective departments of Journalism, Tourism and English. The following student interns worked in the "trenches" transcribing, in-putting, designing charts, and generally infusing my surroundings with positive energy: Caroline Schoepp, Maureen Cole, Suzanne Booth, Lee Wilkinson, Sally Price, Elena Wilkinson, Bret Lampman, Rich Zimmerman and Craig Nelson. I would also like to thank the following people for their special help and consideration: Lindy Boyes of the Honolulu HVB; Roger Rose and Elisa Johnston of the Bishop Museum; Lee Wild, Hawaiian Mission Houses Museum; Marilyn Nicholson, State Foundation of Culture and Arts; Jan DeLuz, National Car Rental; Glenn Masutani, Hawaiian Pacific Resorts; Bill Gough, Royal Hawaiian Airlines; Lindsey Pollock, Hawaiian Air; Hal Corbett, pilot, Polynesian Air. Also, many thanks to my friends who shared their special Hawaii with me: Donna and Ray Barnett; Jim and John Costello; Sharon and Gary Turner; Dr. Terry and Nancy Carolan; and Nasisu Rehnborg Kahalewai. Finally, Sandy B. whose after-school hugs and kisses gave her dad that boost of energy needed to keep going, and to my wife Marlene, married, God help her, to an emotional Italian writer.

PHOTOS AND ILLUSTRATIONS

photos: **J.D. Bisignani:** 3, 23, 28, 31, 33, 58, 68, 70, 73, 87, 91, 96, 100, 102, 110, 123, 125, 131, 133, 134, 135, 136, 138, 139, 144, 145, 149, 150, 151, 153, 158, 159, 160, 161, 167, 172, 180, 182, 183, 188, 189, 193, 194, 197, 199, 200, 206, 207, 210, 211, 213, 217; **Gary Quiring:** 108, 137; **Bob Cowan:** 121, 198, 203; **Hawaii State Archives:** 18, 27, 29, 50, 62, 78, 88, 176, 205; **Hawaii Visitors Bureau:** 6. *illustrations:* **Diana Lasich Harper:** 1, 5, 9, 10, 11, 13, 16, 17, 24, 45, 48, 49, 51, 74, 77, 79, 80, 96, 107, 116, 129, 162, 195, 214; **Louise Foote:** 12, 14, 15, 21, 25, 26, 43, 52, 83, 94, 95, 155, 190; **Mary Ann Abel:** 12, 32, 42, 47, 54, 55, 120, 132, 146, 209, 215, 218; **Sue Strangio:** 7, 20, 46, 56, 75, 115, 147, 163, 170, 177, 185, 186, 191.

CONTENTS

LIST OF MAPS

TABLES AND CHARTS

INTRODUCTION

The *Kumulipo,* the ancient genealogical chant of the Hawaiians, sings of the demigod Maui, a half-human mythological sorcerer known and revered throughout Polynesia. Maui was a prankster on a grand scale who used guile and humor to create some of the most amazing feats of "derringdo" ever recorded. A Polynesian combination of Paul Bunyan and Hercules, Maui's adventures were known as "strifes." He served mankind by fishing up the islands of Hawaii from the ocean floor, securing fire from a tricky mud hen, lifting the sky so humans could walk upright, and slowing down the sun god by lassoing his genitals with a braided rope of his sister's pubic hair. Maui accomplished this last feat on the summit of the great mountain Haleakela ("House of the Sun"), thus securing more time in the day to fish and to dry *tapa.* Maui met his just but untimely end between the legs of the great goddess, Hina. This final prank, in which he attempted to crawl into the sleeping goddess' vagina, left his feet and legs dangling out, causing uproarious laughter among his comrades, a band of warrrior birds. The noise awakened Hina, who saw no humor in the situation. She unceremoniously squeezed Maui to death. The island of Maui is the only island in Hawaii and throughout Polynesia named after a god. With such a legacy the island couldn't help but become known as *"Maui no ka oi,"* "Maui is the best!"

AN OVERVIEW

In a land of superlatives, it's quite a claim to call your island *the* best, but Maui has a lot to back it up. Maui has more miles of swimmable beach than any of the other islands. Haleakala, the massive mountain that *is* East Maui, is the largest dormant volcano in the world, and its hardened lava rising over 30,000 feet from the sea floor makes it one of

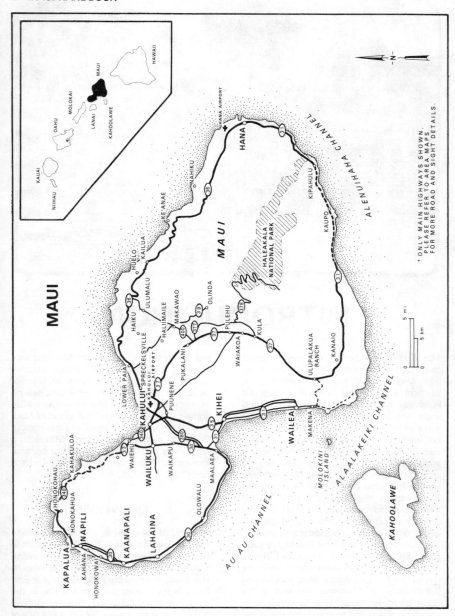

MAUI

HAWAII
MAUI
MOLOKAI
OAHU
LANAI
KAHOOLAWE
KAUAI
NIIHAU

—N—

* ONLY MAIN HIGHWAYS SHOWN
  PLEASE REFER TO AREA MAPS
  FOR MORE ROAD AND SIGHT DETAILS.

ALENUIHAHA CHANNEL

HANA AIRPORT

HANA

NAHIKU

KEANAE

KAILUA

HUELO

ULUMALU

HAIKU

SPRECKELSVILLE

KAHULUI

WAILUKU

WAIEHU

WAIHEE

KAHAKULOA

HONOKOHAU

KAPALUA
HONOKAHUA
KAHANA
NAPILI
HONOKOWAI
KAANAPALI
LAHAINA

OLOWALU

MAALAEA

WAIKAPU

PUUNENE

LOWER PAIA

HALIIMAILE

MAKAWAO

OLINDA

PULEHU

PUKALANI

WAIAKOA

KULA

WAILEA

KIHEI

MAKENA

ULUPALAKUA RANCH

KANAIO

HALEAKALA NATIONAL PARK

MAUI

KIPAHULU

KAUPO

MOLOKINI ISLAND

KAHOOLAWE

AU AU CHANNEL

ALALAKEIKI CHANNEL

5 mi
5 km
0

the heaviest concentrated masses on the face of the earth. There are legitimate claims that Maui grows the best onions and potatoes, but the boast of the best *pakalolo,* may only be a pipe dream, since all islands have great soil, weather and many enterprising gardeners. Some even claim that Maui gets more sunshine than the other islands, but that's hard to prove.

Maui's body

If you look at the silhouette of Maui on a map, it looks like the head and torso of a man bent at the waist and contemplating the uninhabited island of Kahoolawe. The head is West Maui. The profile is that of a wizened old man whose wrinkled brow and cheeks are the **West Maui Mountains.** The highest peak here is **Puu Kukui,** at 5,778 feet, located just about where the ear would be. If you go to the top of the head, you'll be at **Kapalua,** a resort community recently carved from pineapple fields. Fleming Beach begins a string of beaches that continues down over the face, stopping at the neck, and picking up again on the chest which is SE Maui. **Kaanapali** is the

forehead; this massive beach continues almost uninterrupted for four miles. In comparison, this area alone would take in all of Waikiki, from Diamond Head to Ala Moana. Sugarcane fields fringe the mountain side of the road, while condos are strung along the shore. The resorts here are cheek to jowl, but the best are tastefully done with views and access to the beach.

Lahaina would be located at the Hindu "third eye." This town is where it's "happening" on Maui, with concentrations of crafts, museums, historical sites, restaurants and night spots. Lahaina has always been somewhat of a playground, used in times past by royal Hawaiian *ali'i* and then by Yankee whalers. The "good-times" mystique still lingers. At the tip of the nose is **Olowalu,** where a lunatic Yankee trader, Simon Metcalf, decided to slaughter hundreds of curious Hawaiians paddling toward his ship just to show them he was boss. From Olowalu you can see four islands: Molokai, Lanai, Kahoolawe, and a faint hint of Hawaii far to the south. The back of Maui's head is an adventurer's paradise, complete with a

West Maui Mountains

tourist-eliminating rugged road posted with overexaggerated "Proceed No Farther" signs. Back here are tremendous coastal views, bird sanctuaries, *heiau,* and **Kahakuloa,** a tiny fishing village reported to be a favorite stomping ground of great Maui himself.

The isthmus

A low flat isthmus planted primarily in sugar cane is the neck that connects the head of West Maui to the torso of East Maui, which is **Haleakala.** The Adam's apple is the little port of **Maalaea,** which has a good assortment of pleasure and fishing boats, and provides an up-close look at a working port not nearly as frenetic as Lahaina. The nape of the neck is made up of the twin cities of **Wailuku,** the county seat, and **Kahului,** where visitors arrive at Maui's airport. These towns are where the "people" live. Some say the isthmus, dramatically separating east and west, is the reason Maui is called "The Valley Isle." Head into **Iao Valley** from Wailuku, where the West Maui Mountains have been worn into incredible peaked monolithic spires. This stunning valley area played a key role in Kamehameha's unification of the Hawaiian Islands, and geologically seems to be a more fitting reason for Maui's nickname.

East Maui/Haleakala

Once you cross the isthmus you're on the immensus of Haleakala. This mountain is a true microcosm and makes up the entire bulging, muscled torso. Its geology encompasses alpine, desert, jungle, pastureland, and wasteland. The temperature, determined by altitude, ranges from sub-freezing to subtropical. If you head E along the spine, you'll find world-class sailboarding beaches, artist villages, last-picture-show towns, and a few remaining family farms planted in taro. Route

360, the only coastal road, rocks and rolls you over its more than 600 documented curves, and shows you more waterfalls and pristine pools than you can count. After crossing more than 50 bridges, you come to **Hana.** Here, the "dream" Hawaii that people seek still lives. Farther along is **Oheo Stream** and its pools, erroneously known as "The Seven Sacred Pools." However, there is no mistaking the amazing energy vibrations in the area. Close by is where Charles Lindbergh is buried, and many celebrities have chosen the surrounding hillsides as their special retreats and hideaways.

On Haleakala's broad chest are macho cowboy towns complete with wild west rodeos contrasting with the gentle but riotous colors of carnation and protea farms. Polipoli State Park is here, a thick forest canopy with more varieties of imported trees than anywhere else in Oceania. A weird cosmic joke places **Kihei** just about where the armpit would be. Kihei is a mega-growth condo area ridiculed as an example of what developers shouldn't be allowed to do. Oddly enough, **Wailea,** just down the road, exemplifies a reasonable and aesthetic planned community and is highly touted as a "model" development area. Just at the belly button, close to the *kundalini,* is **Makena,** long renowned as Maui's "alternative beach." It's the island's last "free" beach with no restrictions, no park rangers, no amenities, and sometimes, no bathing suits.

Finally, when you pilgrimage to the summit of **Haleakala,** it'll be as if you've left the planet. It's another world: beautiful, mystical, raw, inspired, and freezing cold. When you're alone on the crater rim with the world below garlanded by the brilliance of sunrise or sunset, you'll know that you have come at last to great Maui's heart.

THE LAND

The modern geological theory concerning the formation of the Hawaiian Islands is no less fanciful than the Polynesian legends sung about their origins. Science maintains that 30 million years ago the Earth was little more than a mudball. While the great continents were being geologically tortured into their rudimentary shapes, the Hawaiian Islands were a mere ooze of bubbling magma 20,000 feet below the surface of the primordial sea. For millions of years this molten rock flowed up from fissures in the sea floor. Slowly, layer upon layer of lava was deposited until an island rose above the surface of the sea. The great weight then sealed the fissure, whose own colossal forces progressively crept in a southwestern direction, then burst out again and again to build the chain. At the same time the entire Pacific plate was afloat on the giant sea of molten magma, and it slowly glided to the northwest carrying the newly formed islands with it.

In the beginning the spewing crack formed Kure and Midway Islands in the extreme northwestern sector of the Hawaiian chain. Today, more than 130 islands, islets and shoals make up the Hawaiian Islands, stretching 1600 miles across an expanse of the North Pacific. Some geologists maintain that the "hot spot" now primarily under The Big Island remains relatively stationary, and the 1600-mile spread of the Hawaiian Archipelago is only due to a northwest drifting ef-

fect of about three to five inches per year. Still, with the center of activity under The Big Island, Mauna Loa and Kilauea volcanoes regularly add more land to the only state in the Union that is literally still growing. About 30 miles southeast of the Big Island is Loihi Sea Mount, waiting 3000 feet below the waves. Frequent eruptions bring it closer and closer to the surface until one day it will emerge and become the newest Hawaiian Island.

Maui features

Maui is the second largest and second youngest of the main Hawaiian Islands, next to Hawaii. It is made up of two volcanoes: the West Maui Mountains and Haleakala. The West Maui Mountains are geologically older than Haleakala, but the two were joined by subsequent lava flows that formed a connecting low, flat isthmus. Puu Kukui at 5,778 feet is the tallest peak of the West Maui Mountains. It's the lord of a mountain domain whose old weathered face has been scarred by an inhospitable series of deep crags, valleys and gorges. Haleakala, in comparison, is an adolescent with smooth, rounded features. This precocious kid looms 10,023 feet above sea level, and is four times larger than West Maui. Its incredible mass as it rises over 30,000 feet from the ocean floor is one of the densest on Earth. Its gravitational pull is staggering and it was considered a primary power spot in old Hawaii. The two parts of Maui combine to form 728.8 square miles of land with 120 linear miles of coastline. At its widest, Maui is 25 miles from north to south, and 40 miles east to west. The coastline has the most swimmable beaches in Hawaii, and the interior is a miniature continent with almost every conceivable geological feature evident.

Island builders

The Hawaiians worshiped Madame Pele, the fire goddess. Her name translates equally as "volcano," "fire pit," or "eruption of lava." When she was angry, she complained by spitting fire which cooled and formed land. Volcanologists say that the islands are huge mounds of cooled basaltic lava surrounded by billions of polyp skeletons which have formed coral reefs. The Hawaiian Islands are shield volcanoes that erupt gently and form elongated domes much like turtle shells. Maui, like the rest, is a perfect example of this. Once above the surface of the sea, the tremendous weight of lava seals the fissure below. Eventually the giant tube that carried lava to the surface sinks in on itself and forms a caldera, as evidenced atop Haleakala, whose huge depression could hold all of Manhattan Island. More eruptions occur periodically, and they cover the already existing island like frosting on a titanic cake. Wind and water next take over and relentlessly sculpt the raw lava into deep crevices and cuts that become valleys. The once smooth West Maui Mountains are now more a mini-mountain range due to this process. Great Haleakala is being chiseled too, as can be seen in the Kaupo Gap, and the valleys of Kipahulu and Keanae.

Lava

Lava flows in two distinct types, for which the Hawaiian names have become universal geological terms: *a'a'* and *pa'hoehoe.* They're easily distinguished in appearance, but chemically they're the same. *A'a'* is extremely rough and spiny, and will quickly tear up your shoes if you do much hiking over it. Also, if you have the misfortune to fall down, you'll immediately know why they call it *a'a'.* *Pa'hoehoe* is billowy ropy lava that looks like burned pancake batter which can mold itself

Recent lava flows centered on the Big Island regularly add more land to the state of Hawaii.

into fantastic shapes. Examples of both are frequently encountered on various hikes throughout Maui. Other lava oddities that you may spot on Maui are peridots, green gem-like stones called "Maui Diamonds," clear feldspar, and gray lichens covering the older flows known as "Hawaiian Snow."

Rivers and lakes

Maui has no navigable rivers but there are hundreds of streams. The two largest are Palikea Stream that runs through Kipahulu

Valley forming Oheo Gulch, and Iao Stream that has sculpted the amazing monoliths in Iao Valley. A few reservoirs dot the island, but the only natural body of water is the 41-acre Kanaha Pond, a major bird and wildlife sanctuary on the outskirts of Kahului. Hikers should be aware of the uncountable streams and rivulets that can quickly turn from trickles to torrents, causing flash floods in valleys that were the height of hospitality only minutes before.

Tsunami

Tsunami is the Japanese word for tidal wave. It ranks up there with the worst of them in causing horror in human beings. If you were to count up all the people in Hawaii who have been swept away by tidal waves in the last 50 years, the toll wouldn't come close to those killed on bicycles in only a few mainland cities in just five years. A Hawaiian tsunami is actually a seismic sea wave that has been generated by an earthquake that could easily have had its origins thousands of miles away in South America or Alaska. Some waves have been clocked at speeds up to 500 miles per hour. The safest place, besides high ground well away from beach areas, is out on the open ocean where even an enormous wave is perceived only as a large swell—a tidal wave is only dangerous when it is opposed by land. The worst tsunami to strike Maui in modern times occurred on April 1, 1946. The Hana Coast of windward East Maui bore the brunt with a tragic loss of many lives as entire villages were swept away.

Earthquakes

These rumblings are also a concern in Hawaii and offer a double threat because they cause tsunami. If you ever feel a tremor and are close to a beach, get as far away as fast as possible. The Big Island, because of its active volcanoes, experiences hundreds of technical earthquakes, although 99 percent can only be felt on very delicate equipment. The last major quake occurred on The Big Island in late November 1975, reaching 7.2 on the Richter Scale and causing many millions of dollars worth of damage in the island's southern regions. The only loss of life was when a beach collapsed and two people

from a large camping party were drowned. Maui, like the rest of the state, has an elaborate warning system against natural disasters. You will notice loudspeakers high atop poles along many beaches and coastal areas; these warn of tsunami, hurricanes and earthquakes. They are tested at 11:00 a.m. on the first working day of each month. All island telephone books contain a Civil Defense warning and procedures section with which you should acquaint yourself. Note the maps showing which areas traditionally have been inundated by tsunami, and what procedures to follow in case an emergency occurs.

CLIMATE

Maui has similar weather to the rest of the Hawaiian Islands, though some afficionados claim that it gets more sunshine than the rest. The weather on Maui depends more on where you are than on what season it is. The average yearly daytime temperature hovers around 80 degrees F and is moderated by the tradewinds. Nights are just a few degrees cooler. Since Haleakala is a main feature on Maui, you should remember that altitude drastically affects the weather. Expect an average drop of 3 degrees for every 1,000 feet of elevation. The lowest temperature ever recorded in Hawaii was atop Haleakala in 1961 when the mercury dropped well below freezing to a low, low 11 degrees.

Precipitation

Rain on Maui is as much a factor as it is in all of Hawaii. On any day, somewhere on Maui it's raining, while other areas experience drought. A dramatic example of this phenomenon is to compare Lahaina with Mount Puu Kukui, both on West Maui and separated by only seven miles. Lahaina, which translates as "Merciless Sun," is hot, arid, and gets 17 inches of rainfall annually, while Puu Kukui can receive close to 40 *feet* of rain! This rivals Mt. Waialeale on Kauai as the wettest spot on earth. The windward (wet) side of Maui, outlined by the Hana Road, is the perfect natural hothouse. Here, valleys sweetened with blossoms house idyllic waterfalls and pools that visitors treasure when they happen upon them. On the leeward (dry) side are Maui's best beaches: Kapalua, Kaanapali, Kihei, Wailea and Makena. They all sit in Haleakala's "rain shadow." If it happens to be raining at one, just move a few miles down the road to the next. Anyway, the rains are mostly gentle and the brooding sky, especially at sundown, is even more spectacular than normal.

When to go
The prime tourist season starts two weeks before Christmas and lasts until Easter. It picks up again with summer vacation in early June and ends once more in late August. If possible, avoid these times of year. Hotel, airline and car reservations, which are a must, can be hard to coordinate. Everything is usually booked solid and the prices are inflated. You can save between 10 and 50 percent of the cost and a lot of hassling if you go in the artificially created off-season, from September to early December, and from mid-April (after Easter) until early June. You'll not only find the prices better, but the beaches, hikes, campgrounds, and even restaurants will be less crowded, and the *people* will be happier to see you, too!

AVERAGE MAXIMUM / MINIMUM TEMPERATURE AND RAINFALL

LOCATION		J	F	M	A	M	J	J	A	S	O	N	D
Lahaina	high	80	80	81	81	82	83	84	85	84	83	82	81
	low	62	60	63	65	68	68	70	70	70	68	65	61
	rain	3	2	1	1	0	0	0	0	0	1	1	1
Hana	high	79	79	79	79	80	80	80	82	81	80	80	79
	low	60	60	60	61	62	63	64	67	65	62	61	61
	rain	9	6	7	5	2	3	4	4	5	6	7	9
Kahului	high	80	79	80	82	84	86	86	87	87	86	83	80
	low	64	64	64	66	67	69	70	71	70	69	68	66
	rain	4	3	3	1	1	0	0	0	0	1	2	3

* Rainfall in inches; temperature in F°.

FLORA AND FAUNA

Maui's indigenous and endemic plants, trees and flowers are both fascinating and beautiful. Unfortunately, they, like everything else that was native, are quickly disappearing. The majority of flora found interesting by visitors was either introduced by the original Polynesians or later by white settlers. Maui is blessed with state parks, gardens, undisturbed rainforests, private reserves and commercial nurseries. Combined, they add brilliant and dazzling colors to the landscape.

Protea

These exotic flowers are from Australia and South Africa. Because they come in almost limitless shapes, sizes and colors, they captivate everyone who sees them. They are primitive, almost otherworldly in appearance, and they exude a life force more like an animal than a flower. The slopes of leeward Haleakala between 2,000 and 4,000 feet is heaven to protea — the growing conditions could not be more perfect. Here are found the hardiest, highest quality protea in the world. The days are warm, the nights are cool and the well-drained volcanic soil has the exact combination of minerals that protea thrive on. Haleakala's crater even helps by creating a natural air flow which produces cloud cover, filters the sun, and protects the flowers. Protea make excellent gifts that can be shipped anywhere. As fresh-cut flowers they are gorgeous, but they have the extra benefit of drying superbly. Just hang them in a dark, dry, well-ventilated area and they do the rest. You can see protea, along with other botanical specialties, at the following: **Kula Botanical Garden** (see "Botanical Gardens" below for more info), **Upcountry Protea Farm** on Upper Kimo Drive one mile off Haleakala Hwy. (Rt. 377), **Hawaii Protea Coop**, near Kula Lodge on Crater Rd. and **Protea Gardens of Maui**, on Hapapa Road off Rt. 377 not far from Kula Lodge.

Silversword

Maui's official flower is a tiny pink rose called a *lokelani*. Its unofficial symbol, however, is the silversword. The Hawaiian name for silversword is *ahinahina* which translates as "gray gray," and the English name derives from a silverfish, whose color it's said to resemble. The silversword is from a remarkable plant family that claims 28 members, with five in the specific silversword species. It's kin to the common sunflower, and botanists say the entire family

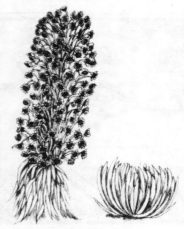

silversword

evolved from a single ancestral species. The members of the silversword family can all hypothetically interbreed and produce remarkable hybrids. Some plants are shrubs, while others are climbing vines, and some even become trees. They grow anywhere from desert conditions to steamy jungles. On Maui, the silversword is only found on Haleakala, above the 6,000-foot level, and is especially prolific in the crater. Each plant lives from five to 20 years and ends its life by sprouting a gorgeous stalk of hundreds of purplish-red flowers. It then withers from a majestic six-foot plant to a flat gray skeleton. An endangered species, silverswords are totally protected. They protect themselves, too, from radiation and lack of moisture by growing fuzzy hairs all over their swordlike stalks. You can see them along the Haleakala Park Road at **Kalamaku Overlook,** or by hiking along **Silversword Loop** on the floor of the crater.

Carnations

If protea aren't enough to dazzle you, how about fields of carnations? Most mainlanders think of carnations stuck in a groom's lapel, or perhaps have seen a table dedicated to them in a hothouse, but fields full of carnations! The Kula area produces carnations that grow outside nonchalantly, in rows, like cab-

bages. They fill the air with an unmistakable perfume, and they are without doubt a joy to behold. You can see family and commercial plots throughout the upper Kula area.

Prickly pear cactus

Interspersed in countless fields and pastures on the windward slope of Haleakala, adding that final nuance to cattle country, are clusters of prickly pear cactus. The Hawaiians call them *panini* which translates as "very unfriendly," undoubtedly because of the sharp spines covering the flat thick leaves. These cactus are typical of those found in Mexico and the southwestern U.S. They were introduced to Hawaii before 1810 and established themselves, coincidently, in conjunction with the cattle being brought in at that time. It's assumed that Don Marin, a Spanish advisor to Kamehameha I, was responsible for bringing in the cactus. Perhaps the early *paniolo* felt lonely without them. The *panini* can grow to heights of 15 feet and are now considered a pest, but nonetheless look as if they belong. They develop small pear-shaped fruit which are quite delicious. Hikers who decide to pick them should be careful of small yellowish bristles that can burrow under the skin and become very irritating. The fruit turns into beautiful yellow and orange flowers.

Botanical Gardens/
Parks and State Forests

Those interested in the flora of Maui would find a visit to any of the following both educational and entertaining. In the Kula area visit: **Kula Botanical Gardens,** clearly marked along Rt. 377 (Haleakala Hwy.) just a mile from where Rt. 377 joins Rt. 37 at the south end, tel. 878-1715. Three acres of plants and trees including *koa* in their natural settings. Open daily 9:00 a.m. to 4:00 p.m., $2.50, self-guided tour. **U. of Hawaii Experimental Station,** just north of the south junction of Rt. 377 and Rt. 37 on Copp Road. Open Mon. to Fri., 7:30 a.m. to 3:30 p.m., closed for lunch, free. Twenty acres of constantly changing plants that are quite beautiful even though the grounds are uninspired, scientific, rectangular plots.

Polipoli Springs State Recreation Area, the finest upcountry camping and trekking area on Maui. At south end of Rt. 377, turn onto Waipoli Road for 10 miles of bad road. Overnight camping is recommended. Native and introduced birds, magnificent stands of redwoods, conifers, ash, cypress, sugi, cedar and various pine. Known for delicious methley plums that ripen in early June. For more info contact Division of State Parks in Wailuku, tel. 244-4354.

Keanae Arboretum, about 15 miles west of Hana on the Hana Hwy (Rt. 360). Always open, no fee. Native, introduced, and exotic plants, including Hawaiian food plants, are in a natural setting with walkways, identifying markers, tropical trees and mosquitoes. Educational, a must. **Helani Gardens,** one mile west of Hana, open daily 10:00 a.m. to 3:30 p.m., adults $2.00. These 60 acres of flowerbeds and winding jeep trails are the lifetime project of Howard Cooper, lovingly tended, exotic jungle, terrific!

Maui Zoo and Botanical Garden, in Wailuku, is easily accessible. Get a basic introduction to flora at this tiny zoo, good for tots, and mildly interesting. In central Maui try: **Kepaniwai Park,** on Rt. 32 leading to Iao Needle. This tropical setting displays formalized gardens from different nations. Daily, no fee. Finally, for an extremely civilized treat visit the formal gardens of the **Hyatt Regency Hotel** in Kaanapali, open to the public. The architecture and grounds are impeccable.

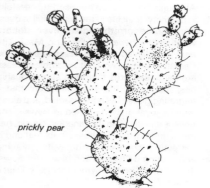

prickly pear

MAUI'S ENDANGERED BIRDS

Maui suffers the same fate as the other islands. Its native birds are disappearing. Maui is the last home of the crested honeycreeper *(akohe'kohe)*. It lives only on the windward slope of Haleakala from 4500 to 6500 feet. It once lived on Molokai, but no longer. Its rather a large bird, averaging over seven inches long, and predominantly black. Its throat and breast are tipped with gray feathers with a bright orange on its neck and underbelly. A distinctive fluff of feathers forms a crown. It primarily eats *ohia* flowers and it's believed that the crown feathers gather pollen and help to propagate the *ohia.* The parrotbill is another endangered bird found only on the slopes of Haleakala above 5000 feet. It has an olive-green back and a yellow body. Its most distinctive feature is its parrot-like bill which it uses to crack branches and pry out larvae.

Two waterbirds found on Maui are the Hawaiian stilt *(aeo)* and the Hawaiian coot *(alae ke'oke'o).* The stilt is about 16 inches tall and lives on Maui at Kanaha and Kealia ponds. Primarily black with a white belly, its sticklike legs are pink. The adults will pretend to be hurt, putting on an excellent performance of the "broken wing" routine, in order to lure predators away from their nests. The Hawaiian coot is a web-footed water bird that resembles a duck. It's found on all the main islands but largely on Maui and Kauai. Mostly a dull gray, it has a white bill and tail feathers. It builds a big floating nest and vigorously defends its young.

The darkrumped petrel is slightly different from other primarily marine birds. This petrel is found around the Visitor's Center at Haleakala Crater about one hour after dusk from May through October. The *amakihi* and the *iiwi* are endemic birds that aren't endangered at the moment. The *amakihi* is one of the most common native birds. It's a yellowish-green bird that frequents the high branches of the *ohia, koa,* and sandalwood looking for insects, nectar or fruit. It's less specialized than most other Hawaiian birds, the main reason for its continued existence. The *iiwi* is a bright red bird with a salmon-colored, hooked bill. It's found only on Maui, Hawaii and Kauai in the forests above 2000 feet. It, too, feeds on a variety of insects and flowers. The *iiwi* is known for its harsh voice that sounds like a squeaking hinge, but is also capable of a melodious song.

Other indigenous birds that are found on Maui are the wedge-tailed sheerwater, the white-tailed tropic bird, the black noddy, the American plover, and a large variety of escaped exotic birds.

Pueo

This Hawaiian owl is found on all of the main islands, but mostly on Maui, especially in Haleakala Crater. The *pueo* is one of the oldest examples of an *aumakua* (family-protecting spirit) in Hawaiian mythology. It was an especially benign and helpful guardian. Old Hawaiian stories abound in which a *pueo* came to the aid of a warrior in distress or a defeated army, which would head for a tree in which a *pueo* had alighted. Once there, they were safe from their pursuers and were under the protection of "the wings of an owl." There are many introduced barn owls in Hawaii, easily distinguished from a *pueo* by their distinctive heart-shaped faces. The *pueo* is about 15 inches tall with a mixture of brown and white feathers. The eyes are large, round and yellow and the legs are heavily feathered, unlike a barn owl. *Pueo* chicks are a distinct yellow color.

pueo

nene

Nene

The *nene,* or Hawaiian goose, deserves special mention because it is Hawaii's state bird and is making a comeback from the edge of extinction. The *nene* is found only on the slopes of Mauna Loa and Mauna Kea on the Big Island and in Haleakala Crater on Maui. It was extinct on Maui till a few birds were returned there in 1957. *Nenes* are raised at the Wildfowl Trust in Slimbridge, England, which provided the first birds at Haleakala, now they're also raised at the Hawaiian Fish and Game Station at Pohakuloa on Hawaii. By the 1940s there were less than 50 birds living in the wild, now approximately 125 birds are on Haleakala, and 500 on the Big Island. Although the birds can be raised successfully in captivity, their life in the wild is still in question. Some ornithologists even debate whether the *nene* ever lived on Maui. The *nene* is believed to be a descendant of the Canadian goose, which it resembles. Geese are migratory birds that form strong kinship ties, mating for life. It's speculated that a migrating goose became disabled, and along with its loyal mate remained in Hawaii. The *nene* is smaller than its Canadian cousin, has lost a great deal of webbing in its feet and is perfectly at home away from water, foraging and nesting on rugged and bleak lava flows. The *nene* is a perfect symbol for Hawaii: let it be and it will live!

HAWAIIAN SEASHELLS

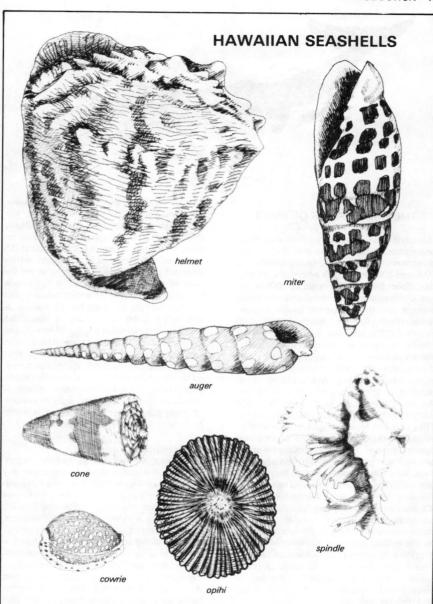

helmet

miter

auger

cone

spindle

cowrie

opihi

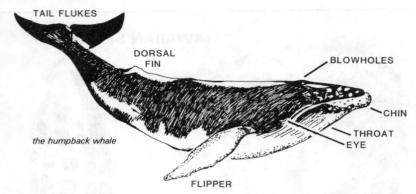

TAIL FLUKES

DORSAL FIN

BLOWHOLES

CHIN

THROAT

EYE

the humpback whale

FLIPPER

THE HUMPBACKS OF MAUI

Humpbacks are named from their style of exposing the dorsal fin when they dive, which gives them a humped appearance. Between 7000 and 8000 humpback whales are alive today, down from an estimated 100,000 at the turn of the century. The remaining whales are divided into three separate global populations: North Atlantic, North Pacific, and South Pacific groups. About 500 North Pacific humpbacks migrate from coastal Alaska starting in November. They reach their peak in February, congregating mostly in the waters off Maui, with a smaller group heading for the waters off Kona on Hawaii. An adult humpback is 45 feet long and weighs in at a svelte 40 tons (80,000 pounds). They come to Hawaii mainly to give birth to single 2000-pound, relatively blubberless calves. Females nurse these young for about one year and become impregnated again the next. While in Hawaiian waters humpbacks generally don't eat, but wait until returning to Alaska where they gorge themselves on krill. It's estimated that they can live off their blubber without peril for six months. An enormous mouth stretching ⅓ the length of their bodies is filled with over 600 rows of baleen, a prickly, fingernail-like substance. Humpbacks have been known to blow air under water, creating giant bubble-nets that help to corral krill, then rush in with mouth agape and dine on their catch.

Like all cetaceans they breathe consciously, not involuntarily the way humans do; like other baleen whales they feed in relatively shallow waters and therefore sound (dive) for periods lasting a maximum of about 15 minutes. In comparison, a sperm whale (toothed bottom-feeder) can stay down for over an hour. On the surface, a humpback will breathe about once every two minutes and will sometimes sleep on the surface or just below it for two hours. A distinctive feature of the humpback is the 15-foot flipper which it can bend over its back. The flippers and tail flukes have white markings that always differ between individuals and are used to recognize the humpbacks from year to year. The humpback is the most aquabatic of all whales and it is a thrilling sight to see one of these playful giants leap from the water and create a monumental splash.

The humpback's song

All whales are fascinating, but the humpbacks have a special ability to sing unlike any others. They create their melodies by grunting, shrieking and moaning. No one knows exactly what the songs represent, but it's clear they're a definite form of communication. The singers appear to be "escort males" that tag along with, and seem to guard, a mother and her calf. The songs are exact renditions that last 20 minutes or more and are repeated over and over again for hours. Amazingly, all the whales know and sing the same song, and the song changes from year to year. The notes are so forceful that they can be heard above and below the water for miles. Some of the deep base notes will even carry underwater for 100 miles! Scientists devote careers to recording and listening to the humpbacks' songs. As yet they're unexplained, but anyone who hears their eerie tones knows that he is privy to a wonderful secret and that the songs are somehow a key to understanding the consciousness of the great humpback.

The Bark *Carthaginian II*
Just to the right of the Loading Dock in Lahaina Harbor is a restored 19th C. square-masted ship, the *Carthaginian*. It's a floating museum dedicated to whales and whaling and features an excellent audio-visual display narrated by actor Richard Widmark. The *Carthaginian* ($2) is open daily 9:30 a.m. to 5:00 p.m., but to enjoy the entire display allow at least an hour. As you descend into the hold of the ship and bright sunlight fades to cool shadow, you become a visitor into a watery world of the humpback whale. The haunting, mysterious "songs" of the humpback provide the background music and set the mood. Sit on comfortable captain's chairs and watch the display. The excellent photos of whales are by Flip Nicklin, courtesy of the National Geographic Society. The *Carthaginian* is a project of the Lahaina Restoration Foundation, P.O. Box 338, Lahaina, HI 96761 (tel. 661-3262). The Foundation is a non-profit organization dedicated to educational and historical restoration in Lahaina.

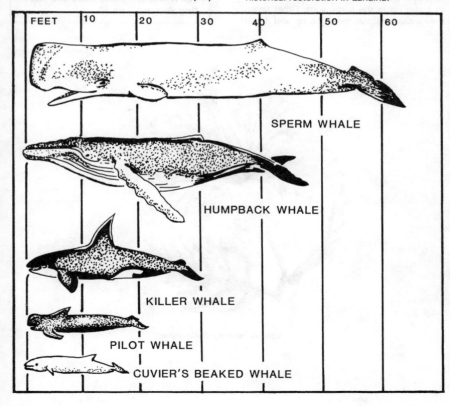

FEET | 10 | 20 | 30 | 40 | 50 | 60

SPERM WHALE

HUMPBACK WHALE

KILLER WHALE

PILOT WHALE

CUVIER'S BEAKED WHALE

Whale-watching

If you're in Hawaii from late Nov. to early May, you have an excellent chance of spotting a humpback. You can often see a whale from a vantage point on land but this is nowhere as thrilling as seeing them close-up from a boat. Either way, binoculars are a must. Telephoto and zoom lenses are also useful and you might even get a nifty photo in the bargain. But don't waste your film unless you have a fairly high-powered zoom: fixed-lens cameras give pictures with a lot of ocean and a tiny black speck. If you're lucky enough to see a whale "breach" (jump clear of the water), keep watching—they often repeat this a number of times. If a whale dives and lifts its fluke high in the air, expect it to be down for quite a while (15 minutes) and not to come up in the same spot. Other times they'll dive shallow, then bob up and down quite often. From shore you're likely to see whales anywhere along Maui's south coast. If you're staying at any of the hotels or condos along Kaanapali or Kihei and have an ocean view, you can spot them from your *lanai* or window. A good vantage spot is Papawai Point along Rt. 30 and up the road heading west just before the tunnel. Maalaea Bay is another favorite nursing ground for mothers and their calves; you also get to see a small working harbor up close. An excellent viewpoint is Makena Beach on the spit of land separating Little and Big Beaches (local names). If you time your arrival near sunset, even if you don't see a whale you'll have a mind-boggling light show.

For whale watching tours see "Getting Around," pg.69.

hibiscus, Hawaii's State flower

HISTORY

The *Kumulipo* sings that Maui was the second island child of *Wakea* and *Papa*. Before the coming of the white man and his written record, it's clear that the island was a powerful kingdom. Wars raged throughout the land and kings ruled not only Maui, but the neighbor islands of Lanai and Kahoolawe. By the 16th C., a royal road called the *Alaloa* encircled the island and signified unity. Today, on West Maui, the road is entirely obliterated: only a few portions remain on East Maui. When the white men began to arrive in the late 1700s, Maui became their focal point. Missionaries, whalers and the new Hawaiian kings of the Kamehameha line all made Lahaina their seat of power. For about 50 years, until the mid-19th C., Maui blossomed. Missionaries built the first permanent stone structures in the islands. An exemplary New England-style school at Lahainaluna attracted students even from California cities. Here, too, a famous printing press brought not only revenue but refinement through the written word. The sugar industry began in secluded Hana and fortunes were made; a new social order under the "Plantation System" began. But by the turn of this century, the "glory years" were over. The whal-

ing industry faded away and Oahu took over as the central power spot. Maui slipped into obscurity. It revived in the 1960s when tourists rediscovered what others had known: Maui is a beauty among beauties.

Maui's great kings
Internal turmoil raged in Hawaii just before discovery by Capt. Cook in 1778. Shortly after contact, the great Kamehameha would rise and consolidate all the islands under one rule, but in the 1770s a king named Kahekili ruled Maui. (Some contend that Kahekili was Kamehameha's father!) The Hana district, however, was ruled by Kalaniopuu of Hawaii. He was the same king who caused the turmoil on the day that Capt. Cook was killed at Kealakekua. Hana was the birthplace of Queen Kaahumanu, Kamehameha's favorite wife. She was the most instrumental *ali'i* in bringing Hawaii into the new age initiated by foreign discovery. In 1776, Kalaniopuu invaded Maui, but his forces were annihilated by Kahekili's warriors at Sand Hill near Wailuku, which means "Bloody Waters." On November 26, 1778 Capt. Cook spotted Maui, but bypassed it because he could find no suitable anchorage. It wasn't until May 28,

Kamehameha I as drawn by Louis Choris, ca. 1816. Supposedly, the one and only time that Kamehameha actually sat to have his portrait rendered. (Hawaii State Archives).

1786 that a French expedition led by Commander LaPerouse came ashore near Lahaina after finding safe anchorage at what became known as LaPerouse Bay. Maui soon became a regular port of call. In 1790 Kamehameha finally defeated Kahekili's forces at Iao Needle and brought Maui under his domain. The great warrior Kahekili was absent from the battle, where Kamehameha used a cannon from the *Fair American,* a small ship seized a few years before. Davis and Young, two marooned seamen, provided the technical advice for these horrible but effective new weapons.

Maui's rise

The beginning of the 19th C. brought amazing changes to Hawaii and many of these came through Maui—especially the port of Lahaina. In 1793, Captain Vancouver visited Lahaina and confirmed LaPerouse's report that it was a fine anchorage. In 1802 Kamehameha stopped with his enormous "Pelelu Fleet" of war canoes on his way to conquer Oahu. He lingered for over a year collecting taxes and building his "Brick Palace" at Lahaina. The bricks were poorly made, but this marked the first Western-style structure in the islands. He also built a

fabulous straw house for his daughter Princess Nahienaena that was so well constructed it was later used as the residence of the U.S. Consul. In 1819 the first whaler, *The Bellina,* stopped at Lahaina and marked the ascendancy of Hawaii as the capital of the whaling industry that lasted until the majority of the whaling fleet was lost in the Arctic in 1871. During its heyday, over 500 ships visited Lahaina in one year. Also in 1819, the year of his death, Kamehameha built an observation tower in Lahaina so that he could watch for returning ships, many of which held his precious cargo. In that prophetic year the French reappeared, with a warship this time, and the drama began. The great Western powers of the period maneuvered to upstage each other in the quest for dominance of this Pacific jewel.

Captain James Cook

The missionaries

In 1823 the first Christian mission was built in Lahaina under the pastorage of Rev. Richards, and the great conversion of Hawaii began in earnest. In that year Queen Kapiolani, the first great convert to Christianity, died. She was buried in Lahaina not according to the ancient customs accorded to an *ali'i,* but as a reborn child of Christ. The Rev. Richards and Queen Kaahumanu worked together and produced Hawaii's first Civil Code based on the Ten Commandments. The whalers fought the interference of the missionaries to the point where attempts were made on Rev. Richards' life, including a naval bombardment of his home. Over the next decade, the missionaries, ever hard at work, became reconciled with the sailors, who donated funds to build a Seaman's Chapel. This house of worship was located just next to The Baldwin Home, an early permanent New England-style house which still stands on Front Street. The house originally belonged to the Spaulding Family, but the Baldwins were such an influence that it was known by their name. Lahainaluna High School, situated in the cool of the mountains just north of Lahaina, became the paramount institution of secondary learning west of the Rocky Mountains. Newly wealthy of Hawaii and California sent their progeny here to be educated along with the nobility of the Kingdom of Hawaii.

Maui fades

If the following 30 years of Maui's historical and sociological development were put on a graph, it would show a sharp rise followed by a crash. By mid-century, Maui boasted the *first* Constitution, Catholic Mass, Temperance Union, Royal Palace, and steamship service. A census was taken and a prison built to house reveling seamen. Kamehameha III moved the capital to Honolulu and the 1850s brought a smallpox epidemic, the destruction of Wainee Church by a "ghost wind," and the death of David Malo, a classic historian of pre-contact Hawaii. By the late 1860s, the whaling industry was dead, but sugar would rise to take its place. The first successful sugar plantation was started by George Wilfong in 1849 along the Hana coast, and the first great

sugar mill was started by James Campbell in 1861. The 1870s saw the planting of Lahaina's famous Banyan Tree by Sheriff W.O. Smith, and the first telephone and telegraph cable linking Paia with Haiku.

The 20th century

When the Pioneer Hotel was built in 1901, Lahaina was still important. Claus Spreckles, "King Sugar" himself, had large holdings on Maui and along with his own sugartown, Sprecklesville, built the Haiku Ditch in 1878. This 30-mile ditch brought 50 million gallons of water a day from Haiku to Puunene so that the "green gold" could flourish. Sugar and Maui became one. Then, because of sugar, Lahaina lost its dominance and Paia became *the* town on Maui during the 1930s, where it housed plantation workers in camps according to nationality. Maui slid more and more into obscurity. A few luminaries brought some passing fame: Tandy MacKenzie, for example, born in Hana in 1892, was a gifted operatic star whose career lasted until 1954. In the 1960s, Maui, as well as all of Hawaii, became accessible to the average tourist. It had been previously discovered by men like Sam Pryor, retired vice-president of Pan Am Airlines who made his home in Hana and invited Charles Lindbergh to visit, then to live and finally die in this idyllic spot. In the mid '60s, the Lahaina Restoration Foundation was begun. It dedicated itself to the preservation of Old Lahaina, and to other historical sites on the island, and now attempts to preserve the flavor of what once was, while looking to future growth. Today, Maui is once again in ascendancy, and is the second most visited island in Hawaii, after Oahu.

GOVERNMENT AND ECONOMY

GOVERNMENT

The only difference between the government of the State of Hawaii and other states is that it's "streamlined," and in theory more efficient. There are only two levels of government: the state and the county. With no town or city governments to deal with, the added bureaucracy is eliminated. Hawaii, in anticipation of becoming a state, drafted a constitution in 1950 and was ready to go when statehood came. Politics and government are taken seriously in the "Aloha State," which consistently turns in the best national voting record per capita. For example, in the first state elections 173,000 of 180,000 registered voters voted—a whopping 94 percent of the electorate. In the election to ratify statehood, there was hardly a ballot that went uncast, with 95 percent of the voters opting for statehood. The bill carried every island of Hawaii except for Niihau where, coincidentally, the majority of people (total population 250 or so) are of relatively pure Hawaiian blood. The U.S. Congress passed the

"Hawaii State Bill" on March 12, 1959, and on August 21, 1959, President Eisenhower proclaimed Hawaii the 50th State. The present governor is George Ariyoshi, first Japanese governor in the United States. Mr. Ariyoshi has held this post since 1974.

Maui County

The boundaries of Maui County are a bit oddball, but historically oddball. Maui County encompasses Maui Island, as well as Lanai, Molokai and the uninhabited island of Kahoolawe. The apparent geographical oddity is an arc on East Maui, from Makawao past Hana and along the south coast almost to Kihei, which is a "shared" political area, aligned with the Kohala District of the Big Island since Polynesian times. These two districts were joined with each other, so it's just a traditional carry-over. The real strangeness occurs in Maui's 5th Senatorial District and its counterpart, the 10th Representative District. These two political areas include West Maui and the islands of Lanai and Molokai. West Maui, with Kaanapali, Lahaina and Kapalua, is one of the most developed and financially sound areas in all of Hawaii. It's a favorite area with tourists, and is the darling of developers. On the other hand, Lanai has a tiny population that is totally dependent on a one-company "pineapple economy." Molokai has the largest per capita concentration of native Hawaiians, a "busted economy" with a tremendous share of its population on welfare, and a grass-roots movement determined to preserve the historical integrity of the island and the dignity of the people. You'd have to be a political magician to fairly represent all of the constituents in these widely differing districts.

Maui's Representatives

Hawaii's state legislature is comprised of 76 members, with the House of Representatives having 51 elected seats, and the State Senate 25. Members serve for 2- and 4-year terms respectively. All officials come from 76 separate electorates based on population. Maui is represented by three State Senators, all of whom are currently Democrats, and five State Representatives, four of whom are Democrats, with one Republican.

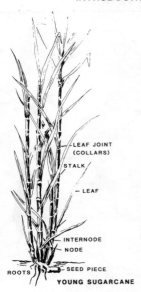

YOUNG SUGARCANE

ECONOMY

Maui's economy is a mirror image of the state's economy: it's based on tourism, agriculture, and government expenditures. The primary growth is in **tourism**, with Maui being the second most frequently chosen Hawaiian destination after Oahu. Over 12,000 rooms are available on Maui in all categories, and they're filled 70 percent of the time. On average, Maui attracts close to a million tourists per year, and on any given day there are about 15,000 visitors enjoying the island. The building trades are still booming, and the majority of the rooms are in Kihei-Wailea, but the Kaanapali area is catching up fast.

Agriculturally, Maui generates revenue through cattle, sugar, pineapples, *pakalolo,* and flowers. Cattle grazing occurs on the western and southern slopes of Haleakala, where 20,000 acres are owned by Ulupala Kua Ranch, and over 32,000 acres by the Haleakala Ranch. The upper slopes of Haleakala around Kula are a gardener's dream. Delicious onions, potatoes, and all

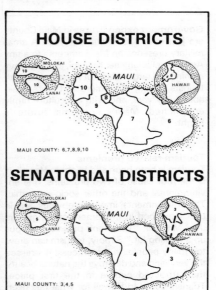

HOUSE DISTRICTS

MAUI COUNTY: 6,7,8,9,10

SENATORIAL DISTRICTS

MAUI COUNTY: 3,4,5

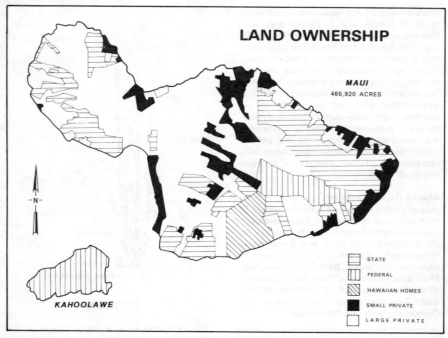

LAND OWNERSHIP

MAUI
465,920 ACRES

KAHOOLAWE

STATE

FEDERAL

HAWAIIAN HOMES

SMALL PRIVATE

LARGE PRIVATE

sorts of garden vegetables are grown, but are secondary to large plots of gorgeous flowers, mainly carnations and the amazing protea. Sugar is still a very important Maui crop. The largest acreage is in the central isthmus area which is virtually all owned by the Alexander and Baldwin Company. There are also large sugar tracts along Kaanapali and the west coast that are owned by Amfac and Maui Land and Pineapple. Those lodging in Kaanapali will become vividly aware of the sugar fields when they're burned off just prior to harvesting. Pineapples are grown in the central east between Paia and Makawao where Alexander and Baldwin own most of the land, and on the far west coast north of Napili where Maui Land and Pineapple control most of the holdings. Renegade entrepreneurs grow patches of *pakalolo* wherever they can find a spot that has the right vibes and is away from the prying eyes of the authorities. Deep in the West Maui Mountains and along the Hana coast are favorite areas.

Government expenditures in Maui County are just over $35 million per year. A small military presence on Maui amounts to a tiny Army installation near Kahului, and the Navy owning the target island of Kahoolawe. With tourists finding Maui more and more desirable every year, and with agriculture firmly entrenched, Maui's economic future is bright.

Tourism-related problems
Tourism is both boon and blight to Hawaii. It is the root cause of two problems: one environmental and the other socio-economic. The environmental impact is obvious, and is best described in the lament of songstress Joni Mitchell: "They took paradise and put up a parking lot." Simply, tourism can draw too many people. In the process, it stresses the very land and destroys the natural beauty that attracted people in the first place. Tourists come to Hawaii for what has been called its "ambient resource"—a balanced

collage of indulgent climate, invigorating waters, intoxicating scenery, and exotic people all wrapped up neatly in one area to both soothe and excite at the same time. It's in the best interest of Hawaii to preserve this resource. Most point to Waikiki as a prime example of development gone mad. Actually two prime examples of the best and the worst development can be found on Maui's south shore at Kihei and Wailea, which are less than 5 miles apart. In the late '60s Kihei experienced a development-inspired "feeding frenzy" that made the real sharks off its shore seem about as dangerous as Winnie the Pooh. Condos were slapped up as fast as cement can dry, their architecture reminiscent of a stack of shoeboxes. Coastline renowned for its beauty was overburdened, and the view was wiped out in the process. Anyone who had the bucks built, and now parts of Kihei look like a high-rise, low-income, federally funded housing project. You can bet that those who made a killing building here don't live here. Conversely, just down the road is Wailea, a model of what development could (and should) be. The architecture is tasteful, low rise, non-obtrusive and done with people and the preservation of the scenery in mind. It's obviously more exclusive, but access points to the beaches are open to everyone, and the view is still there for all to enjoy. It points the way for the development of the future.

Land ownership

Hawaii, landwise, is a small pie, and its slices are not at all well divided. Of 6,425 square miles of land, 98 percent make up the six main inhabited islands. (This figure does not include Niihau, which is privately owned by the Robinson family and inhabited by the last remaining pure-blooded Hawaiians, nor does it include Kahoolawe, the uninhabited Navy bombing target just off Maui's south shore.) Of the 4,045,511 acres that make up the inhabited islands 36 percent is owned by the state, 10 percent by the federal government and the remaining 54 percent is in private hands. But only 40 owners with 5,000 or more acres own 75 percent of all private lands. Moreover, only 10 private concerns own two-thirds of these lands. To be more specific, Castle and Cooke Inc. owns 99 percent of Lanai, while 40-60 percent of Maui, Oahu, Molokai, Kauai and Hawaii is owned by less than a dozen private parties. The largest private landowner is the Kamehameha Schools/Bishop Estate, which has recently lost a Supreme Court battle that allows the State of Hawaii to acquire privately owned land for "the public good." More than in any other state, Hawaii's landowners tend to lease land instead of selling it, and many private homes are on rented ground. Many feel that with land prices going up all the time, only the very rich land developers will be able to purchase, and the "people" of Hawaii will become even more land-poor.

This unwieldy looking vehicle gently plucks pineapples.

THE PEOPLE

Nowhere else on Earth can you find such a kaleidoscopic mixture of people. Every major race is accounted for, and over 50 ethnic groups are represented throughout the islands. Hawaii is the most racially integrated state in the Union. Its population of one million includes 120,000 permanently stationed military personnel and their dependents, and it's the only state where whites are not the majority. About 60 percent of the people living in Hawaii were born there, 25 percent were born on the U.S. mainland, and 15 percent of the people are foreign born.

The population of Hawaii has been growing steadily in recent times, but it fluctuated wildly in times past. In 1876 it reached its lowest ebb, with only 55,000 permanent residents in the islands. This was the era of large sugar plantations, and their constant demand for labor was the primary cause for the importation of various peoples from around the world, which is what led to Hawaii's so racially integrated society. WW II saw Hawaii's population swell from 400,000 just prior to

the war, to 900,000 during the war. Naturally, 500,000 were military personnel who left at war's end, but many returned to settle after getting a taste of island living.

Of the 1,000,000 people in the islands today, 800,000 (80 percent) live on Oahu, with over half of these living in the Honolulu Metropolitan Area. The rest of the population is distributed as follows: 93,000 (9.3 percent) on Hawaii, with 36,000 living in Hilo; 63,000 (6.3 percent) on Maui, with the largest concentration in Wailuku/Kahului at 23,000; 40,000 on Kauai, including 230 pure-blood Hawaiians on Niihau; Molokai with 6,000; and Lanai with just over 2,000. The population density is 164 people per square mile, equal to California's. The population is not at all evenly distributed, with Honolulu claiming more than 1,400 people per square mile, and Maui the second most densely populated island with only 105 people per square mile. City dwellers outnumber those living in the country by 4 to 1.

THE HAWAIIANS

The study of the native Hawaiians is ultimately a study in tragedy because it ends in their demise as a viable people: when Capt. Cook first sighted Hawaii in 1778, there were an estimated 300,000 natives living in perfect harmony with their ecological surroundings; within 100 years a scant 50,000 demoralized and dejected Hawaiians existed almost as wards of the state. Today, although 115,000 people claim varying degrees of Hawaiian blood, experts say that less than 1,000 are pure Hawaiian, and this is stretching the point. It's easy to see why people of Hawaiian lineage could be bitter over what they have lost, being strangers in their own land now, much like native American Indians. The overwhelming majority of "Hawaiians" are of mixed heritage, and the wisest take the best from all worlds. From the Hawaiian side comes simplicity, love of the land, and acceptance of people. It is the Hawaiian legacy of *aloha* that remains immortal and adds that special elusive quality that *is* Hawaii.

Polynesian roots

The Polynesians' original stock is muddled and remains an anthropological mystery, but it's believed that they were nomadic wanderers who migrated from both the Indian sub-continent and SE Asia through Indonesia, where they learned to sail and navigate on protected waterways. As they migrated they honed their sailing skills until they could take on the Pacific, and as they moved, they absorbed people from other cultures and races until they had coalesced into what we now know as Polynesians. Abraham Fornander, still considered a major authority on the subject, wrote in his 1885 *Account of the Polynesian Race,* that he believed the Polynesians started as a white (Aryan) race, which had been heavily influenced by contact with the Cushite, Chaldeo-Arabian civilization. He estimated their arrival in Hawaii at A.D. 600, based on Hawaiian genealogical chants. Modern science seems to bear this date out, although it remains skeptical on his other surmises. The intrepid

Polynesians who actually settled Hawaii are believed to have come from the Marquesa Islands, 1000 miles south and a few hundred miles east of Hawaii. The Marquesans were cannibals and known for their tenacity and strength, two attributes that would serve them well. When Capt. Cook stepped ashore on Waimea, Kauai, on the morning of Jan. 20, 1778, he discovered a population of 300,000. Their agrarian society had flourished in the preceeding thousand years.

The caste system

Hawaiian society was divided into rankings by a strict caste system determined by birth, and from which there was no chance of escaping. The highest rank was the *ali'i*, who were the chiefs and royalty. The impeccable genealogies of the *ali'i* were traced back to

The ali'i wore magnificent feathered capes that signified their rank. The noblest colors were red and yellow, provided by highly specialized hunters who snared and plucked just the right birds.

Commoners were required to lie face down when they saw an approaching kahili, *a standard that resembled a huge feather duster. This was so the* mana *of an* ali'i *would not be defiled by their touch, gaze or even their shadow.*

major project was undertaken, such as building a house, hollowing a canoe log or even offering a prayer. The *mo'o kahuna* were the priests of Ku and Lono who were in charge of praying and following rituals. They were very powerful *ali'i* who kept strict secrets and laws concerning their various functions.

Besides this priesthood of *kahuna*, there were other *kahuna* who were not *ali'i* but commoners. The two most important were the healers *kahuna lapa'au,* and the black magicians *kahuna ana'ana,* who could pray a person to death. The *kahuna lapa'au* had a marvelous pharmacopia of herbs and spices that could cure over 250 diseases common to the Hawaiians. The *kahuna ana'ana* could be hired to cast a love spell over a person or cause their untimely death. They seldom had to send out a reminder of payment!

The common people were called the *maka'ainana,* "the people of land"—the farmers, craftsmen and fishermen. The land that they lived on was owned by the *ali'i,* but they were not bound to it. If the local *ali'i* was cruel or unfair, the *maka'ainana* had the right to leave and reside on another's lands. The *maka'ainana* mostly loved their local *ali'i* much as a child loves a parent, and the feeling was reciprocal. All *maka'ainana* formed extended families called *ohana,* who usually lived on the same section of land, called *ahuapua'a.* Those farmers who lived inland would barter their produce with the fishermen who lived on the shore, and thus all shared equally in the bounty of the land and sea.

A special group called *kauwa* was a landless, untouchable caste confined to living on reservations. Their origins were obviously Polynesian, but they appeared to be descendants of castaways who had survived and become perhaps the aboriginals of Hawaii before the main migrations. It was *kapu* for anyone to go onto *kauwa* lands, and doing so meant instant death. If a human sacrifice was needed, the *kahuna* would simply summon a *kauwa,* who had no recourse but to mutely comply. To this day, to call someone *kauwa,* which now supposedly only means servant, is still considered a fight-provoking insult.

the gods themselves, and the chants *(mo'o ali'i)* were memorized and sung by professionals (called *ku'auhau),* who were themselves *ali'i.* Ranking passed from both father and mother and custom dictated that the first mating of an *ali'i* be with a person of equal status. A *kahuna* was a highly skilled person whose advice was sought before any

Kapu and day-to-day life

There were occasional horrible wars, but mostly the people lived a quiet and ordered life based on a strict caste society and the *kapu* (taboo) system. Famine was known but only on a regional level, and the population was kept in check by birth control, crude abortions, and the distasteful practice of infanticide, especially of baby girls. The Hawaiians were absolutely loving and nurturing parents under most circumstances, and would even take in an adopted *hanai* (child or oldster), a lovely practice that lingers to this day. A strict division of labor existed among men and women. Men were the only ones permitted to have anything to do with taro: this foodstuff was so sacred that it had a greater *kapu* than man himself. Men pounded *poi* and served it to the women. Men also were the fishermen and the builders of houses, canoes, irrigation ditches and walls. Women tended to other gardens and shoreline fishing, and were responsible for making *tapa* cloth. The entire family lived in the common house called *hale noa*.

Certain things were *kapu* between the sexes. Primarily, women could not enter the *mua* (man's house) nor could they eat with men. Certain foods such as pork and bananas were forbidden to women, and it was *kapu* for a man to have intercourse before going fishing, engaging in battle, or attending a religious ceremony. Young boys lived with the women until they underwent a circumcision called the rite of *pule ipu*. After this was performed, they were required to keep the *kapu* of men.

Fatal flaws

Less than 100 years after Capt. Cook's arrival, King Kalaukaua found himself with only 48,000 Hawaiian subjects, down more than 80 percent. Wherever the King went, he would beseech his people, *Hooulu lahui,* "increase the race," but it was already too late. It was as if nature herself had turned her back on these once proud people. Many of their marriages were barren and in 1874 when only 1,400 children were born, a full 75 percent died in infancy. The Hawaiians sat around and could do nothing as their race faded from existence.

The causes

The ecological system of Hawaii has always been exceptionally fragile and this included its people. When the white man came he

Ship's artist Jacques Arago depicts the harsh verdict delivered to a kapu *breaker, ca. 1819 (Hawaii State Archives).*

a modern couple of mixed ethnic background

found a great people who were large, strong and virile, but when it came to fighting off the most minor diseases they proved as delicate as hothouse flowers. To exacerbate the situation, the Hawaiians were totally uninhibited toward sexual intercourse between willing partners, and they engaged in it openly and with abandon. Unfortunately, the sailors who arrived were full of syphilis and gonorrhea. The Hawaiian women brought the diseases es home and, given the nature of Hawaiian society at the time, they spread like wild-fire. By the time the missionaries came in 1820 and helped to halt the unbridled fornication, they estimated the native population at only 140,000, fully half of what it had been only 40 years since initial contact! In the next 50 years measles, mumps, influenza and tuberculosis further ravaged the people. Hawaiian men were excellent sailors and it's estimated that during the whaling years, at least 25 percent of all able-bodied Hawaiian men sailed away, never to return.

But the *coup de grace* that really ended the Hawaiian race, as such, was that all racial newcomers to the islands were attracted to the Hawaiians and the Hawaiians were in turn attracted to them. With so many interracial marriages, the Hawaiians literally bred themselves out of existence. By 1910, there were still twice as many full-blooded Hawaiians as mixed bloods, but by 1940 mixed-blooded Hawaiians were the fastest growing group, and full-blooded the fastest declining.

Hawaiians today

Many of the Hawaiians who moved to the cities became more and more disenfranchised. Their folk society stressed openness and a giving nature, but downplayed the individual and the ownership of private property. These cultural traits made them easy targets for the users and schemers until they finally became either apathetic or angry. Most surveys reveal that although Hawaiians number only 12 percent (16,000) of the population, they account for almost 50 percent of the financially destitute families, and similarly, about half of arrests and illegitimate births. Niihau, a privately owned island, is home to about 250 pure-blood Hawaiians, representing the largest concentration of them, per capita, in the islands. The Robinson family, which owns the island, restricts visitors to invited guests only.

The second largest concentration is on Molokai, where 2,700 Hawaiians, living mostly on 40-acre *kuleana* of Hawaiian Homes Lands, make up 45 percent of that island's population. The majority, 80,000 or so, live on Oahu, where they are particularly strong in the hotel and entertainment fields. People of Hawaiian extraction are still a delight to meet, and anyone so lucky as to be befriended by one long regards this friendship as the highlight of his travels. The Hawaiians have always given their *aloha* freely to all the peoples of the world, and it is we who must acknowledge this precious gift.

THE CHINESE

Next to Yankees from New England, the Chinese are the oldest migrant group in Hawaii, and their influence has far outshone their meager numbers. They brought to Hawaii, along with their individuality, Confucianism, Taoism and Buddhism, although many have long since become Christians. The Chinese population at 57,000 makes up only 6 percent of the state's total, and the majority (52,000) reside on Oahu. As an ethnic group they have the least amount of crime, the highest per capita income, and a disproportionate number of professionals.

The first Chinese

No one knows his name, but an unknown Chinaman is credited with being the first person in Hawaii to refine sugar. This Oriental wanderer tried his hand at crude refining on Lanai in 1802. Fifty years later the sugar plantations desperately needed workers, and the first Chinese brought to Hawaii under the newly passed Masters and Servants Act were 195 coolies from Amoy who arrived in 1852. These conscripts were contracted for 3 to 5 years and given $3 per month plus room and board. This was for 12 hours a day, 6 days a week, and even in 1852 these wages were the pits. The Chinese almost always left the plantations the minute their contracts expired. They went into business for themselves and promptly monopolized the restaurant and small shop trades.

The Chinese niche

Although almost all people in Hawaii considered the Chinese the same, they were actually quite different. The majority came from Kwangtung Province in southern China. They were two distinct ethnic groups: the Punti made up 75 percent of the immigrants, and the Hakka made up the remainder. In China, they remained separate from each other, never mixing; in Hawaii, they mixed out of necessity. For one, hardly any Chinese women came over at first, and the ones who followed were at a premium and gladly accepted as wives, regardless of ethnic background. The Chinese were also one of the first groups who willingly intermarried with the Hawaiians, from whom they gained a reputation for being exceptionally caring husbands. The Chinese accepted the social order and kept a low profile. For example, during the turbulent labor movements of the 1930s and '40s in Hawaii, the Chinese community produced not one labor leader, radical intellectual, or left-wing politician. When Hawaii became a state, one of the two senators elected was Hiram Fong, a racially mixed Chinese. Since statehood, the Chinese community has carried on business as usual as they continue to rise both economically and socially.

Women of many races worked the plantations of the 1890s.

THE JAPANESE

Most scholars believe that (inevitably) a few Japanese castaways floated to Hawaii long before Capt. Cook arrived, and might have introduced iron, which the islanders seemed to be familiar with before the white men arrived. The first official arrivals were ambassadors sent by the *shogun* to negotiate in Washington; they stopped enroute at Honolulu in March, 1860. But it was as plantation workers that the Japanese were brought to the islands. A small group arrived in 1868, and mass migration started in 1885. In 1886, because of famine, the Japanese government allowed farmers mainly from southern Honshu, Kyushu, and Okinawa to emigrate. Among these were members of Japan's little-talked-about untouchable caste, called *eta* or *burakumin* in Japan and *chorinbo* in Hawaii. They gratefully seized this opportunity to better their lot, an impossibility in Japan. The first Japanese migrants were almost all men. Between 1897 and 1908 migration was steady, with about 70 percent men and 30 percent women arriving. Afterwards, migration slowed because of a "Gentlemen's Agreement," a euphemism for racism against the "yellow peril." By 1900 there were over 60,000 Japanese in the islands, constituting the largest ethnic group.

AJAs, Americans of Japanese Ancestry
Parents of most Japanese children born before WW II were *issei* (first generation), who considered themselves apart from other Americans and clung to the notion of "We Japanese." Their children, the *nisei* or second generation, were a different matter altogether. In one generation they had become Americans, and they put into practice the high Japanese virtues of obligation, duty and loyalty to the homeland, and that homeland was now unquestionably America. After Pearl Harbor was bombed, the FBI kept close tabs on the Japanese community and the menace of the "enemy within" prompted the decision to place Hawaii under martial law for the duration of the war. It has since been noted that not a single charge of

espionage or sabotage was ever reported against the Japanese community in Hawaii during the war.

AJAs as G.I.s
Although Japanese had formed a battalion during WW I, they were insulted by being considered unacceptable as American soldiers in WW II. Some American-Japanese volunteered to serve in labor battalions, and because of their flawless work and loyalty, it was decided to put out a call for a few hundred volunteers to form a combat unit. Over 10,000 signed up! AJAs formed two distinguished units in WW II: the 100th Infantry Battalion, and later the 442nd Regimental Combat Team. They landed in Italy at Salerno and even fought from Guadalcanal to Okinawa. They distinguished themselves by becoming *the* most decorated unit in American military history.

the AJAs return
Many returning AJAs took advantage of the G.I. Bill and received college educations. The "Big 5 Corporations" for the first time accepted former AJA officers as executives and the old order was changed. Many Japanese became involved with Hawaiian politics and the first elected member to Congress was Daniel Inouye, who had lost an arm fighting in WW II. Hawaii's present governor, George Ariyoshi, is the country's first Japanese-American ever to reach such a high office. Most Japanese, even as they

Governor Ariyoshi

climb the economic ladder, tend to remain Democrats. Today, one out of every two political offices in Hawaii is held by 'a Japanese-American. In one of those weird quirks of fate, it is now the Hawaiian Japanese who are accused by other ethnic groups of engaging in unfair political practices—nepotism and reverse discrimination. Many of these accusations against AJAs are undoubtedly motivated by jealousy, but the AJA's record with social fairness issues is not without blemish; true to their custom of family loyalty, they do stick together. There are now 240,000 people in Hawaii of Japanese ancestry, 25 percent of the state's population. They are the least likely of any ethnic person to marry outside of their group—especially the men—and they enjoy a higher-than-average standard of living.

CAUCASIANS

White people have a distinction from all other ethnic groups in Hawaii: they are all lumped together as one. You can be anything from a Protestant Norwegian dock worker to a Greek Orthodox shipping tycoon, but if your skin is white, in Hawaii, you're a *haole*. What's more, you could have arrived at Waikiki from Missoula, Montana in the last 24 hours, or your *kamaaina* family can go back five generations, but again: if you're white, you're a *haole*. The word *haole* has a floating connotation that depends upon the spirit in which it's used. It can mean everything from a derisive "honky or cracker" to nothing more than "white person." The exact Hawaiian meaning is clouded, but some say it meant "a man of no background," because white men couldn't chant a genealogical *kanaenae* telling the Hawaiians who they were. *Haole* then became euphemised into "foreign white man" and today, simply "white person."

White History
Next to Hawaiians themselves, white people have the oldest stake in Hawaii. They've been there as settlers in earnest since the missionaries of the 1820s, and were established long before any other migrant group.

a typical haole?

From last century until statehood, old *haole* families owned and controlled everything, and although they were benevolent, philanthropic, and paternalistic, they were also racist. They were established *kamaaina* families, many of whom made up the boards of the "Big 5" corporations, or owned huge plantations and formed an inner social circle that was closed to the outside. Many managed to find mates from among close family acquaintances. Their paternalism, which they accepted with grave responsibility, at first only extended to the Hawaiians, who saw them as replacing their own *ali'i*. Orientals were considered "primarily as instruments of production." These supremacist attitudes tended to drag on in Hawaii until quite recent times. They are today responsible for the sometimes sour relations between white and non-white people in the islands. Today, all individual white people are resented to a certain degree because of these past acts, even though they personally were in no way involved.

White plantation workers

In the 1880s the white land-owners looked around and felt surrounded and outnumbered by Orientals, so they tried to import white people for plantation work. None of their schemes seemed to work out. Europeans were accustomed to a much higher wage scale and better living conditions than what was provided on the plantations. Although only workers, and not considered the equals of the ruling elite, they still were expected to act like a special class. They were treated preferentially, which meant higher wages for the same job performed by an Oriental. Some of the imported workers included: 600 Scandinavians in 1881; 1400 Germans 1881-85; 400 Poles 1897-98; and 2,400 Russians 1909-12. Many proved troublesome, like the Poles and Russians who staged strikes after only months on the job. Many quickly moved to the mainland. A contingency of Scots, who first came as mule skinners, did become successful plantation managers and supervisors. The Germans and Scandinavians were well received and climbed the social ladder rapidly, becoming professionals and skilled workers.

The Depression years, not as economically bad in Hawaii as in the continental U.S., brought many mainland whites seeking opportunity, mostly from the South and the West. These new people were even more racist toward brown-skinned people and Orientals than the *kamaaina haoles,* and they made matters worse. They also competed more intensely for jobs. The racial tension generated during this period came to a head in 1932 with the infamous "Massie Rape Case."

The Portuguese

The last time anyone looked, Portugal was still attached to the European continent, but for some anomalous reason they weren't considered *haole* in Hawaii for the longest time. About 12,000 arrived from 1878 to 1887 and even 6,000 came from 1906 to 1913. Accompanied during this period by 8,000 Spanish, they were considered one and the same. Most of the Portuguese were illiterate peasants from Madeira and the Azores, and the Spanish hailed from Andalusia. They

Portugese plantation workers maintained their own ethnic identity.

were very well received, and because they were white but not *haole* they made a perfect "buffer" ethnic group. Committed to staying in Hawaii, they rose to be skilled workers—the "*luna* class" on the plantations. They, however, spent the least amount on education and became very racist toward Orientals, regarding the Asians as a threat to their own job security. By 1920 the 27,000 Portuguese made up 11 percent of the population. After that they tended to blend with the other ethnic groups and weren't counted separately. Portuguese men tended to marry within their ethnic group, but a good portion of Portuguese women married other white men and became closer to the *haole* group, while another large portion chose Hawaiian mates and grew further away. Although they didn't originate pidgin English (see "Language"), the unique melodious quality of their native tongue did give pidgin that certain lilt it has today. Also, the *ukelele* (jumping flea) was closely patterned after the *cavaquinho,* a Portuguese stringed folk instrument.

The white population

Today all white people together make up the largest racial, if not ethnic, group in the islands at 33 percent (about 330,000) of the population. There are heavy white concentrations on the Kihei and Kaanapali coast of Maui. The white population is the fastest growing in the islands, because most people resettling in Hawaii are white Americans predominently from the West Coast.

FILIPINOS AND OTHERS

The Filipinos who came to Hawaii brought high hopes of making a fortune and returning home as rich heroes: for most it was a dream that never came true. Filipinos had been American nationals ever since the Spanish-American War of 1898, and as such weren't subject to immigration laws that curtailed the importation of Oriental workers at the turn of this century. The first to arrive were 15 families in 1906, but a large number came in 1924 as strike-breakers. The majority were illiterate peasants called *Ilocano* from the northern Phillipines, with about 10 percent Visayans from the central cities. The Visayans were not as hard working or thrifty, but much more sophisticated. From the first, they were looked down upon by all the other immigrant groups, and were considered particularly uncouth by the Japanese. They put the least amount of value on education of any group, and even by 1930 only about half could speak rudimentary English, the majority remaining illiterate. They were billeted in the worst housing, performed the most menial jobs and were the last hired and first fired.

One big difference with Filipinos was that they had no women to marry, so they clung to the idea of returning home. In 1930 there were 30,000 men and only 360 women. This hopeless situation led to a great deal of prostitution and homosexuality; many of these terribly lonely bachelors would feast and drink on weekends and engage in their gruesome but exciting pastime of cockfighting on Sundays. When some did manage to find wives, their mates were inevitably part-Hawaiian. Today, there are still plenty of old Filipino bachelors who never managed to get home, and the Sunday cockfights remain a way of life. The Filipinos constitute 14 percent of Hawaii's population (140,000) with almost 90 percent living on Oahu. Many visitors to Hawaii mistake Filipinos for Hawaiians because of their dark skin, and this is a minor irritant to both groups. Some streetwise Filipinos even claim to be Hawaiians, because being Hawaiian is "in" and goes over well with the tourists, especially the young women tourists. For the most part, these people are hardworking dependable laborers who do tough work for little recognition. They still remain low man on the social totem pole and have not yet organized politically to stand up for their rights.

Because of their dark complexions, Filipinos are often mistaken for Hawaiians by visitors to the islands.

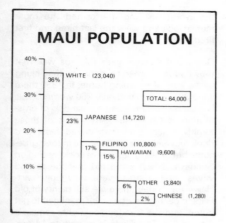

MAUI POPULATION

40%

36% WHITE (23,040)

30%

TOTAL: 64,000

23% JAPANESE (14,720)

20%

17% FILIPINO (10,800)
15% HAWAIIAN (9,600)

10%

6% OTHER (3,840)
2% CHINESE (1,280)

Minor groups
About 10 percent of Hawaii's population is made up of a conglomerate of small ethnic groups. Of these, the largest is Korean with 14,000 people. About 8,000 Koreans came to Hawaii from 1903 until 1905, when their own government halted emigration. During the same period about 6,000 Puerto Ricans arrived, but they have become so assimilated that only 4,000 people in Hawaii today consider themselves Puerto Rican. There were also two attempts made last century to import other Polynesians to strengthen the dying Hawaiian race, but they were failures. In 1869 only 126 Central Polynesian natives could be lured to Hawaii, and from 1878 to 1885 2,500 Gilbert Islanders arrived. Both groups became immediately disenchanted with Hawaii. They pined away for their own islands and departed for home as soon as possible.

Today, however, 12,000 Samoans have resettled in Hawaii and with more on the way are the fastest growing minority in the state. For unexplainable reasons, Samoans and native Hawaiians get along extremely poorly and have the worst racial tensions and animosity of any groups. The Samoans ostensibly should represent the archetypal Polynesians that the Hawaiians are seeking, but it doesn't work that way. Samoans are criticized by Hawaiians for their hot tempers, lingering feuds and petty jealousies. They're clannish and often are the butt of "dumb" jokes. This racism seems especially ridiculous, but that's the way it is. Just to add a bit of exotic spice to the stew, there are about 10,000 blacks, a few thousand American Indians and a smattering of Vietnamese refugees.

THE LANGUAGE

Hawaii is America and people speak English there, but that's not the whole story. If you turn on the TV to catch the evening news, you'll hear "Walter Cronkite" English unless, of course, you happen to tune in a Japanese language broadcast designed for tourists from that country. You can easily pick up a Chinese-language newspaper, or groove to the music on a Filipino radio station, but let's not confuse the issue. All your needs and requests at airports, car rental agencies, restaurants, hotels, or wherever you happen to travel will be completely understood, as well as answered, in English. However, when you happen to overhear "islanders" speaking, what they're saying will sound somewhat familiar, but you won't be able to pick up all the words, and the beat and melody of the language will be noticeably different. Hawaii, like New England, the Deep South, and the Midwest, has its own unmistakable linguistic regionalism. All the ethnic peoples who make up Hawaii have enriched the English spoken there with words, expressions, and subtle shades of meaning that are commonly used and understood throughout the islands. The greatest influence on English has come from the Hawaiian language itself, and words such as *aloha, kapu,* and *muumuu* are familiarly used and understood by most Americans. Other migrant people, especially the Chinese, Japanese and Portuguese, influenced the local dialect to such an extent that the simplified plantation lingo that they spoke has become known as "pidgin." A fun and enriching part of the "island experience" is picking up a few words of Hawaiian and pidgin. English is the official language of the state, business, education, and perhaps even the mind; but pidgin is the language of the people, the emotions and life, while Hawaiian remains the language of the heart and the soul.

PIDGIN

The dictionary definition of pidgin is: a simplified language with a rudimentary grammar used as a means of communication between people speaking different languages. Hawaiian pidgin is a little more complicated than that. It had its roots during the plantation days of last century when white owners and *luna* had to communicate with recently arrived Chinese, Japanese, and Portuguese laborers. It was designed as a simple language of the here and now, and was primarily concerned with the necessary functions of working, eating and sleeping. It has an economical noun-verb-object structure (not necessarily in that order). Hawaiian words make up most of pidgin's non-English vocabulary. There is a good smattering of Chinese, Japanese, Samoan, and the distinctive rising inflection is provided by the melodious Mediterranean lilt of the Portuguese. Pidgin is not a stagnant language. It's kept alive by hip new words introduced by people who are "so radical," or especially by slang words introduced by teenagers. It's a colorful English, like "jive" or "ghettoese" spoken by American blacks, and is as regionally unique as the speech of Cajuns from Louisiana's bayous. *Maka'aina* of all socio-ethnic backgrounds can at least understand pidgin. Most islanders are proud of it, while some consider it a low-class jargon. The Hawaiian House of Representatives has given pidgin an official sanction, and most people feel that it adds a real local style and should be preserved.

Pidgin lives

Pidgin is first learned at school where all students, regardless of background, are exposed to it. The pidgin spoken by young people today is "fo' real" different than that of their parents. It's no longer only plantation talk, but has moved to the streets and picked up some sophistication. At one time there was an academic movement to exterminate it, but that idea died away with the same thinking that insisted on making left-handed people write with their right hands. It is strange, however, that pidgin has become the unofficial language of Hawaii's grassroots movement, when it actually

CAPSULE PIDGIN

The following are a few commonly used words and expressions that should give you an idea of pidgin. It really can't be written properly, merely approximated, but for now, *"brah, study da kine an' bimbye you be hele on, brah! O.K.? Lesgo."*

an' den—and then?; big deal; so what's next; how boring.

blalah—brother, but actually only refers to a large, heavy-set, good-natured Hawaiian man.

brah—all the bro's in Hawaii are brahs; other; pal. Used to call someone's attention. One of the most common words used even among people who are not acquainted. After a fill-up at a gas station, a person would say "Tanks, brah."

bimbye—after a while; bye and bye. "Bimbye, you learn pidgin."

cockaroach—steal; rip off. If you really want to find out what *cockaroach* means, just leave your camera on your beach blanket when you take a little dip.

da' kine—a catch-all word of many meanings that epitomizes the essence of pidgin. *Da' kine* is easily used as a euphemism for pidgin and is substituted whenever the speaker is at a loss for a word or just wants to generalize. It can mean: you know?; watchamacallit; of that type.

geev um—give it to them; give them hell; go for it. Can be used as an encouragement. If a surfer is riding a great wave, the people on the beach might yell, "Geev um, brah!"

hana ho—again; especially after a concert the audience shouts "hana ho" (one more!).

hele on—right on!; hip; with it; groovy.

howzit?—as in "howzit brah?"; what's happening; how is it going. The most common greeting, used in place of the more formal "How do you do?"

hu hu—angry! "You put the make on the wrong da' kine wahine brah, and you in da' kine trouble, if you get one big Hawaiian blalah plenty hu hu."

kapu—a Hawaiian word meaning forbidden. If *kapu* is written on a gate or posted on a tree it means "No trespassing." *Kapu*-breakers are still very unpopular in the islands.

lesgo—Lets go! Do it!

li'dis an' li'dat—like this or that; a catch-all grouping especially if you want to avoid details; like, ya' know?

lolo buggah—stupid or crazy guy (person). Words to a tropical island song go, "I want to find the lolo who stole my pakalolo (marijuana)."

mo' bettah—real good!; great idea. An island sentiment used to be, "mo'bettah you *come* Hawaii." Now it has subtly changed to, "mo'bettah you *visit* Hawaii."

ono—number one! delicious; great; groovy. "Hawaii is ono, brah!"

pakalolo—literally "crazy smoke"; marijuana; grass; reefer. "Hey, brah! Maui-wowie da' kine ono pakalolo."

pakiki head—stubborn; bull-headed.

pau—a Hawaiian word meaning finished; done; over and done with. *Pau hana* means end of work or quitting time. Once used by plantation workers, now used by everyone.

stink face—basically frowning at someone; using facial expression to show displeasure. Hard looks. What you'll get if you give local people a hard time.

swell head—burned up; angry.

talk story—spinning yarns; shooting the breeze; throwing the bull; a rap session. If you're lucky enough to be around to hear *kapuna* (elders) "talk story," you can hear some fantastic tales in the tradition of old Hawaii.

tita—sister, but only used to describe a fun-loving, down-to-earth country girl.

waddascoops—what's the scoop?; what's up?; what's happening?

began as a white owner's language which was used to supplant Hawaiian and all other languages brought to the islands. Although hip young *haole* use it all the time, it has gained some of the connotation of being the language of the non-white locals, and is part of the "us against them" way of thinking. All local people, *haole* or not, do consider pidgin their own island language, and don't really like it when it's used by *malihini* (newcomers). If you're in the islands long enough, you don't have to bother learning pidgin; it'll learn you. There's a book sold all over the islands called *Pidgin to da Max*, written by (you guessed it), a *haole* from Nebraska named Doug Simonson. You might not be able to understand what's being said by locals speaking pidgin (that's usually the idea), but you should be able to feel what's being meant.

HAWAIIAN

The Hawaiian language sways like a palm tree in a gentle wind. Its words are as melodious as a love song. Linguists say that you can learn a lot about people through their language: when you hear Hawaiian you think of gentleness and love, and it's hard to imagine the ferocious side so evident in Hawaii's past. With many Polynesian root words that are easily traced to Indonesian and Malayan, it's evident that Hawaiian is from this same stock. The Hawaiian spoken today is very much different from old Hawaiian. Its greatest metamorphosis occurred when the missionaries began to write it down in the 1820s. There is a movement to re-establish the Hawaiian language, and courses are offered in it at the University of Hawaii. Many scholars have put forth translations of Hawaiian, but there are endless, volatile disagreements in the academic sector about the real meanings of Hawaiian words. Hawaiian is no longer spoken as a language except on Niihau, and the closest tourists will come to it is in place names, street names and in words that have become part of common usage, such as *aloha* and *mahalo*. A few old Hawaiians still speak it at home and there are sermons in Hawaiian at

THE ALPHABET.

VOWELS.		SOUND.	
	Names.	*Ex. in Eng.*	*Ex. in Hawan.*
A a	--- â	as in *father,*	la—sun.
E e	--- a	— *tele,*	hemo—cast off.
I i	--- e	— *marine,*	marie—quiet.
O o	--- o	— *over,*	ono—sweet.
U u	--- oo	—*rule,*	nui—large.

CONSONANTS.	*Names.*	CONSONANTS.	*Names.*
B b	be	**N n**	nu
D d	de	**P p**	pi
H h	he	**R r**	ro
K k	ke	**T t**	ti
L l	la	**V v**	vi
M m	mu	**W w**	we

The following are used in spelling foreign words:

F f	fe	S s	se
G g	ge	Y y	yi

cover page of the first Hawaiian primer

some local churches. Kawaiahao Church in downtown Honolulu is the most famous of these. (See Capsule Hawaiian, pp. 38-41, for commonly used Hawaiian words.)

Wiki Wiki Hawaiian

Thanks to the missionaries, the Hawaiian language is rendered phonetically using only 12 letters. They are the five vowels, a-e-i-o-u, sounded as they are in Italian, and seven consonants, h-k-l-m-n-p-w, sounded exactly as they are in English. Sometimes "w" is pronounced as "v," but this only occurs in the middle of a word and always follows a vowel. A consonant is always followed by a vowel, forming two letter syllables, but vowels are often found in pairs or even triplets. A slight oddity about Hawaiian is the "glottal stop." This is merely an abrupt break in sound in the middle of a word such as "oh-oh" in English, and is denoted with an apostrophe ('). A good example is *ali'i* or even better, the Oahu town of Ha'iku which actually means "abrupt break."

Pronunciation key

For those unfamiliar with the sounds of Italian or a romance language, the vowels are sounded as follows:

A - in stressed syllables, long "a" as in "Ah" (that feels good!). (Hah lay ah kah lah.) Unstressed syllables get a short "a" as in "again," or "above." (**Ka**mehameha).

E—short **e** as in pen or dent. (Hale). Long **e** sounded as "ay" as in sway or day. For example the Hawaiian goose (**Ne ne**) is a "nay nay", not a "knee knee."

I—a long **i** as in see or we. (Hawaii or pali).

O—round **o** as in no or oh. (koa, or ono).

U—round **u** like do or stew. (kapu, or puna).

Dipthongs

There are also eight vowel pairs known as "diphthongs" (ae-ai-ao-au-ei-eu-oi-ou). These are sounds made by gliding from one vowel to another within a syllable. The stress is placed on the first vowel. In English, examples would be **soil** and **eu**phoria. Common examples in Hawaiian are *lei* (lay) and *heiau*.

Stress

The best way to learn which syllables are stressed in Hawaiian is just by listening closely. It becomes obvious after a while. There are also some vowel sounds that are held longer than others and these can occur at the beginning of a word such as the first "a" in *aina* or in the middle of a word like the first "a" in *lanai*. Again, it's a matter of tuning your ear and paying attention. No one is going to give you a hard time if you mispronounce a word. It's good, however, to pay close attention to the pronunciation of street and place names because many Hawaiian words sound alike and a misplaced vowel here or there could be the difference in getting to where you want to go and getting lost.

CAPSULE HAWAIIAN

The following lists are merely designed to give you a "taste" of Hawaiian and to provide a basic vocabulary of words in common usage which you are likely to hear. Becoming familiar with them is not a strict necessity, but they will definitely enhance your experience and make it more congenial when talking with local people. You'll soon notice that many islanders spice their speech with certain words especially when they're speaking "pidgin," and you too can use them just as soon as you feel comfortable. You might even discover some Hawaiian words that are so perfectly expressive, that they'll become a regular part of your vocabulary. Many Hawaiian words have actually made it into the English dictionary. Place names, historical names, and descriptive terms used throughout the text may not appear in the lists below, but will be sited in the "Glossary" at the back of the book. Also see "Pidgin," "Food," and "Getting Around" for applicable Hawaiian words and phrases in these categories. The definitions given are not exhaustive, but are generally considered the most common.

BASIC VOCABULARY

a'a—rough clinker lava; *a'a* has become the correct geological term to describe this type of lava found anywhere in the world.

ae—yes

akamai—smart; clever; wise.

ali'i—a Hawaiian chief or nobleman.

aloha—the most common greeting in the islands. Can mean both hello and good-bye, welcome or farewell. It also can mean romantic love, affection or best wishes.

aole—no

(continued)

hale — house or building; often combined with other words to name a specific place such as Haleakala (House of the Sun), or Hale Pai at Lahainaluna meaning "printing house."

hana — work; combined with *pau* means end of work or quitting time.

haole — a word that at one time meant foreigner, but now means a white person or Caucasian. Many etymological definitions have been put forth, but none satisfy everyone. Some feel that it signified a person without a background, because the first white men could not chant their genealogies as was common to Hawaiians.

hapai — pregnant. Used by all ethnic groups when a *keiki* is on the way.

hapa — half, as in a mixed blooded person being referred to as *hapa haole*.

heiau — a traditional Hawaiian temple. A platform made of skillfully fitted rocks, upon which structures were built and offerings made to the gods.

holomu — a long ankle length dress that is much more fitted than a *muumuu*, and which is often worn on formal occasions.

hoolaulea — any happy event, but especially a family outing or picnic.

hoomalimali — sweettalk; flattery.

huhu — angry; irritated; mad.

huli huli — barbeque, as in *huli huli* chicken.

hula — a native Hawaiian dance where the rhythm of the islands is captured in swaying hips and the story is told by lyrically moving hands.

hui — a group; meeting; society. Often used to refer to Chinese businessmen or family members who pooled their money to get businesses started.

imu — underground oven filled with hot rocks and used for baking. The main cooking feature at a *luau* used to steam-bake the pork and other succulent dishes. Traditionally the tending of the *imu* was for men only.

ipo — sweetheart; lover; girl or boyfriend.

kalua — roasted underground in an *imu*. A favorite island food is *kalua* pork.

kamaaina — a child of the land; an old timer; a long time island resident of any ethnic background; a resident of Hawaii or native son. Oftentimes hotels and airlines offer discounts called *kamaaina rates* to anyone who can prove island residence.

kane — means man, but actually used to signify a relationship such as husband or boyfriend. Written on a door means "Men's Room."

kapu — forbidden; tabu; Keep out; Do not touch.

kaukau — slang word meaning food or chow; grub. Some of the best eating in Hawaii is from "kaukau wagons," which are trucks from which plate lunches and other morsels are sold.

keiki — child or children; used by all ethnic groups. "Have you hugged your *keiki* to-day?"

kokua — help. As in "Your *kokua* is needed to keep Hawaii free from litter."

kona wind — a muggy sub tropical wind that blows from the south and hits the leeward side of the islands. Usually brings sticky hot weather. One of the few times when air conditioning will be appreciated.

kupuna — a grandparent or old timer; usually means someone who has gained wisdom. The statewide school system now invites *kupuna* to talk to the children about the old ways and methods.

lanai — veranda or porch. You'll pay more for a hotel room if it has a *lanai* with an ocean view.

lei — a traditional garland of flowers or vines. One of Hawaii's most beautiful customs. Given at any auspicious occasion, but especially when arriving or leaving Hawaii.

limu — edible seaweed of various types. Gathered from the shoreline and makes

(continued)

an excellent salad. Used to garnish many island dishes and is a favorite at a *luau.*

lomilomi — traditional Hawaiian massage; also, raw salmon made up into a vinegared salad with chopped onion and spices.

lua — the toilet; the head; the bathroom.

luau — an Hawaiian feast featuring *poi, imu* baked pork and other traditional foods. Good ones provide some of the best gastronomical delights in the world.

mahalo — thanks; thank you ; "mahalo nui", big thanks or thank you very much.

mahu — a homosexual; often used derisively like "fag" or "queer."

makai — towards the sea. Used by most islanders when giving directions.

malihini — what you are if you have just arrived. A newcomer; a tenderfoot; a recent arrival.

manauahi — free; gratis; extra.

manini — stingy; tight. A Hawaiinized word taken from the name of Don Francisco "Marin" who was instrumental in bringing many fruits and plants to Hawaii. He was known for never sharing any of the bounty from his substantial gardens on Vineyard Street.

mauka — towards the mountains. Used by most islanders when giving directions.

mauna — mountain. Often combined with other words to be more descriptive as *Mauna Kea*, (White Mountain).

moana — the ocean; the sea. Many businesses and hotels as well as place names have *moana* as part of their name.

muumuu — the garment introduced by the missionaries to cover the nakedness of the Hawaiians. A "mother hubbard"; a long dress with a high neckline that has become fashionable attire for almost any occasion in Hawaii.

ohana — a family; the fundamental social division; extended family. Now used to denote a social organization with "grass roots" overtones as in the "Save Kahoolawe Ohana."

okolehau — literally "iron bottom"; a traditional booze made from *ti* root; okole means your "rear end" and "hau" means iron, which was descriptive of the huge blubber pots that it was made in. Also, if you drink too much it'll surely knock you on your *okole.*

ono — delicious; delightful; the best. *Ono ono* means "extra or absolutely" delicious.

opu — belly; stomach.

pahoehoe — smooth ropey lava that looks like spilled and burned pancake batter. *Pahoehoe* is now the correct geological term used to describe this type of lava found anywhere in the world.

pakalolo — "crazy smoke;" marijuana; grass; smoke; dope.

pali — a cliff; precipice. Hawaii's geology makes them quite common. The most famous are the Pali of Oahu where a major battle was fought.

paniolo — an Hawaiian cowboy. Derived from the Spanish *espaniola*. The first cowboys brought in during the early 19th century were Mexicans from California.

pau — finished; done; completed. Often combined into *pau hana* which means end of work or quitting time.

pilau — stink; smells bad; stench.

pilikia — trouble of any kind, big or small; bad times.

pono — righteous or excellent.

poi — a glutinous paste made from the pounded corm of taro which ferments slightly and has a light sour taste. Purplish in color, and a staple at a *luau,* where it is called "one, two, or three finger" poi depending upon the thickness of it.

puka — a hole of any size. *Puka* is used by all island residents and can be employed when talking about a tiny *puka* in a rubber boat or a *puka* (tunnel) through a mountain.

punee — bed; narrow couch. Used by all ethnic groups. To recline on a *punee* on a breezy *lanai* is a true island treat.

(continued)

pupule—crazy; nuts; out of your mind.

pupu— appetizer; a snack; hors d'oeuvres; can be anything from cheese and crackers to *sushi*. Oftentimes, bars or nightclubs offer them free.

tapa—a traditional paper cloth made from beaten bark. Intricate designs were stamped in using beaters, and color was added with natural dyes. The tradition was lost in Hawaii, but is now making a come-back, and provides some of the most beautiful folk art in the islands

tutu—grandmother; granny; older woman. Used by all as a term of respect and endearment.

ukulele—literally *uku* means "flea" and *lele* means "jumping" or "jumping flea." The way the Hawaiians perceived the quick finger movements on the banjo-type Portuguese folk instrument called a *cavaquinha*. The ukelele quickly became synonymous with the islands.

wahine—young woman; female; girl; wife. Used by all ethnic groups. When written on a door means "Women's Room."

wai—fresh water; drinking water.

wela—hot. "*wela kahao*' is a "hot time" or "making whoopy."

wiki—quickly; fast; in a hurry. Often seen as *wiki wiki* (very fast), as in "Wiki wiki Messenger Service."

USEFUL PHRASES

aloha ahiahi—Good evening.
aloha au ia oe—I love you!
aloha kakahiaka—Good morning.
aloha nui loa—much love; fondest regards.
hauoli la hanau—Happy Birthday.

hauoli makahiki hau—Happy New Year.
komo mai—please come in; enter; welcome.
mele kalikimaka—Merry Christmas.
okole maluna—bottoms up; salute'; cheers; kampai.

RELIGION

The Lord saw fit to keep His island paradise secret from mankind for a few million years, but once we finally arrived we were awfully thankful. Hawaii sometimes appears like a floating tabernacle; everywhere you look there's a church, temple, shrine, or *heiau*. The Islands are either a very holy place, or there's a powerful lot of sinning going on that would require so many houses of prayer. Actually, it's just America's "right to worship" concept fully employed... in microcosm. All the peoples who came to Hawaii brought their own form of devotion. The Polynesian Hawaiians praised the primordial creators, Wakea and Papa, from whom their pantheon of animistically inspired gods sprang. Obviously to a modern world these old gods would never do. Unfortunately for the old gods, there were simply too many of them, and belief in them was looked upon as mere superstition, the folly of semi-civilized pagans. So the famous missionaries of the 1820s brought Congregational Christianity and the "true path" to heaven.

Inconveniently, the Catholics, Mormons, Reformed Mormons, Adventists, Episcopalians, Unitarians, Christian Scientists, Lutherans, Baptists, Jehovah's Witnesses, Salvation Army, and every other major and minor denomination of Christianity that followed in their wake brought their own brand of enlightenment and never quite agreed with each other. The Chinese and Japanese migrants came and established all the major sects of Buddhism, Confucianism, Taoism, and Shintoism. Allah is praised, the Torah is canted in Jewish synagogues, and nirvana is available at a variety of Hindu temples. If the spirit moves you, a Hare Krishna devotee will be glad to point you in the right direction and give you a free flower for only a dollar or two. If the world is still too much with you, you might find peace at a Church of Scientology, or meditate at a Kundalini Yoga institute, or perhaps find relief at a local assembly of Baha'i. Anyway, rejoice, because in Hawaii you'll not only find paradise, but you might even find salvation.

THE WATERS OF KANE

The Polynesian Hawaiians worshipped nature. They saw its forces manifested in a multiplicity of forms to which they ascribed god-like powers, and daily life was based on this animistic philosophy. Hand-picked and specially trained storytellers chanted the exploits of the gods. These ancient tales, kept alive in a special oral tradition called *moolelo,* were recited only by day. Entranced listeners encircled the chanter; in respect for the gods and in fear of their wrath, they were forbidden to move once the tale was begun. This was serious business where a man's life could be at stake. It was not like the telling of *kaao* which were simple fictions, tall tales and yarns of ancient heroes, merely related for amusement and to pass the long nights. Any object, animate or inanimate, could be a god. All could be infused with *mana,* especially a dead body, or a respected ancestor.

Ohana had personal family gods called *aumakua* whom they called on in times of danger or strife. There were children of gods called *kupua* who were thought to live among men and who were distinguished either for their beauty and strength or for their ugliness and terror. It was told that processions of dead *ali'i,* called "Marchers of the Night," wandered through the land of the living and unless you were properly protected it could mean death if they looked upon you. There were simple ghosts known as *akua lapu* who merely frightened people. Forests, waterfalls, trees, springs and a thousand forms of nature were the manifestations of *akua li'i,* "little spirits," who could be invoked at any time for help or protection.

Behind all of these beliefs was an innate sense of natural balance and order. It could be interpreted as positive-negative, yin-yang, plus-minus, life-death, light-dark, whatever, but the main idea was that everything had its opposite. The time of darkness when only the gods lived was *po.* When the great gods descended to the earth and created light, this was *ao* and man was born. All of these *moolelo* are part of the *Kumulipo,* the great chant that records the Hawaiian version of creation. From the time the gods descended and touched Earth at Ku moku on Lanai, the genealogies were kept. Unlike the Bible, these included the noble families of female *ali'i* as well as males.

THE STRIFES OF MAUI

Of all the heroes and mythological figures of Polynesia, Maui is the best known. His "strifes" are like the great Greek epics, and they make excellent tales of daring that elders loved to relate to youngsters around the evening campfire. Maui was abandoned by his mother, "Hina of Fire," when he was an infant. She wrapped him in her hair and cast him upon the sea where she expected him to die, but in heroic fashion he lived and returned home to become her favorite. She knew then that he was a born hero and had strength far beyond that of ordinary mortals. His first exploit was to lift the sky. In those days the sky hung so low that men had to crawl around on all fours. Then a seductive young woman approached Maui and asked him to use his great strength to lift the sky. In fine heroic fashion, the big boy agreed, if the beautiful woman would euphemistically "give him a drink from her gourd." He then obliged her by lifting the sky, and he might even have made the earth move for her once or twice.

Kapu *sticks, like six foot swabs, crossed at the entrance of a house meant, "Forbidden, do not enter."*

More land

The territory of man was small at that time. Maui decided that more land was needed, so he conspired to "fish up islands." He descended into the land of the dead and petitioned an ancestress to fashion him a hook out of her jawbone. She obliged, and created the mythical hook, *Manai ikalani*. Maui then secured a sacred *alae* bird that he intended to use for bait and bid his brothers to paddle him far out to sea. When he arrived at the deepest spot, he lowered *Manai ikalani* baited with the sacred bird, and his sister, "Hina of the Sea," placed it into the mouth of "Old One Tooth," who held the land fast to the bottom of the waters. Maui then exhorted his brothers to row, but warned them not to look back. They strained at the oars with all their might and slowly a great land mass arose. One brother, overcome by curiosity, looked back, and when he did so, the land shattered into all of the islands of Polynesia.

Further exploits

Maui still desired to serve mankind. People were without fire, whose secret was held by the sacred *alae* birds which learned it from Maui's far distant mother. "Hina of Fire" gave Maui her burning finger nails, but he oafishly kept dropping them into streams until all had fizzled out and he had totally irritated his generous progenitor. She pursued him, trying to burn him to a cinder; Maui chanted for rain to put out her scorching fires. When she saw that they were all being quenched she hid her fire in the barks of special trees and informed the mud hens where they could be found, but first made them promise never to tell men. Maui knew of this and captured a mud hen, threatening to wring its scrawny, traitorous neck unless it gave up the secret. The bird tried trickery and told Maui first to rub together the stems of sugar cane, then banana and even taro. None worked, and Maui's determined rubbing is why these plants have hollow roots today. Finally, with Maui's hands tightening around the mud hen's gizzard, the bird confessed that fire could be found in the *hau* tree and also the sandalwood, which Maui named *ili aha* ("fire bark") in its honor. He then rubbed

the feathers off the mud hen's head for being so deceitful, which is why their crowns are featherless today.

The sun is snared

Maui's greatest deed, however, was in snaring the sun and exacting a promise that it would go slower across the heavens. The people complained that there were not enough daylight hours to fish or farm. Maui's mother could not dry her *tapa* cloth because the sun rose and set so quickly. She asked her son to help. Maui went to his blind grandmother, who lived on the slopes of Haleakala and was responsible for cooking the sun's bananas, which he ate every day in passing. She told him to personally weave 16 strong ropes with nooses out of his sister's hair. Some say these came from her head, but other versions insist that it was no doubt Hina's pubic hair that had the power to hold the Sun God. Maui positioned himself with the rope, and as each of the 16 rays of the sun came across Haleakala, he snared them until the sun was defenseless and had to bargain for his life. Maui agreed to free him if he promised to go more slowly. From that time forward the sun agreed to move slowly and Haleakala ("The House of the Sun") became his home.

ANCIENT WORSHIP

Heiau and idols

A *heiau* is an Hawaiian temple. The basic *heiau* was a masterfully built and fitted rectangular stone wall that varied in size from as large as a basketball court to the size of a football field. Once the restraining outer walls were built, the interior was backfilled with smaller stones and the top dressing was expertly laid and then rolled, perhaps with a log, to form a pavement-like surface. All that remains of Hawaii's many *heiau* are the stone platforms. The buildings upon them, made from perishable wood, leaves and grass, have long disappeared. Some *heiau* were dreaded temples where human sacrifices were made. Tradition says that this barbaric custom began at *Wahaula Heiau* on the Big

Island in the 12th C. and was introduced by a ferocious Tahitian priest named Paao. Other *heiau,* such as *Puuhonua o Honaunau,* also on the Big Island, were temples of refuge where the weak, widowed, orphaned, and vanquished could find safety and sanctuary.

Idols

All the people worshipped gods who took the form of idols fashioned from wood, feathers, or stone. The eyes were made from shells and until they were inlaid, the idol was dormant. The hair used was often human hair, and the arms and legs were usually flexed. The mouth was either gaping or formed a wide figure-eight lying on its side, and more likely than not, it was lined with glistening dog teeth. There were small figures made of woven basketry that were expertly covered with feathers. Red and yellow were favorite colors which were taken from specific birds by men whose only work was to roam the forests in search of them. It made no difference who or what you were in old Hawaii, the gods were ever present and they took a direct and active role in your life.

Kukailimoku, Kamehameha's war god, was 30 inches tall. Fashioned from feathers, it presented a horrible sight with its gaping mouth of dog's teeth and was reputed to utter loud cries while battle was being waged.

Opukahaia (Mission Houses Museum)

MISSIONARIES ONE AND ALL

In Hawaii, when you say "missionaries," it's taken for granted you're referring to the small and determined band of Congregationalists who arrived aboard the Brig *Thaddeus* in 1820, and the follow-up groups called "companies" or "packets" that reinforced them. They were sent from Boston by the American Board of Commissioners for Foreign Missions (ABCFM), which learned of the supposed sad and godless plight of the Hawaiian people through returning sailors and especially from the few Hawaiians who had come to America to study. The person most instrumental in bringing the missionaries to Hawaii was a young man named Opukahaia. He was an orphan befriended by a ship's captain and taken to New England, where he studied theology. Obsessed with the desire to return home and save his people from certain damnation, his accounts of life in Hawaii were published and widely read. These accounts were directly responsible for the formation of the Pioneer Company to the Sandwich Islands Missions in 1819. Unfortunately, Opukahaia died in New England from typhus the year before they left.

"Civilizing" Hawaii

The first missionaries had the straightforward task of bringing the Hawaiians out of paganism and into Christianity and civilization. They met with terrible hostility—not from the natives, but from the sea captains and traders who were very happy with the open debauchery and wanton whoremongering that was status quo in the Hawaii of 1820. Many incidents of direct confrontation between these two factions even included the cannonading of missionaries' homes by American sea captains, who were denied the customary visits of island women, thanks to meddlesome "do-gooders." The most memorable incident of this type involved "Mad Jack" Percival, the captain of the USS *Dolphin*. In actuality, the truth of the situation was much closer to the sentiments of James Jarves who wrote, "The missionary was a far more useful and agreeable man than his Catholicism would indicate; and the trader was not so bad a man as the missionary would make him out to be." The missionaries' primary aim might have been conversion, but the most fortuitous by-product was education, which raised the consciousness of every Hawaiian, regardless of his religious affiliation. The American Board of Missions officially ended its support in 1863, and in 40 short years Hawaii was considered a civilized nation well on its way into the modern world.

Non-Christians

By the turn of the century, both Shintoism and Buddhism, brought by the Japanese and Chinese, were firmly established in Hawaii. The first official Buddhist Temple was Hongpa Hongwanji, established on Oahu in 1889. All the denominations of Buddhism account for 17 percent (170,000 parishioners) of the island's religious total, and there are about 50,000 Shintoists. The Hindu religion has perhaps 2,000 adherents, and there are about the same number of Jewish people living throughout Hawaii with only one synagogue, Temple Emanuel, on Oahu. The largest number of people in Hawaii (300,000) remain unaffiliated, and about 10,000 people are in new religious movements and lesser-known faiths such as Bahai'i and Unitarianism.

ARTS AND CRAFTS

Wild Hawaiian shirts or bright *muumuus,* especially when worn on the mainland, have the magical effect of making wearers "feel" like they're in Hawaii, while at the same time eliciting spontaneous smiles from passers-by. Maybe it's the colors, or perhaps it's just the "vibe" that signifies "party time" or "hang loose," but nothing says Hawaii like *aloha* wear does. There are more than a dozen fabric houses in Hawaii turning out distinctive patterns, and many dozens of factories creating their own personalized designs. Oftentimes these factories have attached retail outlets, but in any case you can find hundreds of shops selling *aloha* wear. *Aloha* shirts were the brilliant idea of a Chinese merchant in Honolulu, who used to hand-tailor them and then sell them to the tourists who arrived by ship in the glory days before WW II. They were an instant success. *Muumuus* or "Mother Hubbards" were the idea of missionaries, who were appalled by Hawaiian women running about *au natural* and insisted on covering their new Christian converts from head to foot. Now the roles are

reversed, and it's mainlanders who come to Hawaii and immediately strip down to as little clothing as possible.

Aloha wear
At one time exclusively made of cotton, or from man-made yet naturally based rayon, these materials were and still are the best for any tropical wear. Beware, however: polyester has slowly crept into the market! No material could possibly be worse than polyester for the island climate, so when buying your *aloha* wear make sure to check the label for material content. *Muumuus* now come in various styles and can be worn for the entire spectrum of social occasions in Hawaii. *Aloha* shirts are still basically cut the same, but the patterns have undergone changes, and apart from the original flowers and ferns, modern shirts might depict an island scene giving the impression of a silkscreen painting. A basic good quality *muumuu* or *aloha* shirt starts at about $25 and is guaranteed to be worth its price in good times and happy smiles. The connoisseur might want to pur-

chase *The Hawaiian Shirt, Its Art and History,* by R. Thomas Steele. It's illustrated with more than 150 shirts that are now considered works of art by collectors the world over.

Scrimshaw

This art of etching and carving on bone and ivory has become an island tradition handed down from the times of the old whaling ships. Although scrimshaw can be found throughout Hawaii, the center remains in the old whaling capital of Lahaina. Here along Front Street are numerous shops specializing in scrimshaw. Today, pieces are carved on fossilized walrus ivory that is gathered by Eskimos and shipped to Hawaii. It comes in a variety of shades from pure white to mocha, depending upon the mineral content of the earth in which it was buried. Elephant ivory or whale bone is no longer used because of ecological considerations, but there is a "gray market" in Pacific walrus tusks. Eskimos can legally hunt the walrus. They then make a few minimal scratches on the tusks which technically qualifies them to be "Native American Art," and free of most governmental restrictions. The tusks are then

sent to Hawaii as art objects, but the superficial scratches are immediately removed and the ivory is reworked by artisans. Scrimshaw is made into everything from belt buckles to delicate earrings and even into coffee table centerpieces. The prices can go from a few dollars up into the thousands.

Woodcarvings

One Hawaiian art that has not died out is woodcarving. This art was extremely well developed among the old Hawaiians and they almost exclusively used *koa* because of its density, strength,and natural luster. It was turned into canoes, woodware and furniture used by the *ali'i. Koa* is becoming increasingly scarce, but many items are still available, though costly. Milo and monkeypod are also excellent woods for carving and have largely replaced *koa.* You can buy *tikis,* bowls, and furniture at numerous shops. Countless inexpensive carved items are sold at variety stores, such as little hula girls or salad servers, but most of these are imported from Asia or the Philippines and can be bought at any variety store.

Weaving

The minute you arrive in Hawaii you should shell out $2 for a woven beach mat. This is a necessity, not a frivolous purchase, but it definitely wasn't made in Hawaii. What is made in Hawaii is *lauhala.* This is traditional Hawaiian weaving from the leaves *(lau)* of the pandanus *(hala)* tree. These leaves vary greatly in length, with the largest over six feet, and they have a thorny spine that must be removed before they can be worked. The color ranges from light tan to dark brown. The leaves are cut into strips from one-eighth to one inch wide and are then employed in weaving. Any variety of items can be made or at least covered in *lauhala.* It makes great purses, mats, baskets, and table mats.

Woven into a hat, it's absolutely superb but should not be confused with a palm-frond hat. A *lauhala* hat is amazingly supple and even when squashed will pop back into shape. A good one is expensive ($25) and with proper care will last for years. All *lauhala* should be given a light application of mineral

has placed strict limits and guidelines on the firms and divers involved.

Pink coral has long been treasured by man. The Greeks considered it a talisman for good health, and there's even evidence that it has been coveted since the Stone Age. Coral jewelry is on sale at many shops throughout Hawaii and the value comes from the color of the coral and the workmanship. *Puka* (shells with little naturally occurring holes) and *opihi* shells are also made into jewelry. Many times these items are very inexpensive, yet they are authentic and great purchases for the price. Hanging macrame planters festooned with seashells are usually quite affordable and sold at roadside stands along with shells.

Hawaii produces some unique food items that are appreciated by most people. Various-sized jars of macadamia nuts and butters are great gifts, as are tins of rich, gourmet quality Kona coffee, the only coffee produced in the U.S. Guava, pineapple, passion fruit, and mango are often gift-boxed

oil on a monthly basis especially if it's exposed to the sun. For flat items, iron over a damp cloth and keep purses and baskets stuffed with paper when not in use. Palm fronds, also, are widely used in weaving. They, too, are a great natural raw material, but not as good as *lauhala*. Almost any item such as a beach bag woven from palm makes a good authentic yet inexpensive gift or souvenir. There are countless items like these available in countless shops.

Gift items
Jewelry is always an appreciated gift, especially if it's distinctive, and Hawaii has some of the most unique. The sea provides the basic raw materials of pink, gold, and black coral, and it's so beautiful it holds the same fascination as gem stones. Harvesting the coral is very dangerous work. The Lahaina beds off Maui have one of the best black coral lodes in the islands, but unlike reef coral these trees grow at depths bordering the outer limits of a scuba diver's capabilities. Only the best can dive 180 feet after the black coral, and about one diver per year dies in pursuit of it. Conservationists have placed great pressure on the harvesters of these deep corals and the state of Hawaii

shell macrame

into assortments of jams, jellies and spicy chutneys. And for that special person in your life, you can bring home island fragrances in bottles of perfumes and colognes in the exotic odors of gardenia, plumeria, and even ginger. All of the above items are reasonably priced, lightweight and easy to carry.

A dancing woman of Maui captured by ship's artist Jacques Arago. (Hawaii State Archives).

HULA AND LEI

Hawaiian *hula* was never performed in grass skirts; *tapa* or *ti*-leaf skirts were worn. Grass skirts came to Hawaii from the Gilbert islands, so if you see grass or cellophane skirts in a "hula revue," you'll know that it's not traditional. *Hula,* like all art forms, has its own highly specialized techniques. A dancer has to learn how to control every part of his body including the facial expressions, which become very important and help to set the mood. The hands are extremely important and provide instant background scenery. For example, if the hands are thrust outwardly in an aggressive manner, this can be a battle; if they sway gently overhead, they refer to the gods or the early time of creation. They can

easily become rain, or clouds or the sun, sea or moon. You must watch the hands to get the gist of the story, but the best comeback to this advice was the classic wisecrack, "You watch the parts you like, and I'll watch the parts I like." Swaying hips, depending upon their motion, can be a long walk, a canoe ride or sexual intercourse. The foot motion can portray a battle, a walk or any kind of movement or conveyance. The overall effect is multi-directional synchronized movement. The correct chanting of the *mele* is an integral part of the performance. These story-chants, combined with the various musical instruments that accompany the dance, make the *hula* very much like opera, and are especially similar in the way the tale is unfolded.

Language of the *lei*

Every major island of Hawaii is symbolized by its own *lei,* made from a distinctive flower, shell, or fern. Each island has its own official color as well, which doesn't necessarily correspond to the color of the island's *lei*. Maui is the pink island and its *lei* is the corresponding small pink rose called the *lokelani*. These flowers are not native, but were imported and widely cultivated at one time. In recent years they've fallen prey to a rose beetle and sometimes when they're scarce, a substitute *roselani* is used for Maui's *lei*.

MUSEUMS, GARDENS, ETC.

Alexander & Baldwin Sugar Museum, 3957 Hansen Rd., tel. 871-8050.

Baldwin House, Front St., Lahaina, Maui 96761. Open daily from 9:30 a.m. to 5:00 p.m., tel. 661-3262. Two-story home of medical missionary Dwight Baldwin.

Brig Carthaginian Floating Museum, Lahaina Harbor, Lahaina. Open daily, 9:00 a.m. to 5:00 p.m. Replica of a 19th C. brig. Features whaling artifacts and exhibits of the humpback whale.

Hale Hoikeke Museum, 2375 A Main, Wailuku, tel. 244-3326. Hawaiian history museum. Art gallery featuring Kahoolawe artifacts and the renowned paintings of Edward Bailey.

Hale Pa'i Printshop Museum, P.O. Box 338, Lahaina, HI, 96761, tel. 667-7040. Located on grounds of Lahainaluna school. Operational relics of original printing press. Original Lahainaluna press publications, exhibit of Lahainaluna school past and present.

Hana Cultural Center, Box 27, Hana, HI 96713, tel. 248-8070. Preserves and restores historical sites, artifacts, photos, documents, etc. Construction of museum facilities in Hana.

Kula Botanical Gardens, Hwy. 377 to Upper Kula Road, tel. 878-1715. Open daily, 9:00 a.m. to 4:00 p.m. Excellent arrangements of tropical plants and flowers.

Lahaina Arts Society, P.O. Box 991, Lahaina, HI 96761, tel. 661-0111. To perpetuate and further Hawaiian culture, the arts, crafts. Two galleries, annual scholarship, traveling exhibitions, help maintain Lahaina district courthouse.

Lahaina Restoration Foundation, P.O. Box 991, Lahaina, HI, 96761, tel. 661-3262. James C. Luckey, director. Open Mon. to Sat., 10:00 a.m. to 4:00 p.m. Organization dedicated to the preservation of historical Lahaina. Sponsors restorations, archaeological digs and renovation of cultural and historical sites. Operates Baldwin Home, Brig *Carthaginian,* among others.

Maui Historical Society, P.O. Box 1018, Wailuku, HI 96793. 244-3326. Open 25 hours per week. Same as or part of Hale Hoikeke museum. Promotes interest in and knowledge of history of Hawaii and Maui County. Six free lectures per year.

Whaler's Village Museum, Whaler's Village Shopping Center, Kaanapali, tel. 667-9564. Whaling artifacts, 30-foot sperm whale skeleton set among gift shops. Self guided learning experience while you shop.

ART INFORMATION

Arts Council of Hawaii, P.O. Box 50225, Honolulu, HI 96850, tel.   524-7120, Karl Ichida, Exec. Director. This is a citizen's advocacy group for the arts, which provides technical assistance and information to individuals and groups. It publishes the *Cultural Climate,* a newsletter that covers what's happening in the arts of Hawaii. It includes a calendar of events, plus feature articles, and editorials. Anyone interested in Hawaiian arts can become a member of ACH for only $15 which entitles you to receive the *Cultural Climate.* Non-members can pick it up for 50 cents an issue.

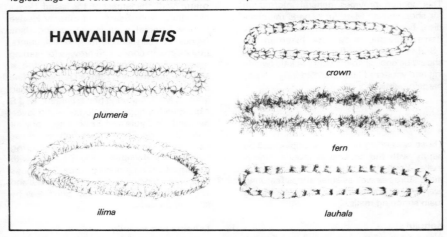

HAWAIIAN *LEIS*

plumeria

ilima

crown

fern

lauhala

Pacific Handcrafters Guild, P.O. Box 15491, Honolulu, HI 96818, tel. 923-5726. The guild's focus is on developing and preserving handcrafts in Hawaii and the Pacific. They sponsor four major craft fairs, two guild-sponsored fairs, and two gallery shows annually.

State Foundation on Culture and the Arts, 335 Merchant Street, Room 202, Honolulu, HI 96813, tel. 548-4145. Begun by state legislature in 1965, its goals are to preserve Hawaii's diverse cultural heritage, promote the arts and artists, and to make cultural and artistic programs available to the people. Their budget includes the purchasing of art works. (One percent of cost of building any state buildings goes for art.) Many of their purchases hang for a time in the Governor's office. They publish the very complete *Hawaii Cultural Resource Directory,* which lists most of the art organizations, galleries, councils, co-ops, and guilds throughout Hawaii.

carved koa *bowl, traditional style*

SHOPPING

This section provides general information for shopping on Maui for general merchandise, books, arts and crafts and specialty items. Specific shops are listed in the "Sights" section of each chapter. This should be enough to get your pockets twitching and your credit cards smoldering! Happy bargain hunting!

SHOPPING MALLS

Those who enjoy one-stop shopping will be happy with the choices in Maui's various malls. You'll find regularly known department stores as well as small shops featuring island-made goods. The following are Maui's main shopping malls.

Kahului
Along Kaahumanu Ave., you'll find **Kaahu-**manu Mall, the largest on the island. Here's everything from **Sears** and **Liberty House** to **Sew Special,** a tiny store featuring island fabrics. You can eat at numerous restaurants, buy ice cream cones, and browse for reading material in the **Book Cache.** Here too is **Village Cinema,** and **Idini's Deli** with a fine selection of wine and spirits. Down the road is **Maui Mall,** featuring photo centers, **M J S Music** with a huge selection of island favorites, and the **Cycle and Sport Shop** for your outdoor needs. Sandwiched between these two modern facilities is **Kahului Shopping Center.** It's definitely "down home" with old-timers sitting around outside. The shops here aren't fancy, but they are authentic and you can make some off-beat purchases by strolling through.

Lahaina and vicinity
Lahaina has the best shopping on Maui in

various little shops strung out along Front St. (see "Shopping" in the Lahaina section). The following are the local malls: **The Wharf** on Front St. has a multitude of eating establishments, as well as stores and boutiques in its multi-level shopping facility. Some of the more interesting stores include **The Royal Art Gallery, Ecology House,** and the **Woodpecker,** all featuring distinctive art works and novelty items. When you need a break, get a coffee at **Upstart Crow Bookstore,** great selections and a top-notch snack bar. **Lahaina Market Place,** tucked away on Front St., features established shops along with open air-stalls. **Lahaina Shopping Center** between Rt. 30 and Front St. has various shops, but check out Cliff McQueen at the **Wizard of Aah's** where you can eat an organic frozen yogurt while talking sports in this combo yogurt-tennis shop. **Whalers' Village** is a Kaanapali mall which features a decent open-air, self-guided museum as you walk around. There are various eateries, bottle shops, **The Book Cache** and a cinema. It's a great place to stroll, buy, and learn a few things about Maui's past. The **Sheraton** and **Marriot Hotel** both have shopping, but the best is at the **Hyatt Regency.** You'll need a suitcase stuffed with money to buy anything, but it's a blast just walking around the grounds and checking out the big-ticket items.

Kihei and Wailea

Azeka Place is just along Kihei Road. There's food shopping, a **Liberty House, Mediterranean House,** a dive shop and activities center along with others. **Wailea Shopping Village** has a wide assortment of boutiques in this exclusive mall just near the Intercontinental and Stouffer's Resorts.

SPECIALTY STORES

Some truly nifty and distinctive stores are wedged in among Maui's run-of-the-mill shopping centers, but for real treasures you'll find the solitary little shop the best. Lahaina's Front St. has the greatest concentration of top-notch boutiques, but others are dottted here and there around the island. The follow-ing is only a sampling of the best; many more are listed in the individual chapters.

Hana Highway

Along this route, the **Maui Crafts Guild** is an exemplary crafts shop that displays the best in local island art. All artists must be selected by active members before their works can be displayed. All materials used must be natural, with an emphasis on those found only in Hawaii. The **Guild** grew from a great idea originated by **Touchstone Ceramics,** which is still located around back. A wide variety of handcrafted items, open 7 days, 10:00 a.m. to 5:30 p.m. Located on Rt. 36, on the left as you enter Paia from the west heading toward Hana. **The Shell Stop!** is located near mile marker 18 along the Hana Highway. It's in an agricultural area—the taro patches of Wailuanui, to be exact—so no signs are allowed along the highway. The Shell Stop! is owned by Anna Kapuana. Here, three Hawaiian families gather *opihi,* whose flesh they send to Oahu, but whose shells they fashion into distinctive jewelry. All shells used are from Hawaii, no imports from the S. Pacific or Philippines. Check "Hana Highway" for exact directions.

Makawao

This upcountry town is known for rodeos and cowboys; you'll find both, and some good shopping, too! Along Makawao Ave. check out: Dana, Peter or Lyn at **Upcountry Downunder,** importers of top-quality New Zealand woolens, crafts, and fleece products. Just down the street is **Makawao Leather and Gift Shop** where you can buy custom-made, tooled leather products. Across the street is **Outdoor Sports,** basically outdoor outfitters with a western flair. If you've ever wanted to visit a general store from out of a cowboy movie, this is the place. If new purchases don't excite you, see Peter at **Grandma's Attic.** Browse through *Life* magazines from the '40s, or spin a few records on the old Victrola.

Wailuku/Kahului

Near Kahului visit the **Pink and Black Coral Factory.** Local craftsmen make distinctive coral jewelry from the amazing corals found under Maui's seas. Divers lose their lives yearly while harvesting these fantastic corals. **Maui Swap Meet** at Maui County Fairgrounds, in Kahului off Puunene Ave. (Hwy. 35); open every Sat., 8:00 a.m to 1:00 p.m. Admission $ .50. Great junk! In Wailuku, check out two odd little shops on Market St.: **Maui Wholesale Gold and Treasure Imports,** adjacent to each other. They deal in eelskin artifacts from belts to briefcases.

Lahaina

You can't beat Lahaina's Front St. for shopping. There are great little shops shoulder to shoulder. The following are some good ones: **High as a Kite** sells kites and other delights. **Vagabond** for backpacks, daypacks, beach

bags and T-shirts. **Lahaina Scrimshaw Factory**, touristy but still terrific; great scrimshaw from $ .50 baubles to works of fine art. **Jade and Jewels** offers rubies, emeralds, sapphires, ivory sculptures and brass work from India; great stuff, but costly. **Waterfront Gallery and Gifts,** lovely jewelry with ocean and Hawaiian motifs, and great models of tall-masted ships that'll thrill kids of all ages. **Tropical Boutique** sells *batik* apparel from Indonesia. **Silks of Lahaina**, on the far end of Front St. heading east, sells top-quality designer silks for women. **Skin Deep Tatooing,** if you want to be your own indelible souvenir from Maui. On Lahainaluna St., they specialize in Polynesian and "new age" primal tatoos.

top: "...one small step for man..." (Gary Quiring);
bottom left: the silverswords of Haleakala Crater (JDB);
botom right: Oheo Stream meets the sea (JDB)

top left: Captain Dave Ventura and friend, Molokini Crater (JDB); top right Winona, tattoo artist of Lahaina (JDB); bottom left: contented Buddah, Jodo Mission, Lahaina (Gary Quiring); bottom right: Jungle John at Makena Harbor (JDB)

EVENTS

American national holidays and Hawaiian state events are all celebrated and commemorated on Maui, but several other unique happenings occur only on The Valley Isle. If you happen to be visiting when any of the following is in progress, be sure to attend!

March
The month for marathons. The "Valley Island Runners" sponsor the **Maui Marathon** in early March from Wailuku to Lahaina. Later the **Kukini Run** follows an ancient trail through Kahakuloa Valley on Maui's NW coast. The **LPGA Womens Kemper Open** is a world-class match at Kaanapali Golf Course.

July
Go to the coolness of upcountry Makawao for the annual 4th of July rodeo. *Paniolos* are an old and very important tradition in Hawaiian life. Held at the Oskie Rice Arena.

August
Late July or early August offers *the* most difficult marathon in the world. **The Run to the Sun** takes runners from sea level to the top of Haleakala (10,000 feet) over 37 long grueling miles. Also, a good-time music festival featuring local entertainers is held in Kapalua.

September
Back up to Makawao for another excellent **Maui County Rodeo,** and plenty of good happenings during the statewide **Aloha Week.**

October
Visit the **Maui County Fair** held at the fairgrounds in Kahului. Old-fashioned fair with Western and homespun flavor. Wild costumes and outlandish behavior islandwide for Halloween. Lahaina's Pioneer Inn is H.Q. for the **Lahaina Jackpot Fishing Tournament,** where the biggest marlin landed can bring prize money of $50,000.

November
This month remembers Maui of old with the **Na Mele O Maui** festival in Lahaina and Kaanapali. Hawaiian music, dance, arts and crafts are featured.

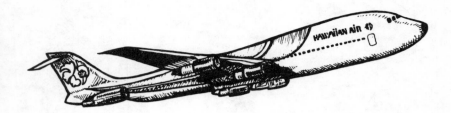

GETTING THERE

Maui, the Hawaiian destination second only to Oahu, attracts over a million visitors per year. A range of direct flights from the mainland are offered by United and Western, with a few flights flown by American Airlines. All other airlines servicing Hawaii, both domestic and foreign, land at Honolulu International Airport and then offer connecting flights on "inter-island carriers" from there; in most cases they're part of the original ticket price with no extra charge. Different airlines have "interline" agreements with different Hawaiian carriers so check with your travel agent. All major and most smaller inter-island carriers service Maui from throughout Hawaii with over 100 flights per day in and out of Kahului Airport.

Maui's airports
There are now two commercial airports on Maui, but the vast majority of travelers will only be concerned with **Kahului Airport**, which 99 percent of the flights in and out of Maui use. Kahului Airport is only minutes from Kahului town, on the northcentral coast of Maui. A full-service facility with most amenities, it has car rental agencies, information booths, lockers, and limited public and private transportation. Major roads lead from Kahului Airport to all primary destinations on Maui. The other airport is at Hana on the NE coast. **Hana Airport** is commercially serviced only by Royal Hawaiian Air Service, and is an isolated strip just west of Hana with no amenities, facilities or transportation. People flying into Hana Airport generally plan to

vacation in Hana for an extended period and have made prior arrangements for being picked up.

Non-stop mainland flights
Until recently, **United Airlines** was the only carrier that offered non-stop flights to Maui from the mainland. Now, there are two competitors, **American Airlines** and **Western Airlines** that operate non-stop daily flights to Maui, both from Los Angeles. United flies to Maui from Chicago, Portland, Seattle, San Francisco and Los Angeles. All United flights passing through Denver fly to Maui via San Francisco. Call, United 1-800-652-1211; American 1-800-252-0421; Western 1-800-227-6105.

INTER-ISLAND CARRIERS

Hawaiian Air offers more flights to Maui than any other inter-island carrier. The majority of flights are to and from Honolulu (average flight time 30 minutes), with over 30 per day in each direction. Hawaiian Air flights to Maui from Honolulu begin at 6:10 a.m., with flights thereafter about every 30 minutes until 7:50 p.m. Flights from Maui to Honolulu begin at 7:03 a.m. and go all day until 9:00 p.m. Hawaiian Air flights to and from Kauai (over 20 per day in each direction, about 35 minutes) begin at 7:00 a.m. and go until 7:00 p.m. There are three flights to/from Hilo daily, two in the morning and one in midafternoon. Kona, on the Big Island, is serviced with five daily flights. Flights from Maui begin at 7:30 a.m. with the last at 4:39 p.m.; from Kona at 9:50 a.m. with the last at 7:32 p.m. There are two flights from Molokai at 10:15 a.m and 2:35 p.m., both on Dash 7s. Six flights from Maui to Molokai begin at 7:00 a.m. with the last at 3:11 p.m. One flight to Lanai goes at 4:25 p.m., and two flights from Lanai at 7:10 a.m. and 6:00 p.m. Aircraft flown are either DC-9 jets, or Dash 7 turbo props. Hawaiian Air tel. 1-(800) 367-5320; on Maui tel. 244-9111.

Aloha Airlines' all-jet fleet of 737s flies from Honolulu to Maui over 20 times per day beginning at 6:10 a.m. with the last flight at 7:50 p.m.; to Honolulu at 6:58 a.m., last at 8:35 p.m. Multiple flights throughout the day from Kauai begin at 6:59 a.m. until 7:05 p.m.; to Kauai at 6:58 a.m. and throughout the day until 7:05 p.m. From Hilo, two flights in mid-morning and the last at 5:10 p.m.; to Hilo four flights interspersed from 9:30 a.m. until 4:20

p.m. From Kona at 9:50 a.m. and two in the afternoon with the last at 3:15 p.m.; to Kona five flights from 8:45 a.m. until 4:05 p.m. Aloha Airlines tel. 1-(800) 367-5250; on Maui, 877-2025.

Mid Pacific offers flights to and from Maui on its fleet of turbo prop YS11s. Their more than 30 daily departures from Maui to Honolulu begin at 7:15 a.m. and go throughout the day until 8:55 p.m.; from Honolulu starting at 6:15 a.m. until 7:55 p.m. More than a dozen flights are offered to and from Kauai beginning at 7:10 a.m., with the last flight at 6:05 p.m. There are three flights to and from Kona at midmorning and early and late afternoon with 2 flights to/from Hilo at midmorning and late afternoon. Mid Pacific, tel. 1-(800) 367-7010; on Maui 242-4906.

Fares for these three major airlines are always very competitive, with each offering special

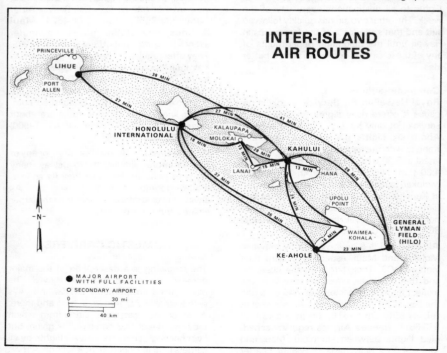

Try a "commuter airline" like Royal Hawaiian for an up-close look at the islands.

service or amenities to sweeten the deal. Mid Pacific instigated a one-price fare on all flights to all destinations every day of the week. The other two airlines quickly followed suit and that's the state of the fare prices in Hawaii until the marketing departments of any of these airlines comes up with a better idea.

Commuter airlines

Royal Hawaiian Air Service is unique because it offers daily flights to Maui which service not only Kahului, but Hana as well. About six flights per day run Honolulu/ Kahului with the earliest at 4:30 a.m. and the latest at 5:30 p.m.; to Hana at 8:00 a.m., last 4:30 p.m. Flights to and from Kona, Hilo, Molokai, Lanai and Kamuela land and depart at Kahului on a daily basis with at least one flight in the morning and one in the afternoon. Contact Royal Hawaiian at tel. 1-(800) 367-2652; on Oahu 836-2200.

Air Molokai is a great way to fly between Molokai and Maui, especially aboard their vintage DC3. Their fares are the cheapest and they fly three times per day with the earliest flight from Molokai at 7:45 a.m. and the last at 5:10 p.m. Contact Air Molokai at tel. 1-(800) 352-3616, or in Hawaii at 536-6611. **Reeves Air** has regularly scheduled flights between Honolulu, Maui and Molokai on a daily basis as well as charter

service to get you there when you want to go. Their prices are higher, but it's like hiring your own private air taxi. Call Reeves Air at Oahu 833-9555; Maui, 871-4624. **Maui Airlines**, one of the newest commuter airlines in Hawaii, got off the ground in 1985. They offer regularly scheduled flights from/to Kahului/Honolulu as well as specialty air tours. They fly 17-passenger Twin Otter aircraft. Their regularly scheduled flights are more expensive than the established commuter lines, while their air tours are about average. Call Maui Airlines at tel. 1-(800) 367-2920; Maui, 871-6201.

Whenever you fly **Royal Hawaiian**, or any of the commuter airlines, try to get as many stops as possible. Because they fly so low, it's like getting a free flightseeing tour. As always the costs are a bit more than the larger airlines, but it's more fun.

DOMESTIC CARRIERS

The following is a description of the major domestic carriers to and from Hawaii. The planes used are primarily DC10s and 747s with a smaller 727 thrown in here and there. A list of the "gateway" cities from which they fly "direct and non-stop" is given, but "connecting" cities are not. All flights by all carriers land at Honolulu International Airport except for American and Western which have a few direct flights, and United which flies direct to all major islands. The following lists only the established companies; entrepreneurial small airlines such as the now-defunct Hawaii Express pop up now and again and specialize in dirt cheap fares. There is a hectic frenzy to buy their tickets. Business is great for a while, then the established companies lower their fares and the gamblers fold.

United Airlines
Since their first island flight in 1947, United has become "top dog" in flights to Hawaii. Having just bought all of **Pan American's** Pacific routes, they'll dominate the field even more. Their mainland routes connect over 100 cities to Honolulu. The main gateways are direct flights from San Francisco, Los Angeles, San Diego, Seattle, Portland, Chicago, New York, Denver and Toronto. They also offer direct flights from San Francisco, Chicago, Portland, and Los Angeles to Maui; San Francisco and Los Angeles to Kauai and Kona on the Big Island; with a Los Angeles run to Hilo. United offers a number of packages ranging from a first-class "Classic Hawaii" to their more moderate "Affordable Hawaii." They interline with **Aloha Airlines** and offer special deals with **National Car Rental** among others. They're the "big guys" and they intend to stay that way—their packages are hard to beat. Call 1-(800) 652-1211.

Hawaiian Air
One of Hawaii's own domestic airlines has entered the mainland market. As of now, they operate a daily flight from Los Angeles and S.F. to Honolulu on 325-passenger L1011s. The "common fare" ticket price includes an on-going flight to any of the "Neighbor Islands," and if leaving from Hawaii, a free flight from a "Neighbor Island" to the link-up in Honolulu. Hawaiian has plans to expand, but for now they offer these reasonable flights from other cities in California. These are available through Sun-Trips at 1-(800) 662-9292. Other charter agents for Hawaiian include **International Travel Arrangers** for the Midwest, and

Conquest Tours of Toronto for Canada. Hawaiian flies from Honolulu to American Samoa and Tonga. Call Hawaiian at 1-(800) 367-5320.

World Airways
They still offer the cheapest air fares to Hawaii. The gateway cities are Los Angeles and Oakland with flights on a daily basis. Connecting flights come in from Kansas City and Newark and a lay-over may be necessary. Call 1-(800) 225-2500.

Pan American
The first commercial airline to fly the Pacific, they've been offering "Clipper Service" to Hawaii since 1936. United is taking over their Pacific routes, but as of now they still fly to the following. They connect with many mainland cities and offer flights from San Francisco and Los Angeles to Honolulu. They also connect Honolulu with Australia, New Zealand, Japan, the Philippines, Hong Kong and Guam. Call 1-(800) 652-1186.

American Airlines
Offers direct flights to Honolulu from Los Angeles, San Francisco, Dallas, and Chicago. They also fly from Los Angeles to Maui. Call 1-(800) 252-0421.

Western Airlines
They have a large share of the Hawaii market and offer numerous connecting flights from all over the country. Their gateway cities to Honolulu are Los Angeles, San Francisco, San Diego, Anchorage and Vancouver. Western now flies non-stop flights to Maui from Los Angeles departing daily at 1:40 p.m. Tel. 1-(800) 227-6105.

Continental
Flights to Honolulu from Los Angeles, Houston and Chicago. Also offers flights from Australia and New Zealand via Fiji. Connects with Air Micronesia to Guam. Call 1-(800) 525-0280.

Northwest Orient
Flights from Los Angeles, San Francisco, and Seattle via Portland. Onward flights to Tokyo, Osaka, Okinawa, Manila, Hong Kong, Taipei and Seoul. Call 1-(800) 225-2525.

Delta Airlines
In 1985, Delta entered the Hawaiian market

with non-stop flights to Honolulu from Atlanta and Dallas/Ft. Worth. Call 1-(800) 652-1330.

FOREIGN CARRIERS

The following carriers operate throughout Oceania but have no U.S. flying rights. This means that in order to vacation in Hawaii using one of these carriers, your flight must originate or terminate in a foreign city. You can have a stopover in Honolulu with a connecting flight to a "Neighbor Island." For example, if you've purchased a flight on Japan Airlines from San Francisco to Tokyo, you can stop in Hawaii, but you then must carry on to Tokyo. Failure to do so will result in a stiff fine, and the balance of your ticket will not be refunded.

Canadian Pacific Air
Flights from Canada to Honolulu originate in Vancouver, Edmonton, Toronto, and Calgary. Canadian Pacific also continues on to Fiji and Australia. Call 1-(800) 426-7007.

Air New Zealand
Flights link New Zealand, Australia and Fiji with Los Angeles via Honolulu. There is also a remarkable advance purchase fare (APEX) offered at a very reasonable price, which takes you from Los Angeles to Honolulu, with 11 stopovers throughout Oceania before deplaning in New Zealand. Call 1-(800) 262-1234.

Japan Air Lines
The Japanese are the second largest group, next to our fellow Americans, to visit Hawaii. JAL flights to Honolulu originate in Tokyo and Osaka. There are no JAL flights to or from the mainland from Hawaii. **Note:** both Japan's **All Nippon Airways** and Hawaii's **Aloha Airlines** are seeking expansion into this territory through bilateral agreements. Call 525-3663.

Philippine Airlines
Flights to and from Los Angeles and San Francisco to Manila via Honolulu. Connections in Manila to most Asian cities. Call 227-4600.

Qantas
Multiple weekly flights from San Francisco and Los Angeles to Sydney via Honolulu. Stopovers possible in New Caledonia, New Zealand, Fiji, and Tahiti. Call 622-0850.

China Airlines
They maintain routes from Los Angeles to Taipei with stopovers in Honolulu and Tokyo possible, but they are not available year-round. Connections from Taipei to most Asian capitals. Call 652-1428.

Korean Airlines
Some of the least expensive flights to Asia. Free stopovers from Los Angeles and San Francisco in both Honolulu and Tokyo on a RT ticket. One-way ticket allows only one stopover. Connections to many Asian cities. Call 421-8200.

Singapore Airlines
Flights to and from San Francisco and Los Angeles to Singapore via Honolulu. Free stopover. Additional stopovers in Taipei and Hong Kong, nominal fee. Call 742-3333.

Air Tungaru
Limited flights from Kiribati to Honolulu via Christmas Island and Tarawa. In Hawaii, call (808) 839-4561.

Air Niugini
Weekly flight from Honolulu to Papua New Guinea with connections to Japan, Australia, Hong Kong, Manila, and Singapore. In Hawaii, call (808) 531-5341.

Air Nauru
The South Pacific's richest island offers flights throughout Polynesia including most major islands with connections to Japan, Taipei, Hong Kong, Manila, Singapore, and Australia. In Hawaii, call (808) 531-9766.

South Pacific Island Airways
Grounded for awhile because of lack of sound-muffling "hush kits," SPIA is back in the air. Flights to Honolulu from Guam, Tahiti, American Samoa, Vancouver and Anchorage. Connecting flights to Port Moresby (Papua New Guinea), Belau, Pago Pago (American Samoa), Tonga, and Saipan. In Hawaii, call (808) 526-0844.

Samoa Airlines
Operates twice weekly flights to American Samoa from Honolulu. They're also trying for rights to Tonga and Tahiti. In Hawaii call (808) 537-2098.

Hawaiian Air

This domestic carrier operates flights to American Samoa and Tonga. Call (800) 367-5320; in Hawaii call (808) 537-5100.

Polynesian Airlines

Another domestic Hawaiian airlines is inaugurating flights to Western Samoa. In Hawaii call (808) 836-3838.

TOUR COMPANIES

Many tour companies offering packages to Hawaii appear in large city newspapers every week. They advertise very reasonable air fares, car rentals and accommodations. Without trying, you can get RT airfare from the West Coast and a week in Hawaii for $400 using one of these companies. The following are tour companies that offer great deals, and have excellent reputations. This list is by no means exhaustive.

Council Travel Services

These "full service" budget travel specialists are a subsidiary of the non-profit Council on International Educational Exchange, and the official U.S. representative to the International Student Travel Conference. They'll custom design their trips and programs for everyone from senior citizens to college students. Groups and business travelers are also welcome. They are dedicated to providing all of their clients with reliable low-cost transportation and travel services. They're simply the best in the business with offices coast to coast. For full information write to the main office of Council Travel Services, 919 Irving St., #102, San Francisco, CA 94122, tel. (415) 566-6222.

Student Travel Network

You don't have to be a student to avail yourself of their services. Their main office is at 2500 Wilshire Blvd., #920, Los Angeles, CA 90057, call (213) 380-2184. In Honolulu at 1831 S. King St., Honolulu, HI 96826, call (808) 942-7755. STN also maintains offices in San Diego, San Francisco, and Northridge, California, as well as throughout Australia.

Nature Expeditions International

These quality tours have nature as the theme. Their guides are experts in their fields and give personable and attentive service. Contact Nature Expeditions International at 474 Willamette, P.O. Box 11496, Eugene, OR 97440, tel. (503) 484-6529.

SunTrips

This California-based tour and charter company sells vacations all over the world. They're primarily a wholesale company, but will work with the general public. Contact SunTrips, 100 Park Center, P.O. Box 18505, San Jose, CA 95158, tel. (800) 662-9292.

Pacific Outdoor Adventures

This truly remarkable tour company offers the best in nature tours. The emphasis is on the outdoors with hiking, camping, and kayaking central. Prices are very hard to beat. Contact Pacific Outdoor Adventures, P.O. Box 61609, Honolulu, HI 96822, tel. (808) 988-3913.

Island Odysseys

A new company full of vim and vigor and out to please. They try to take care of everyone, offering everything from camping to sailing to luxury condos. Their prices are very competitive, with flights on Northwest Orient and Hawaiian Air. Contact Island Odysseys, 46-018 Kam Hwy., Suite 205, Kaneohe, HI 96744. In Hawaii, tel. (808) 235-6696, or toll free, 1-(800) 367-5696.

Island Holiday Tours

An established Hawaiian-based company that offers flights with United and American. Contact Island Holiday Tours, 2255 Kuhio Ave., Honolulu, HI 96815, call 1-(800) 448-6877.

Pleasant Hawaiian Holidays

A California-based company specializing in Hawaii. At 150 Powell St., Suite 406, San Francisco, CA 94102, call 1-(800) 242-9244.

Hawaiian Holidays

An Hawaiian-based company with plenty of experience. Featuring United, Hawaiian Air and National Car Rental. Contact Hawaiian Holidays, 2222 Kalakaua Ave, Honolulu, HI 96815, tel. 1-(800) 367-5040; in Hawaii, (808) 923-6548.

(Hawaii State Archives)

GETTING AROUND

If it's your intention to *see* Maui when you visit, and not just to lie on the beach in front of your hotel, the only efficient way is to rent a car. Limited public transportation, a few free shuttles, taxis, and the good old thumb are available, but all these are flawed in one way or another. Other unique and fun-filled ways to tour the island include renting a bike or moped, or hopping on a helicopter, but these conveyances are highly specialized and are more in the realm of sports than touring.

Public transportation

The **Grayline Airporter**, tel. 877-5507, will pick you up at or deliver you to Kahului Airport. It services all the popular destinations such as Lahaina/Kaanapali and Kihei/Wailea. At about $7 OW it's a slightly expensive but a no-hassle way to deal with arrival and departure, but out of the question for "every day" transportation. The Maui Transit System operates **The Blue Shoreline Bus**, tel. 661-3827, which is adequate in the limited area that it services. It runs primarily along

the SW coast between Lahaina and Kaanapali with connections to Napili and Kapalua. These runs are made every 15 minutes during business hours from 8:00 a.m. until 5:00 p.m., then every 30 minutes until 10:00 p.m. The Blue Shoreline Bus stops at all the Kaanapali resorts except for the Whaler; this westbound run is $1.50 no matter how far you go. Three runs a day go from Lahaina eastward to Wailea, with stops at Maalaea and Kihei enroute, $1.50-$3.50, depending on distance traveled.

There are also very limited shuttles operating in the major resort areas. The **Kaanapali Jitney**, which runs up and down the Kaanapali Beach area from 9:00 a.m. to 9:00 p.m., costs $2 for an all-day pass. The **Kapalua Shuttle** services all of the hotels and condos in Kapalua from 7:00 a.m. to 11:00 p.m. on an "on call" basis. Your hotel desk will make arrangements for you. The **Wailea Resorts Shuttle** is free and stops at all Wailea Beach hotels and condos from 6:30 a.m. until 10:30 p.m.

Taxis

About ten taxi companies on Maui more or less operate in a fixed area. Most, besides providing normal taxi service, also run tours all over the island. Taxis are expensive. For example, a ride from Kahului Airport to Kaanapali is $30 for about six people (about half this much to Kihei). Try Mita Taxi, at the airport, 871-4622; Kahului Taxi at 242-6404; Red and White Cabs in Lahaina at 661-3684; Lahaina Taxi, 661-4147; Wailea Taxi, 879-1059; Kihei Taxi, 879-3000.

Hitchhiking

The old tried-and-true method of hitchhiking — via extended thumb — is "out" on Maui! It's illegal, and if a policeman sees you, you'll be hassled, if not outright arrested. You've got to play the *game.* Simply stand on the side of the road facing traffic with a smile on your interesting face, but put away the old thumb. In other words, you can't actively solicit a ride. People know what you're doing; just stand there. You can get around quite well by thumb, if you're not on a schedule. The success rate of getting a ride to the number of cars that go by isn't that great, but you will get picked up. Locals and the average tourist with family will generally pass you by. Recent residents and single tourists will most often pick you up, and 90 percent of the time these will be white males. Hitching short hops along the resort beaches is easy. People can tell by the way you're dressed that you're not going far and will give you a lift. Catching longer rides to Hana or up to Haleakala can be done, but it'll be tougher because the driver will know that you'll be with them for the duration of the ride. Women, under no circumstances, should hitch alone.

RENTAL CARS

Maui has over 30 car rental agencies that can put you behind the wheel of anything from a Mercedes convertible to a used station wagon with chipped paint and torn upholstery. There are national companies, inter-island firms, good local companies and a few fly-by-nights that'll rent you a clunker. More than a dozen companies are clustered in little booths at the Kahului Airport, a few at Kaanapali, and none at Hana Airport, but your Hana hotel can arrange a car for you. The rest are scattered around the island with a heavy concentration on Dairy Rd. near Kahului airport. Those without an airport booth either have a courtesy phone or a number to call; they'll pick you up. Stiff competition tends to keep the prices more or less reasonable. Good deals are offered during off-season, with

The "Lahaina Jitney" is free and will take you to most tourist spots around town.

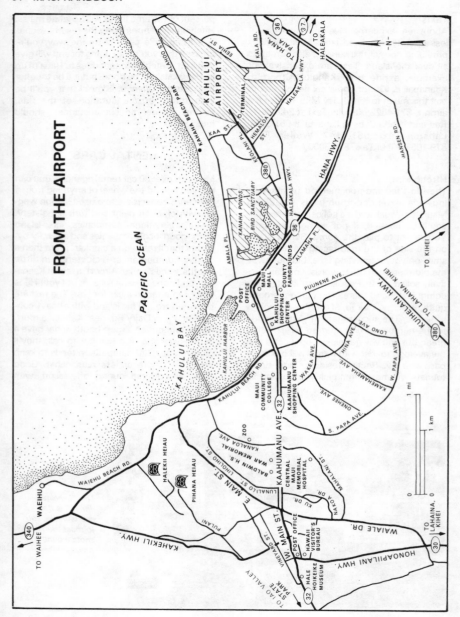

FROM THE AIRPORT

price wars flaring at anytime and making for real savings, but these unfortunately can't be predicted. Even with all these companies, it's best to book ahead. You might not save money, but you can save yourself headaches.

Tips

The best cars to rent on Maui happen to be the cheapest: sub-compacts with standard shift (if you can drive a standard!). Maui's main highways are broad and well paved, just like major roads on the mainland, but the backroads where all the fun is are narrow twisty affairs. You'll appreciate the down-shifting ability of standard transmissions on curves and steep inclines. If you get a big fatso luxury car, it'll be great for "puttin' on the ritz" at the resort areas, but you'll feel like a hippopotamus in the backcountry. If you've got that much money to burn, rent two cars! Try to get a car with cloth seats. Vinyl is too sticky, but sitting on your towel will help. You won't need a/c unless you plan on being in Lahaina a lot. The mile markers on back roads are great for pinpointing sites and beaches, and the lower number on these signs is the highway number, so you can always make sure that you're on the right road. The car rental agencies prohibit travel past Seven Sacred Pools on the other side of Hana, or around the top of the head of Maui. These roads are indeed rugged, but passable; the locals do it all the time. The car companies will warn you that your insurance "might" not cover you on these roads. They're really protecting their cars from being banged around. Traveling these roads is not recommended... for the faint hearted. Be careful, drive slowly and have fun!

Nationally known companies

The following are major firms that have booths at Kahului Airport. **National Car Rental** is one of the best of the nationally known firms. They have GMs, Nissans, Toyotas, Datsuns, vans, jeeps and station wagons. National offers excellent weekly rates especially on standard sub-compacts. All major credit cards are accepted. On Maui, call 877-5347. **Avis** is also located in Kaanapali. They feature late-model GM cars

as well as most imports and convertibles. Call Avis at 871-7575 or in Kaanapali at 661-4588. **Budget** offers competitive rates on a variety of late-model cars. At Kahului call 871-8811, in Kaanapali 661-4660. **Hertz,** perhaps the best known company, offers a wide variety of vehicles with some special weekly rates. Hertz has locations at Kaanapali and Wailea. Call 661-3195 and request the location nearest you. **Dollar** rents all kinds of cars, as well as jeeps and convertibles. At Kahului, call 877-6526; Kaanapali, 661-3037. **Alamo** has good weekly rates. Call 1-(800) 327-9633. For **Holiday,** call 877-2464.

Island companies

The following companies are based in Hawaii and either have a booth at the airport or pick-up service through courtesy phones. **Tropical Rent a Car** has a good reputation for service and prices. Also located at Kaanapali and Kihei, call 877-0002, or 661-0061. **Toms** has a good variety including luxury cars and convertibles. Use marked courtesy phones at the airport or call 871-7721. **El Cheapo** mostly lives up to its name and rents decent vehicles. Use courtesy phones or call 877-5851. **Word of Mouth** has late-model cars with cheaper rates on the older ones. Use courtesy phone or call 877-2436. **Rent a Wreck** has decent rates on late model cars and cheaper rates on older cars, call 877-5600. **Luxury Sports Car Rental** is good for stepping out in Corvettes, Porches, or Mercedes. Expensive; call 661-5646. **24 Karat Cars** has convertibles and luxury cars. Located in Kaanapali at 667-6289. **Roberts** has a good reputation, 877-5038. Others include: **Trans Maui,** 877-5222; **AAA,** 871-4610; **Andres,** 877-5378; **Convertibles Hawaii,** 877-0031; **Klunkers,** variable rates at 877-3197.

4-wheel drive

Though much more expensive than cars, some people might feel safer in them for completely circling Maui. Also unlike cars, the rental companies offering 4WDs put no restrictions on driving past the Sacred Pools or around the head. 4WDs can be had from **El Cheapo,** 877-5851; **Maui Rent a Jeep,**

877-6626; **Maui Sailing Center**, 877-3065; **Hertz**, 877-5167. Variable rates from company to company depend on availability and length of rental.

Camper rentals

A good alternative to staying in hotels or condos. You might also want to rent a camper for an overnight trip to Hana. The convenience will offset the extra cost, and might even save money over staying in a hotel. Unlike cars, campers carry a price per mile charge (about 6 cents). Since most campers sleep at least four people and provide all necessary gear, you might try splitting costs. **Beach Boy Campers** has a good reputation, renting economical Toyota and Nissan models, call 879-5322. Or try **Holo Holo Campers** at 877-5265.

Motorcycles and mopeds

Just for running around town or to the beach mopeds are great, but for real open-road exploring you'll need a cycle. Hourly rates average $5, and expect to pay about $25 for the day or up to $125 for the week. For motorcycles try **Aloha Funway Rentals** in Lahaina, 661-8702. They offer sizes from 185 to 1000cc. For mopeds: **Go Go Bikes** at the Kaanapali Transportation Center, call 661-3063 or 669-6669; **A & B Mopeds** at the Honokawai General Store, call 669-0027. Motorcycles and mopeds are rented by the hour, day or week.

BICYCLES

Bicycle enthusiasts should be thrilled with Maui, but the few flaws might flatten your spirits as well as your tires. The countryside is great, the weather is perfect, but the roads are heavily trafficked and the most interesting ones are narrow and have bad shoulders. Peddling to Hana will give you an up-close personal experience, but for bicycle safety this road is one of the worst. Haleakala is stupendous, but with a rise of more than 10,000 feet in less than 40 miles it is considered one of the most grueling rides in the world. A paved bike path runs from Lahaina to Kaanapali that's tame enough for everyone and you can even arrange a bicycle tour of Lahaina. In short, cycling on Maui as your primary means of transportation is not for the neophyte; because of safety considerations and the tough rides, only experienced riders should consider it.

For bike rentals, try: **Aloha Funway Rentals** in Lahaina at 661-8702; **Go Go Bikes Hawaii** in Kaanapali at 661-3063; **A & B Rentals** in Honokowai at 669-0027; **South Seas Rental** in Lahaina at 661-8655; **Cruiser Bob's** in Lahaina at 667-7717. Bikes rent for about $12 for a 24-hour period, and you can generally get a 3-speed, 10-speed, or a tandem. For bicycle sales, parts and repairs **The Cycle and Sports Shop** is well equipped and generous in their information about touring. They're at 2 locations: Maui Mall in Kahului at 877-5848, and in Lahaina at 661-4191.

Bicycle tours

An adventure on Maui that's quickly becoming famous is riding a specially equipped bike from the top of Mt. Haleakala for 40 miles to the bottom. A pioneer in this field is **Cruiser Bob's**, located at the Lahaina Travelodge (no longer a motel) at 667-7717. A courtesy van fetches you at your lodging, takes you to the summit, providing instructions along the way, and then you're fed a great breakfast. You start your downhill coast, then break for a gourmet lunch. It's as fantastic and fun filled as it sounds, but it costs around $80 and for that price good 'ole Bobby Boy has no trouble "cruising" to the bank! The main competition comes from **Bicycle Tours of Maui** at 879-3374, and **Coast to the Coast** at Captain Nemo's in Lahaina, call 661-4644. Essentially you get the same experience for about the same amount of money. For downhilling you have to be a good rider; those under 16 require parental release. These outfits offer tamer tours of Lahaina and the beach resorts with admissions into historical sites and museums included. There's no gripe with the Haleakala experience; it's guaranteed thrill, but the price is a bummer.

SIGHTSEEING TOURS

Tours are offered that will literally let you cover Maui from head to foot; you can walk it, drive it, sail around it, fly over it, or see it from below the water. Almost every major hotel has a tour desk from which you can book. Plenty of booking agencies are along Lahaina's wharf: on Front St. in Lahaina try **Tom Durkwood's Information Booth**, the only free-standing sidewalk booth in Lahaina, or **Visitor Info & Ticket Center** in the Wharf Shopping Complex at 661-5151. Call **Aloha Activity Center** in Kaanapali and Lahaina at 667-9564; in Kihei a good general purpose activities booth is **Activities Unlimited**, just across the street from Kalama Beach Park on Kihei Rd., 879-3688. **Ocean Activities Center** in Kihei, tel. 879-4485, can also book you into a wide variety of activities. Others are found in Wailea, Kahului and Napili.

Land tours

It's easy to book tours to Maui's famous areas such as Lahaina, Hana, Kula, Iao Valley, and Haleakala. Normally, they're offered on half- or full-day schedules (Hana is always a full day) and range anywhere from $17 to $50 with hotel pickup included. Big bus tours are run by **Grayline**, tel. 877-5507, and **Roberts**, tel. 877-5038. These tours are quite antiseptic as you sit behind tinted glass in an a/c bus. You get more personalized tours in the smaller vans, such as **Holo Holo Tours**, tel. 661-4858. Among other destinations they'll take you to Hana with a continental breakfast for $50. **Personalized Small Group Tours**, tel. 871-9551, goes to Hana for $40, or to Haleakala for $30. **No Kai Oi Tours** hits all the high spots and has competitive prices, tel. 871-9008; **Trans Hawaii Maui** specializes in all-day trips to Hana for $40, bring your own lunch, tel. 877-7308. **Maui Special Tours** shows you the sights with an old Maui hand, Jack Groenewout. His personalized tours are enhanced by a storehouse of information about Maui, tel. 879-9944.

The Sugar Cane Train

This is the most popular tour on Maui. The old steam engine puffs along from Lahaina to Kaanapali, a 25-min. ride each way, and costs $4.25 OW and $6.50 RT adults, $2 OW and $3.25 RT children to age 12. A free bus shuttles between Lahaina Station and the waterfront. The train runs throughout the day from 9:35 a.m. to 4:10 p.m. It's very popular so book in advance. All rides are narrated and there may even be a singing conductor. All kinds of tours are offered as well: some feature lunch, a tour of Lahaina with admission to the Baldwin House and the *Carthaginian,* and even a cruise on a glass-bottom boat. They're tame, touristy and fun. The price is right: the deluxe tour including RT train ride, lunch, Lahaina tour and an all-day Kaanapali Jitney pass for $15. Call the Lahaina Kaanapali and Pacific Railroad at tel. 661-0089.

Air tours

Maui is a spectacular sight from the air. Two small airlines and a handful of helicopter companies swoop you around the island. These joy rides are literally the highlight of many people's experience on Maui, but they are expensive. The excursions vary, but expect to spend at least $100 for a basic half-hour tour. The most spectacular ones take you into Haleakala crater, or perhaps to the remote West Maui mountains where inaccessible gorges lie at your feet. Other tours are civilized; expect a champagne brunch after you visit Hana. Still others take you to nearby Lanai or Molokai to view some of the world's most spectacular sea cliffs and remote beaches. Know, however, that many hikers and trekkers have a beef with the air tours: after they've spent hours, or maybe days, hiking into remote valleys in search of peace and quiet, out of the sky comes the mechanical whir of a chopper.

The two airlines operating from Kahului Airport are **Paragon Air** at 244-3356, and **Central Pacific Airlines** at 242-7894. The helicopter companies include: **Papillon Helicopters**, flying from Pineapple Hill in Kapalua, call 669-4884; **Kenai Helicopter**, which leaves from Kaanapali at 661-4427; **Awesome Maui Helicopter** at 661-8889; **Maui Helicopter Adventures,** located at the Intercontinental Hotel in Wailea, tel. 879-1601. All tours are narrated over specially designed earphones, and all helicopter companies will make special arrangements to drop off and pick up campers in remote areas.

OCEAN TOURS

You haven't really seen Maui unless you've seen it from the sea. Tour boats operating out of Maui's harbors take you fishing, whale watching, dining, diving, and snorkeling. You can find boats that offer all of these, or just sail you around for pure pleasure. Many take day trips to "The Pineapple Island" Lanai, or to Molokai with a visit to Kalaupapa Leper Colony included. Many visit Molokini, a submerged volcano with only half the crater rim above water, that has been designated as a Marine Life Conservation District. The vast majority of Maui's pleasure boats are berthed in Lahaina Harbor and most have a booth right there on the wharf where you can sign up. Other boats come out

of Maalaea with a few companies based in Kihei. If you're interested in snorkeling, scuba, fishing, sailing, water or jet skiing, parasailing, sailboarding, or being captain on your own sailboat, see "Sports" section.

The boats

The following are general tour boats that offer a variety of cruises. **The Lin Wa** is a glass-bottom boat that's a facsimile of a Chinese junk. One of the tamest and least expensive tours out of Lahaina Harbor, it departs six times a day from Slip #3 and charges $9.50 adults and $4.50 children. It gives you a tour just off Maui's shore and even goes for a whale watch in season. It's little more than a sea-going carnival ride. Call the *Lin Wa* at 661-3392, and remember that it's very popular. **The Coral See,** tel. 661-8600, is more of the same only it's a bit larger and offers a snorkel/picnic tour. For $39 (children half price) it provides equipment, lunch and an open bar. It's in Slip #1, Lahaina Harbor.

Trilogy Excursions, tel. 661-4713, is operated by the Coon Family. They run two trimarans: the 50-foot *Trilogy* and the 40-foot *Kailana,* which carries up to 35 passengers to Lanai. For $85 you get breakfast, then fish

waiting to board the Lin Wa

and snorkel on your way to Lanai. Once there you anchor in Manele Bay and after a tour of the island you come back to an excellent barbecue. An all-day affair, it provides a sampling of Maui's ocean activities.

Windjammer Cruises, tel. 667-6834, offers similar trips to Lanai aboard their 65-foot, three-masted schooner. They pack in over 100 passengers and on weekends feature a lunch at the Hotel Lanai in place of the barbecue. **Seabird Cruises,** tel. 661-3643, takes day trips to Lanai or Molokai for $59. Over 100 passengers fit aboard their two 65-foot catamarans, *Aikane II* and *Ono Mana*. They also run the 65-foot *Viajero* that carries 35 passengers. They feature a Kalaupapa Tour on Molokai. Seabird Cruises also offers a sunset cocktail sail for $22 and a snorkel-and-dinner sail for $32. **Unicorn Tours,** tel. 879-6333, takes 50 passengers on *Unicorn I* to Lanai or Molokai on half-day excursions or to both on full-day trips. Prices are $36 to Lanai, $56 to Molokai, and $80 for both. Food and island tours are included. **Captain Nemo's Emporium,** tel. 661-5555, located on Front St., sails *Seasmoke,* a 58-foot catamaran (built for James Arness and reported to be the fastest "cat" on the island) to Lanai on a snorkel and diving run. They leave at 8:00 a.m. and return at 2:00 p.m. and serve breakfast and lunch for $65.

These companies also have dinner sails, cocktail sails and whale watches for much cheaper prices, but they tend to pack them in so tight that they're known derisively as "cattle boats." Don't expect the personal attention you'd receive on smaller boats. However, all the boats going to Molokai or Lanai will take passengers for the OW trip. You won't participate in the snorkeling or the food, but the prices (negotiable) are considerably cheaper. This extra service is offered only if there's room. Talk to the individual captains.

Sunset cruises
These romantic cruises are very popular and are available from many boats. They last for about two hours and cost $20-$30 for the basic cruise. If cocktails or dinner is added

the price goes up. **Alihilani Yacht Charters,** tel. 661-3047, will sail you out of Lahaina at sunset on its teak and mahogany 40-foot yacht for $25. They also trip to Lanai for $52 and will take you snorkeling for $40. **Kaulana Cruises,** tel. 667-2518, offers a dinner sail for $32 and a cocktail sail for $20 (children half price) on its 70-foot catamaran. They also sail a picnic/snorkel to Lanai. **Scotch Mist,** tel. 661-0386, has two racing yachts, *Scotch Mist I* and *II*. They are the oldest sailing charters on Maui (1970) and claim to be the fastest sailboats in the harbor: boasting the lightest boat, the biggest sail and the best crew. They'll cruise, snorkel (varying prices) or take their 19 passengers on a sunset sail complete with champagne for $33 or $25, depending on which boat.

Out of Kihei you might try the **Maui Sailing Center,** tel. 879-5935, which takes six passengers on its Cal 27 for a full-day snorkel sail to Molokini departing from Maalaea harbor. From Wailea's Ulua Beach you can board the 65-foot *Wailea Kai* catamaran along with 90 others for a picnic/snorkel outing to Molokini. They also offer a popular dinner sail. Contact **Ocean Activities Center,** tel. 879-4485. From Kaanapali the **Sea Sails** makes an evening dinner sail from its anchorage at the Sheraton Beach. Contact **Sea Sport Activities Center** at 667-2759.

Whale watching
Anyone on Maui from Nov. to April gets the added treat of watching humpback whales as they frolic in their feeding grounds just off Lahaina, one of the world's major wintering areas for the humpback. Almost every boat in the harbor runs a special whale watch during this time of year. A highly educational whale watch is sponsored by the **Pacific Whale Foundation,** located in Kihei at Azeka Plaza, tel. 879-6530. A non-profit organization dedicated to the study and preservation of the whale, their extremely popular three-hour whale watch takes place only on Sundays aboard *Aikane II,* operated by **Seabird Cruises,** tel. 661-3643.

If you're at all interested in whales, visit **Greenpeace** at 628 Front St., Lahaina, tel.

Doug Duncan of Greenpeace

667-2059. Here, Doug Duncan, the office manager, is full of enthusiasm and information about whales. Greenpeace has an educational video on whales, and can book you on a wide variety of whale watching cruises. It costs no more to book through Greenpeace and part of your ticket price becomes a tax-deductible donation to the **"Save The Whales"** campaign.

Since Lahaina Harbor is an attraction in itself, just go there and stroll along to hand-pick your own boat. Many times the whale watch is combined with a snorkel and picnic sail so prices vary accordingly. Two of the cheapest are aboard the *Lin Wa* and the *Coral See.* Others include the *Mareva,* tel. 661-4522, berthed in Slip #63, a 38-foot sloop which will take you out for a half-day whale watch for $30. *The Kamehameha* is a 15-foot catamaran for snorkeling or whale watching at $17. This "cat" is in Slip #67, tel. 661-4522.

If Lahaina is too frenetic for your tastes, head for Kihei where you can get a boat out of Maalaea. Try booking through **The Dive Shop,** tel. 879-5172. They might book you on the *Maui Diamond,* skippered by Capt. Dave Ventura, berthed in Maalaea Harbor; you couldn't make a better choice of sporting boat. Book through the Dive Shop or through Capt. Dave directly, tel. 879-9119. For further information on whales, see "Flora and Fauna."

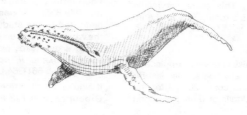

by Fritz Kraft, ca. 1920

ACCOMMODATIONS

With over 12,000 rooms available, and more being built every day, Maui is second only to Oahu in the number of visitors it can accommodate. There's a tremendous concentration of condos on Maui, plenty of hotels, and a growing number of Bed and Breakfasts. Camping is limited to a handful of parks, but what it lacks in number it easily makes up for in quality.

Tips

Maui has an **off-season** like all of Hawaii, which runs from after Easter to just before Christmas, with the fall months being particularly beautiful. During this period you can save 25 percent or more on accommodations. If you'll be staying for over a week, get a condo with cooking facilities or a room with at least a refrigerator; you can save a bundle on food costs. You'll pay more for an ocean view, but along Maui's entire south shore from Kapalua to Wailea, you'll have a cheaper and cooler room if you're mountainside, away from the sun.

Your choices

Over 80 hotels and condos have sprouted on West Maui from Kapalua to Lahaina. The most expensive are in **Kaanapali** and include the Hyatt Regency, Marriott, Maui Surf and Sheraton, strung along some of Maui's best beaches. The older condos just west in Honokawai are cheaper, with a mixture of expensive and moderate as you head toward Kapalua. **Lahaina** itself offers only a handful of places to stay: condos at both ends of town, and the famous non-luxury Pioneer Inn. Most people find the pace a little too hectic, but you couldn't get more in the middle of *it* if you tried. **Maalaea Bay**, between Lahaina and Kihei, has over 20 quiet condos and a few hotels. Prices are reasonable, the beaches are fair, and you're in striking distance of the action in either direction.

Kihei is "condo row," with over 50 of them along the six miles of Kihei Ave., plus a few hotels. This is where you'll find top-notch beaches and the best deals on Maui. **Wailea** just up the road is expensive, but the hotels here are world class and the secluded beaches are gorgeous. **Kahului** often takes the rap for being an unattractive place to stay on Maui. It isn't all that bad. You're smack in the middle of striking out to the best of Maui's sights, and the airport is minutes away for people staying only a short time. Prices are cheaper and Kanaha Beach is a sleeper, with great sand, surf, and few visitors. **Hana** is an experience in itself. You can camp, rent a cabin, or stay at an exclusive hotel. Always reserve in advance and consider splitting your stay on Maui, spending your last few nights in Hana. You can really soak up this wonderful area, and you won't have to worry about rushing back along the Hana Highway.

Hotel Amenities

All hotels have some of them, and some hotels have all of them. Air conditioning is available in most, but under normal circumstances you won't need it. Balmy tradewinds provide plenty of breezes, which flow through louvered windows and doors in many hotels. Casablanca room fans are better. TVs are often included in the rate, but not always. In-room phones are provided, but a service charge is usually tacked on, even for local calls. Swimming pools are very common, even though the hotel may sit right on the beach. There is always a restaurant of some sort, a coffee shop or two, a bar, cocktail lounge, and sometimes a sundries shop. Some hotels also offer tennis courts or golf courses either as part of the premises or affiliated with the hotel; usually an "activities desk" can book you into a variety of daily outings. Plenty of hotels offer laundromats on the premises, and hotel towels can be used at the beach. Bellhops get about $1 per bag, and maid service is free, though maids are customarily tipped between $1-$2 per day and a bit more if kitchenettes are involved. Parking is free. Hotels can often arrange special services like babysitters, all kinds of lessons, and often special entertainment activities. A few even have bicycles and some snorkeling equipment to lend. They'll receive and send mail for you, cash your traveler's cheques and take messages.

Condominiums

The method of paying for and reserving a condo is just about the same as for a hotel. However, requirements for deposits, final payments, and cancellation charges are much stiffer than in hotels. Make absolutely sure you fully understand all of these requirements when you make your reserva-

tions. The main qualitative difference between a condo and a hotel is in amenities. At a condo, you're more on your own. You're temporarily renting an apartment, so there won't be any bellhops, rarely a bar, restaurant or lounge on the premises, though many times you'll find a sundries store. The main lobby, instead of having that grand entrance feel of many hotels, is more like an apartment house entrance, although there might be a front desk. Condos can be efficiencies (one big room), but mostly they are one- or multiple-bedroom affairs with a complete kitchen. Reasonable housekeeping items should be provided: linens, all furniture, and a fully-equipped kitchen. Most have TVs and phones, but remember that what is available is all up to the owner. You can find brand new furnishings that are top of the line, right down to "garage sale" bargains. Inquire about their condition when you make your reservations. Maid service might be included on a limited basis (for example once weekly), or you might have to pay for it if you require a maid.

Condos usually require a minimum stay, although some will rent on a daily basis, like hotels. Minimum stays when applicable are often three days, but seven is also commonplace, and during peak season, two weeks isn't unheard of. Swimming pools are common, and depending on the "theme" of the condo, you can find saunas, weight rooms, jacuzzis, and tennis courts. Rates are about 10-15 percent higher than comparable hotels, with hardly any difference between doubles and singles. A nominal extra is charged for more than two people, and condos can normally accommodate 4 to 6 guests. You can find clean, decent condos for as little as $200 per week, all the way up to exclusive apartments for well over $1000. Their real advantage is for families, friends who want to share, and especially long-term stays where you will always get a special rate. The kitchen facilities save a great deal on dining costs, and it's common to find units with their own mini-washers and dryers. Parking space is ample for guests, and like hotels, plenty of stay/drive deals are offered. You'll find condos all over Hawaii, but they're particularly prevalent on Maui.

Hotel/condominium information

The best source of hotel/condo information is the **Hawaii's Visitors Bureau**. While planning your trip, either visit one nearby or write to them in Hawaii. (Addresses are given in the "Visitor's Bureau" section.) Request a copy of their free and current **Member Accommodation Guide**. This handy booklet lists all the hotel/condo members of the HVB. Listings include the addresses, phone numbers, facilities and rates. General tips are also given.

BED AND BREAKFAST

Bed and Breakfasts are hardly a new idea. The Bible talks of the hospitable hosts who opened the gates of their homes and invited the wayfarer in to spend the night. Bed and Breakfasts (B&Bs) have a long tradition in Europe, and were commonplace in Revolutionary America. Now, lodging in a private home called a Bed and Breakfast is becoming increasingly fashionable throughout America, and Hawaii is no exception. Not only can you "visit" Maui, you can "live" there for a time with a host family and share an intimate experience of daily life.

Points to consider

The primary feature of Bed and Breakfast homes is that every one is privately owned, and therefore uniquely different from any other. The range of B&Bs is as wide as the living standards in America. You'll find everything from semi-mansions in the most fashionable residential areas to little grass shacks offered by a down-home fisherman and his family. This means that it's particularly important for you to choose a host family with whom your lifestyle is compatible. Unlike a hotel or a condo, you'll be living *with* a host and most likely his family, although your room will be private, with private baths and separate entranceways being quite common. You don't just "check in" to a Bed and Breakfast. In Hawaii you go through agencies (listed below) which act as a "go between," matching host and guest. Write to them and they'll send you a booklet with a complete description of the Bed and Breakfast, its general location, the fees charged and a good idea of the lifestyle of your host family. With the reservations application they'll include a questionnaire that will basically determine your profile: are you single? children? smoker? etc., as well as arrival and departure dates and all pertinent particulars. Since Bed and Breakfasts are run by individual families, the times that they will accept guests can vary according to what's happening in their lives. This makes it imperative to write well in advance: three months is good; earlier (six months) is too long and too many things can

Relax and enjoy la dolce vita.

change. Four weeks is about the minimum time required to make all necessary arrangements. Expect a minimum stay (three days is common) and a maximum stay. Bed and Breakfasts are not "long-term" housing, although it's hoped that guest and host will develop a friendship and future stays can be as long as both desire.

B&B Agencies

A top notch B&B agency is **Bed and Breakfast Hawaii**, operated by Evelyn Warner and Al Davis. They've been running this service since 1978. B&B Hawaii has a membership fee of $5 yearly. For this they mail you their "Directory of Homes," a periodic "hot sheet" of new listings, and all pertinent guest applications. Write, Bed and Breakfast Hawaii, Box 449, Kapaa HI 96746. Phone info and reservations at (808) 822-1582. Another B&B agency with a good reputation is **Go Native Hawaii**. They'll send you a directory and all needed informa-

tion by writing to their mainland address at P.O. Box 13115, Lansing MI 48901, or in Hawaii at 130 Puhili St., Hilo HI 96720. **Go Native** will also accept collect calls from travelers already in Hawaii at (808) 961-2080. Another is **Bed and Breakfast Pacific Hawaii**, 19 Kainani Pl., Kailua HI 96734, tel. 262-6026. Information on B&Bs can also be obtained from the **American Board of Bed and Breakfast Assn.**, Box 23294, Washington D.C. 20026.

Home exchanges

One other method of staying in Hawaii, open to homeowners, is to offer the use of their home for a home in Hawaii. This is done by listing your home with an agency that facilitates the exchange and publishes a descriptive directory. To list your home and to find out what is available, write: Vacation Exchange Club, 12006 111 Ave., Youngtown AZ 85363; or, Interservice Home Exchange, Box 87, Glen Echo MD 20812.

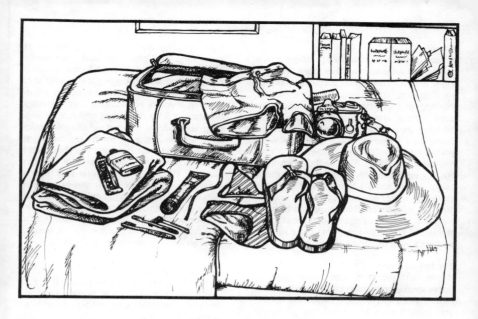

WHAT TO TAKE

It's a snap to pack for a visit to Maui. Everything is on your side. The weather is moderate and uniform on the whole, and the style of dress is delightfully casual. The rule of thumb is to pack lightly: few items, and light clothing both in color and weight. What you'll need will depend largely on your itinerary, and your desires. Are you drawn to the nightlife, the outdoors, or both? If you forget something at home, it won't be a disaster. You can buy everything you'll need in Hawaii. As a matter of fact, Hawaiian clothing, such as *muumuus* and *aloha* shirts, are some of the best purchases you can make, both in comfort and style. It's quite feasible to bring only one or two changes of clothing with the express purpose of outfitting yourself while there. Prices on bathing suits, bikinis and summer wear in general are quite reasonable.

Basic necessities
As previously mentioned, you really have to consider only two "modes" of dressing in Hawaii: beachwear and casual clothing. The following is designed for the mid-range traveler carrying one suitcase or a backpack.

Remember there are laundromats and you'll be spending a considerable amount of time in your bathing suit. Consider the following: one or two pair of light cotton slacks for going out and about, and one pair of jeans for trekking, or better yet, corduroys which can serve both purposes; two to three casual sundresses—*muumuus* are great; three or four pair of shorts for beachwear and for sightseeing; four to five short-sleeved shirts or blouses and one long-sleeved; three to four colored and printed T-shirts that can be worn anytime from trekking to strolling; a beach cover-up with the short terry cloth-type being the best; a brimmed hat for rain and sun—the crushable floppy type is great for purse or daypack; two to three pairs of socks are sufficient, nylons you won't need; two bathing suits, nylon ones dry quickest; plastic bags to hold wet bathing suits and laundry; five to six pairs of underwear; towels (optional, because hotels provide them, even for the beach); a first aid kit (see below), pocket size is sufficient; suntan lotion; insect repellent; a daypack or large beach purse; and don't forget your windbreaker, perhaps a shawl for the evening, and a universal jogging suit.

Shoes

Dressing your feet is hardly a problem. You'll most often wear zoris (rubber thongs) for going to and from the beach, leather sandals for strolling and dining, and jogging shoes for trekking and sightseeing. A few discos require leather shoes, but it's hardly worth bringing them just for that. If you plan on heavy-duty trekking, you'll definitely want your hiking boots. Lava, especially *a'a*, is murderous on shoes. Most backcountry trails are rugged and muddy, and you'll need those good old lug soles for traction. If you plan moderate hikes, you might want to consider bringing rubberized ankle supports to complement your jogging shoes. Most drug stores sell them, and the best are a rubberized sock with toe and heel cut out.

For the camper

If you don't want to take it with you, all necessary camping gear can be purchased or rented while in Hawaii. Besides the above, you should consider taking the following: framed backpack or the convertible packs that turn into suitcases, daypack, matches in a waterproof container, all-purpose knife, mess kit, eating utensils, flashlight (remove batteries), candle, nylon cord, and sewing kit (dental floss works as thread). Take a first aid kit containing bandaids, all-purpose antiseptic cream, alcohol swabs, tourniquet string, cotton balls, elastic bandage, razor blade, telfa pads, and a small mirror to view private nooks and crannies. A light sleeping bag is good, although your fleecy jogging suit with a ground pad and covering of a light blanket or even your rain poncho will be sufficient. Definitely bring a down bag for Haleakala or mountainous areas, and in a film container pack a few nails, safety pins, fish hooks, line and bendable wire. Nothing else does what these do and they're all handy for a million and one uses.

In the cold and rain

Two occasions for which you'll have to consider dressing warm are visiting the top of mountains, and going for boat rides where wind and ocean sprays are a factor. You can conquer both with a jogging suit (sweat suit) and a featherweight, water-resistant windbreaker. If you're intending to visit Haleakala on Maui, it'll be downright chilly. Your jogging suit with a hooded windbreaker/raincoat will do the trick for all occasions. If you're going to camp or trek, you should add another layer, the best being a woolen sweater. Wool is the only fiber that retains most of its warmth-giving properties even if it gets wet. If your hands get cold, put a pair of socks over them. Tropical rain showers can happen at any time, so you might consider a fold-up umbrella; but the sun quickly breaks through and the warming winds blow.

Specialty items

Following is a list of specialty items that you might wish to consider bringing along. They're not necessities but most will definitely come in handy. A pair of binoculars really enhances sightseeing—great for watching birds, sweeping panoramas, and almost a necessity if you're going whale watching. A folding teflon-bottomed travel iron makes up for cotton's one major shortcoming, wrinkles, and you can't always count on hotels having irons. Nylon twine and miniature clothespins for drying garments, especially bathing suits. Commercial and hotel laundromats abound, but many times you'll get by with hand washing a few items in the sink. A transistor radio/tape recorder provides news, weather, entertainment and can be used to record impressions, island music and a running commentary for your slide show. Hair dryer: although the wind can be relied on to dry, it leaves a bit to be desired in the styling department. An inflatable raft for riding waves, along with flippers, mask and snorkel, can easily be bought in Hawaii, but don't weigh that much or take up much space in your luggage.

FOOD AND DRINK

Hawaii is a gastronome's Shangri La, a sumptuous smorgasbord in every sense of the word. The considerable array of ethnic groups that have come to Hawaii in the last 200 years have brought their own special enthusiasm and culture, and lucky for all, they didn't forget their cook pots, hearty appetites, and exotic taste buds. The Polynesians who first arrived found a fertile but barren land. Immediately they set about growing their taro, coconuts and bananas, and raising chickens, pigs, fish, and even dogs, though these were reserved for the nobility. Harvests were bountiful and the islanders thanked the gods with a traditional feast called the *luau*. An underground oven, the *imu*, baked most of the dishes, and participants were encouraged to feast while relaxing on straw mats and enjoying the *hula* and various entertainments. The *luau* is as popular as ever, a treat that's guaranteed to delight anyone with a sense of eating adventure.

Missionaries and sailors came next; their ships' holds carried barrels of ingredients for puddings, pies, dumplings, gravies, and roasts — the sustaining "American foods" of New England farms. The mid-1800s saw the arrival of boatloads of Chinese and Japanese peasants, who wasted no time making rice instead of bread the islands' staple. Chinese added their exotic spices, creating complex Szechuan dishes, as well as workingmen's basics like chop suey, while the Japanese introduced *shoyu, sashimi,* boxed *(bento)* lunches, delicate *tempura,* and rich, filling noodle soups. The Portuguese brought their luscious Mediterranean dishes with tomatoes and peppers surrounding plump spicy sausages, nutritious bean soups, and mouthwatering sweet treats like *malasadas* and *pao dolce* (sweet bread). Koreans carried crocks of zesty *kimchi,* and quickly fired up barbecue pits for *pulgogi,* a traditional marinated beef cooked over an open fire. Filipinos served up their mouthwatering *adobo* stews of fish, meat or chicken in a rich sauce of vinegar and garlic.

Recently, Thai and Vietnamese restaurants have been offering their irresistible dishes side by side with fiery burritos from Mexico and elegant Marsala cream sauces from France. The ocean breezes of Hawaii not only cool the skin, but on them waft some of the most delectable aromas on earth, to make the tastebuds thrill and the spirit soar.

HAWAIIAN FOOD

Hawaiian foods, oldest of all island dishes, are wholesome, well prepared and delicious. All you have to do on arrival is notice the size of some of the local boys (and women) to know immediately that food to them is indeed a happy and serious business. An oft-heard island joke is that "local men don't eat until they're full, they eat until they're tired." Many Hawaiian dishes have become standard fare at a variety of restaurants, eaten one time or another by anyone who spends time in the islands. Hawaiian food in general is called *kaukau,* cooked food is *kapahaki,* and something broiled is called *kaola.* All of these prefixes on a menu will let you know that Hawaiian food is served. Usually inexpensive, it will definitely fill you and keep you going.

Traditional favorites

In old Hawaii, although the sea meant life, many more people were involved with cultivating beautifully tended garden plots of taro, sugarcane, breadfruit, and various sweet potatoes *(uala)* than fishing. They husbanded pigs and barkless dogs *(ilio),* and prized *moa* (chickens) for their feathers and meat, but found eating the eggs repulsive. The only farming implement that they had was the *o'o,* a sharpened hardwood digging stick. The Hawaiians were the best farmers of Polynesia, and the first thing they planted was taro, a tuberous root that was created by the gods at the same time as man. This main staple of the old Hawaiians was made into *poi.* Every *luau* will have poi, a glutinous purple paste made from pounded taro root. It comes in liquid consistencies referred to as "one-, two-, or three-finger *poi.*" The fewer fingers you need to eat it, the thicker it is. *Poi* is one of the most nutritious carbohydrates known, but people unaccustomed to it find it bland and tasteless, although some of the best, fermented for a day or so, has an acidic bite. *Poi* is made to be eaten *with* something, but locals who love it pop it in their mouths and smack their lips. However, those unaccustomed to it will suffer constipation if they eat too much.

A Hawaiian family eating poi *as depicted by A. Plum, ca. 1846 (Hawaii State Archives).*

A tasty popular dessert is *haupia,* a custard made from coconut. *Limu* is a generic term for edible seaweed, which many people still gather from the shoreline and eat as a salad, or mix with ground *kukui* nuts and salt as a relish. A favorite Hawaiian snack is *opihi,* small shellfish (limpets) that cling to rocks. People gather them, always leaving some on the rocks for the future. Cut from the shell and eaten raw by all peoples of Hawaii, as testament to their popularity they sell for $150 per gallon in Honolulu. A general term that has come to mean *hors d'oeuvres* in Hawaii is *pu pu.* Originally the name of a small shell fish, now everyone uses it for any "munchy" that's considered a finger food. A traditional liquor made from *ti* root is *okolehao.* It literally means "iron bottom," reminiscent of the iron blubber pots used to ferment it.

TROPICAL FRUITS AND VEGETABLES

Some of the most memorable taste treats from the islands require no cooking at all: the luscious tropical and exotic fruits and vegetables sold in markets and roadside stands, or found just hanging on trees, waiting to be picked. Make sure to experience as many as possible. The general rule in Hawaii is that you are allowed to pick fruit on public lands, but it should be limited to personal consumption. The following is a sampling of some of Hawaii's best produce.

Passionfruit
Known by their island name of *lilikoi,* they make excellent juice and pies. They're a small yellow fruit (similar to lemons but smooth-skinned) mostly available in summer and fall, and many wild ones grow on vines, waiting to be picked. Slice off the stem end, scoop the seedy pulp out with your tongue, and you'll know why they're called "passionfruit."

Avocados
Brought from South America, avocados were originally cultivated by the Aztecs. They have a buttery consistency and a nutty flavor. Hundreds of varieties in all shapes and

colors are available fresh year-round. They have the highest fat content of any fruit next to the olive.

Coconuts
What tropical paradise would be complete without coconuts? Indeed, these were some of the first plants brought by the Polynesians. When children were born, coconut trees were planted for them so they'd have fruit throughout their lifetime. Truly tropical fruits, they know no season. Drinking nuts are large and green, and when shaken you can hear the milk inside. You get about a quart of fluid from each. It takes skill to open one, but a machete can handle anything. Cut the stem end flat so that it will stand, then bore a hole into the pointed end and put in a straw or hollow bamboo. Coconut water is slightly acidic and helps to balance alkaline foods. Spoon meat is a custard-like gel on the inside of drinking nuts. Sprouted coconut meat is also an excellent food. Split open a sprouted nut, and inside is the yellow fruit, like a moist sponge cake. "Millionaire's salad" is made from the heart of a coconut palm. At one time an entire tree was cut down to get to the heart, which is just inside the trunk below the fronds and is like an artichoke heart except that it's about the size of a watermelon. In a downed tree, the heart stays good for about two weeks.

breadfruit

Breadfruit
This is a staple of the islands that provides a great deal of carbohydrates, but many people find the baked, boiled or fried fruit bland. It grows all over the islands and is really thousands of little fruits growing together to form a ball.

Mangos
These are some of the most delicious fruits known to humans. They grow wild all over the islands; the ones on the leeward sides of the islands ripen from April to June, while the ones on the windward sides can last until October. They're found in the wild on trees up to 60 feet tall, and the problem is to stop eating them once you start!

Papaya
This truly tropical fruit has no real season but is mostly available in the summer. They grow on branchless trees and are ready to pick as soon as any yellow appears. Of the many varieties, the "solo papaya," meant to be eaten by one person, is the best. Split them in half, scrape out the seeds and have at them with a spoon.

Bananas
No tropical island is complete without them. There are over 70 species in Hawaii, with hundreds of variations. Some are for peeling and eating while others are cooked. A "hand" of bananas is great for munching, backpacking, or just picnicking. Available everywhere—and cheap.

common banana

Guava
These small round yellow fruits are abundant in the wild where they are ripe from early summer to late fall. Considered a pest—so pick all you want. A good source of Vitamin C, they're great for juice, jellies, and desserts.

macadamia nuts

The king of nuts was brought from Australia in 1892. Now it's the state's fourth largest agricultural product. Available roasted, candied, or buttered.

litchi

Called nuts but really a small fruit with a thin red shell. They have a sweet and juicy white flesh when fresh, and appear like nuts when dried.

potpourri

Beside the above, you'll find pineapple, oranges, limes, kumquats, thimbleberries, and blackberries, as well as carambolas, wild cherry tomatoes, and tamarinds.

MUNCHIES AND ISLAND TREATS

Certain "finger foods," fast foods, and island treats are unique to Hawaii. Some are a meal in themselves, but others are just snacks. Here are some of the best, and most popular.

Pu pu

Pronounced as in "Winnie the Pooh Pooh," these are little finger foods and *hors d'oeuvres*. They're everything from crackers to cracked crab. Often, they're given free at lounges and bars and can even include chicken drumettes, fish kabobs, and tempura. A good display of them and you can have a free meal.

Crack seed

A sweet of Chinese origin, these are preserved and seasoned fruits and seeds. Some favorites include coconut, watermelon, pumpkin seeds, mango, and papaya. Different tasting, they take some getting used to, but make great "trail snacks." Available in all island markets. Also look for dried fish (cuttlefish) on racks, usually near the "crack seed." These are nutritious and delicious and make a great snack.

Shave ice

This real island institution makes the mainland "snow cone" melt into in-significance. Special machines literally "shave ice" to a fluffy consistency. It's mounded into a paper cone and you choose from dozens of exotic island syrups that are generously poured over it. You're given a straw and a spoon, and just slurp away.

Malasadas and *pao dolce*

Two sweets from the Portuguese. *Malasadas* are holeless donuts and *pao dolce* is sweet bread. They're sold in island bakeries and they're great for breakfast or just as a treat.

Lomilomi salmon

This is a salad of salmon, tomatoes, and onions with garnish and seasonings. Often accompanies "plate lunches" and featured at buffets and *luaus*.

EXOTIC ISLAND DRINKS

To complement the fine dining in the islands, the bartenders have been busy creating their own tasty concoctions. The full range of beers, wines, and standard drinks is served in Hawaii, but for a real treat you should try some mixed drinks inspired by the islands. A locally brewed beer is "Primo." At one time brewed only in Hawaii, it's also made on the mainland now. A serviceable American brew in the German style, like others it lacks that full, hearty flavor of the European beers. "Kona Coffee" is the only coffee grown in America. It comes from the Kona District of the Big Island and is a rich, aromatic, truly fine coffee. If it's offered on the menu, have a cup.

Drinking laws

There are no "state" liquor stores; all kinds of spirits, wines, and beers are available in markets and shops, generally open during normal business hours, seven days a week. The drinking age is 18, and no towns are "dry." Legal hours for serving drinks depend on the type of establishment. Hours generally are: hotels, 6:00 a.m. to 4:00 a.m.; discos, and nightclubs where there is dancing, 10:00 a.m. to 4:00 a.m.; bars, lounges where there is no dancing, 6:00 a.m. to 2:00 a.m. Most restaurants serve alcohol, and in many that don't, you can bring your own.

Exotic drinks

To make your experience complete, you must order one of these colorful island drinks. Most look very innocent because they come in pineapples, coconut shells, or tall frosted glasses. They're often garnished with little umbrellas or sparklers, and most have enough fruit in them to give you your vitamins for the day. Rum is used as the basis of many of them. It's been an island favorite since it was introduced by the whalers of last century. Here are some of the most famous: *mai tai,* a mixture of light and dark rum, orange curacao, orange and almond flavoring and lemon juice; *chi chi,* a simple concoction of vodka, pineapple juice and coconut syrup, real sleeper because it tastes like a milk shake; Blue Hawaii, vodka and blue curacao; Planter's Punch, light rum, grenadine, bitters and lemon juice. Great thirst quencher; Singapore Sling, a sparkling mixture of gin, cherry brandy and lemon juice.

FISH AND SEAFOOD

Anyone who loves fresh fish and seafood has come to the right place. Island restaurants specialize in seafood, and it's available everywhere. Pound for pound, seafood is one of the best dining bargains on Maui. You'll find it served in every kind of restaurant, and often the fresh catch of the day is proudly displayed on ice in a glass case. The following is a sampling of the best.

Mahi mahi

This excellent eating fish is one of the most common and least expensive in Hawaii. It's referred to as a "dolphin," but is definitely a fish, not a mammal at all. *Mahi* can weigh 10-65 pounds; the flesh is light and moist. This fish is broadest at the head. When caught it's a dark olive color, but after a while the skin turns irridescent—blue, green and yellow. Can be served as a main course, or as a patty in a fish sandwich.

A'u

This true island delicacy is a broadbill swordfish or marlin. It's expensive even in Hawaii because the damn thing's so hard to catch. The meat is moist and white and truly superb. If it's offered on the menu, order it. It'll cost a bit more, but you won't be disappointed.

Ono

Ono means "delicious" in Hawaiian so that should tip you off to the taste of this "wahoo," or king mackarel. *Ono* is regarded as one of the finest eating fishes in the ocean, and its white flakey meat lives up to its name.

Manini

These smallish five-inch fish are some of the most abundant in Hawaii and live in about 10 feet of water. They school and won't bite a hook but are easily taken with spear or net. Not often on a menu, but they're favorites with local people who know best.

Ulua

This member of the "Jack Cravelle" family ranges between 15 and 100 pounds. Its flesh is white and has a steak-like texture. Delicious and often found on the menu.

Uku

This is a gray snapper that's a favorite with local people. The meat is light and firm and grills well. *Ahi* is a yellowfin tuna with distinctive pinkinsh meat. A great favorite cooked, or uncooked in sushi bars. *Moi* is the Hawaiian word for "king". It has large eyes and a shark-like head. Considered one of the finest eating fishes in Hawaii, it's best during the autumn months.

Fish potpourri

Some other island seafood found on the menu include *limu,* edible seaweed; *opihi,* small shellfish (limpets) that clings to rocks and is considered one of the best island delicacies, eaten raw; *aloalo,* like tiny lobsters; crawfish, plentiful in taro fields and irrigation ditches; *ahipalaka,* albacore tuna; various octopus (squid or calamari); and shark of various types.

HAWAIIAN GAME FISH

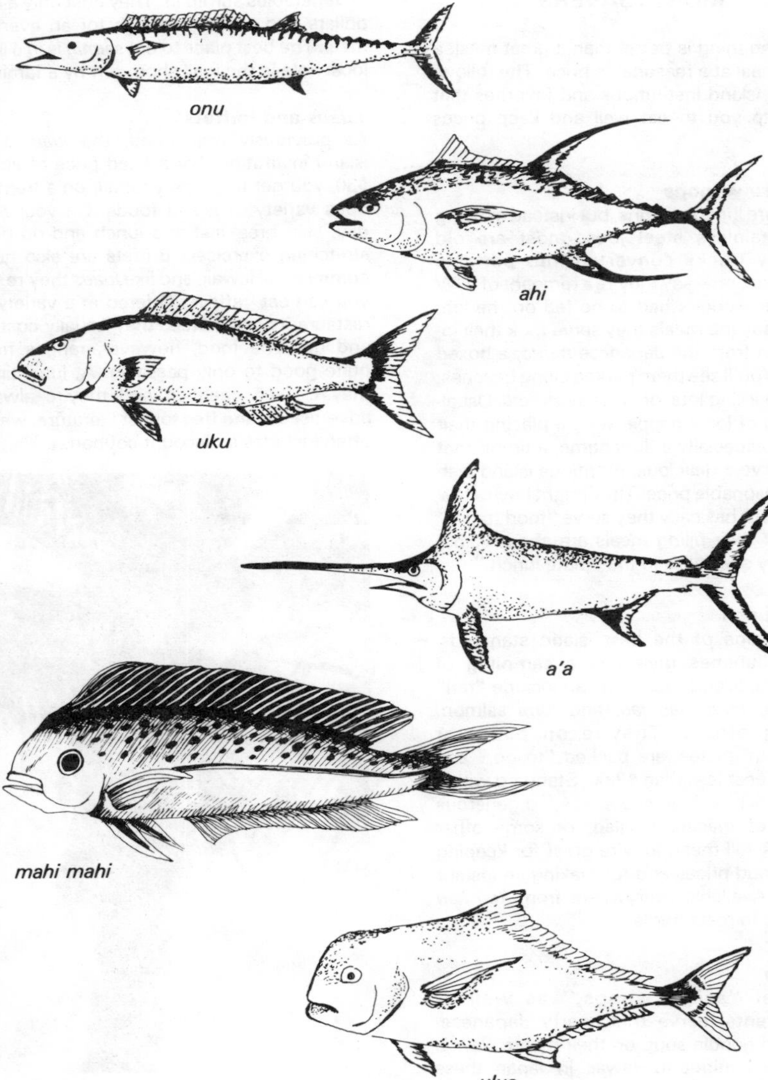

onu

ahi

uku

a'a

mahi mahi

ulua

MONEYSAVERS

Only one thing is better than a great meal: a great meal at a reasonable price. The following are island institutions and favorites that will help you to eat well and keep prices down.

Kau kau wagons

These are lunch wagons, but instead of being slick stainless steel jobs, most are old delivery trucks converted into portable kitchens. Some say they're a remnant of WW II, when workers had to be fed on the job; others say the meals they serve took their inspiration from the Japanese *bento,* a boxed lunch. You'll see them parked along beaches, in city parking lots, or on busy streets. Usually a line of local people will be placing their orders, especially at lunchtime, a tip-off that they serve a delicious, nutritious island dish for a reasonable price. They might have a few tables, but basically they serve "food to go." Most of their filling meals are about $3.50, and they specialize in the "plate lunch."

Plate lunch

This is one of the best island standards. These lunches give you a sampling of authentic island food and can include "teri" chicken, *mahi, lau lau,* and *lomi* salmon, among others. They're on paper or styrofoam plates, are packed "to go," and usually cost less than $3.50. Standard with a plate lunch is "two scoop rice," a generous dollop of macaroni salad, or some other salad. A full meal, they're great for keeping down food prices and for making an instant picnic. Available everywhere from *kau kau* wagons to restaurants.

Saimin

Special "*saimin* shops," as well as restaurants, serve this hearty Japanese-inspired noodle soup on their menu. *Saimin* is a word unique to Hawaii. In Japan, these soups would either be called *ramin* or *soba,* and it's as if the two were combined to

saimin. These are large bowls of noodle soup, in a light broth with meat, chicken, fish or vegetables stirred in. They cost only a few dollars and are big enough for an evening meal. The best place to eat *saimin* is in a little local hole-in-the-wall shop, run by a family.

Luaus and buffets

As previously mentioned, the *luau* is an island institution. For a fixed price of about $30, you get to gorge yourself on a tremendous variety of island foods. On your *luau* day, skip breakfast and lunch and do belly stretching exercises! Buffets are also quite common in Hawaii, and like *luaus* they're "all you can eat" affairs. Offered at a variety of restaurants and hotels, they usually cost $8 and up. The food, however, ranges from quite good to only passable. At lunchtime, they're even cheaper, and they're always advertised in the free tourist literature, which often includes a discount coupon.

Those really determined to save money can always try this!

Tips

Even some of the island's best restaurants in the fanciest hotels offer "early-bird specials" — the regular menu dinners offered to patrons who come in before the usual dinner hour, which is approximately 6:00 p.m. You pay as little as half the normal price, and can dine in luxury on some of the best foods. Often advertised in the free tourist books, coupons for reduced meals might also be included: two for one, or limited dinners at a much lower price. Just clip them out (see below). Maui also has the full contingency of American fast food chains including Jack in the Box, McDonalds, Shakeys Pizza, Kentucky Fried Chicken, and all the rest.

RESTAURANTS

If you love to eat, you'll love Maui. Besides great fish, there's fresh beef from Maui's ranches and fresh vegetables from the highlands. The cuisines offered are as cosmopolitan as the people: Polynesian, Hawaiian, Italian, French, Continental, Mexican, and Oriental.

Classy dining

Four five-star restaurants on Maui are: **The Plantation Veranda** at the Kapalua Bay Hotel, **The Swan Court** at the Hyatt Regency, **La Perouse** at the Maui Intercontinental Wailea, and **Raffles** at Stouffer's Wailea Resort. You won't be able to afford these every day, but for that one-time blow out, take your choice.

Bargains

Great "early-bird specials" are offered at the **Moana Terrace** at Kaanapali's Marriott, the two **Island Fish Houses** in Kahului and Kihei, and at **Leilani's** in the Whalers Village. Also, **Kihei Prime Rib House** offers some dandy specials.

Fill 'er up

For more moderate fare, try these no-atmosphere restaurants that'll fill you up with good food for "at home" prices: **Ma Chan's** in the Kaahumanu Shopping Center; **Hat's**

Restaurant in the Maui Mall and in Paia (especially the $2 breakfast); **Kitada's** in Makawao for the best bowl of *saimin* on the island. For great sandwiches try: **Philadelphia Lou's** in Kahului and Kihei; and the snack bars at all of the island's health food stores, especially **Paradise Fruit Co.** in Kihei.

Can't go wrong

Great Mexican vegetarian food at **Polli's Restaurant** in Kihei and Makawao, and both **La Famiglia's** in Kaanapali and Kihei have a great happy hour, complete with free chips and salsa. **Longhi's** in Lahaina is well established as a gourmet cosmopolitan/Italian restaurant, and **Mama's Fish House** in Paia recieves the highest compliment of being a favorite with the locals. **Piero's** in Paia serves good Italian food and has "open mike" evenings with the best of island color. **Robaire's** is an expensive but authentic French restaurant in Kihei; the breakfast at the Maui Surf's **Eight Bells Restaurant** can't be beat. **Erik's Seafood Grotto** in Kahana is good value, and **Leilani's** and the **Rusty Harpoon** are up-and-comers in the Whaler's Village. The *luau* at the **Maui Lu Hotel** in Kihei is a classic, and the **Maui Beach Hotel** in Kahului has a decent buffet.

FOOD MARKETS

If you're shopping for general food supplies and are not interested in gourmet or specialty items including organic foods, you'll save money by shopping at the big-name supermarkets, located in Lahaina, Kahului, and Kihei, often in malls. Smaller towns have general stores which are adequate, but a bit more expensive. You can also find convenience items at commissaries in many condos and hotels, but these should be used only for snack foods or when absolutely necessary, because the prices are just too high.

Kahului

The greatest number of supermarkets is found in Kahului. They're all conveniently located along Rt. 32 (Kaahumanu Ave.) in three malls, one right after the other.

Foodland, open 7 days, 8:30 a.m. to 10:00 p.m., is in the **Kaahumanu Shopping Center**. Just down the road in the **Kahului Shopping Center** is the ethnic **Ah Fooks**, open 7 days, 8:00 a.m. to 7:00 p.m., closes early Sat. and Sun., specializing in Japanese, Chinese and Hawaiian foods. Farther along in the **Maui Mall** is **Star Market**, open 7 days, 8:30 a.m. to 9:00 p.m., 7:00 p.m. Sunday. Just behind the Maui Mall on E. Kamehameha Ave. is a **Safeway**. Wailuku doesn't have shopping malls, but if you're taking an excursion around the top of West Maui, make a "last chance" stop at **T.K. Supermarket** at the end of N. Market St. in the Happy Valley area. They're open 7 days, but close early on Sunday afternoons.

Kihei

In Kihei you've got a choice of three markets, all strung along S. Kihei Rd., the main drag. **Foodland** in the Kihei Town Center, or **Star Market** just down the road, offer standard shopping. The most interesting is **Azeka's Market** in Azeka Plaza. This market is an institution, and is very famous for its specially prepared (uncooked) ribs, perfect for a barbecue. In Wailea you'll find **Wailea Pantry** in the Wailea Shopping Village, open 7 days, 8:00 a.m. to 7:00 p.m., but it's an exclusive area and the prices will make you sob.

Lahaina and vicinity

In Lahaina you can shop at **Foodland** in Lahaina Square, close to Rt. 30. More interesting is **Nagasako's** in the Lahaina Shopping Center, just off Front Street. They've got all you need, plus a huge selection of Chinese and Japanese items. Nagasako's is open 7 days, 8:00 a.m to 8:00 p.m., 9:00 p.m. Fri. and 5:00 p.m. Saturday. Just west of Lahaina in Honokawai, you'll find the **Honokawai Superette**. Although there are a few sundry stores in various hotels in Kaanapali, this is the only real place to shop. It's open 7 days, 8:00 a.m. to 9:00 p.m. In Napili, pick up supplies at **Napili Village Store**, a bit expensive, but well stocked and convenient. In Olowalu, east of Lahaina, you can pick up some limited items at the **Olowalu General Store**.

Hana

In Hana you have the legendary **Hasegawa's General Store**. They have just about everything, and are geared toward standard American selections. Hasegawa's is open 7 days, 7:30 a.m. to 6:00 p.m., and 9:00 a.m. to 3:30 p.m. on Sunday. Also in Hana is the **Hana Store**, which actually has a better selection of health foods and imported beers. Open 7 days, 7:30 a.m. to 6:00 p.m.

Around and about

Other stores where you might pick up supplies are: **Komoda's** in **Makawao**. They're famous throughout Hawaii for their cream buns, which are sold out by 8:00 a.m, At **Pukalani Superette** in Pukalani, open 7 days, you can pick up supplies and food-to-go including *sushi*. In Paia try **Nagata's** or **Paia General Store** on the main drag. In Kaupakulua you have **Hanzawa's**, a last chance store on the back road (Rt. 365) from Hana to Haleakala.

HEALTH FOOD

Those into organic foods, fresh vegetables, natural vitamins and take-out snack bars have it made on Maui. At many fine health food stores you can have most of your needs met. Try the following: in Wailuku, **Down to Earth** is an excellent health food store complete with vitamins, bulk foods and a snack bar. This Krishna-oriented market, on the corner of Central and Vineyard, is open 7 days, 8:00 a.m. to 6:00 p.m., 5:00 p.m. Sat., 4:00 p.m. Sunday. **Lahaina Natural Foods** is at the far end of Front St., towards Kaanapali. Open 7 days, they're a full-service health food store, featuring baked goods and Herbalife vitamins. **Paradise Fruit Company** on S. Kihei Rd. is terrific. It's not strictly a health food store, but does have plenty of wholesome items. Their food bar is the best. They're open 24 hours, everyday. You can't go wrong! **Tradewinds Natural Foods** in Paia is a full-service health food market. They're open 7 days, 7:00 a.m. to 8:00 p.m.; shorter Sun. hours. You can pick up whatever you need for your trip to Hana. **Maui**

top: Lahaina Harbor (JDB);
bottom left: Kepaniwai Park and Heritage Gardens (JDB);
bottom right: waterfall and pool along the Hana Road (Gary Quiring)

top: an orchid (B. Cowan); middle left: fiddle head ferns (JDB); middle right: plumeria (B. Cowan);
bottom left: hibiscus (B. Cowan); bottom right: passion fruit (Gary Quiring)

Some of the best island treats come from small roadside stands.

Natural Foods in the Maui Mall in Kahului is open 7 days and has a fair selection of fresh foods with a big emphasis on vitamins. **The Silversword Bakery** and the little store right there have a limited but excellent selection of baked goods and natural foods. Many items are on consignment from local kitchens. They're at the Silversword Inn in Kula.

Fresh fruit and fish

What's Hawaii without its fruits, both from the vine and from the sea? For fresh fish try the Fish Market at **Maalaea Harbor**. They get their fish right from the boats, but they do have a retail counter. In Kihei along S. Kihei Rd., just west of Azeka Place, some enterpris-

ing fishermen set up a roadside stand whenever they have a good day. Look for their coolers propping up a sign. **Lahaina Fishery** in the Lahaina Shopping Center has a wide selection and reasonable prices. For fresh fruits and vegetables try **The Farmers' Market**. Gardeners bring their fresh Kula vegetables to makeshift roadside markets on Mon. in Lahaina at Front and Baker Sts.; on Wed. in Napili close to the Napili Kai, and Fri. in Kihei along Kihei Road. Signboards mark the spot. All along the road to Hana are little fruit stands tucked away. Many times no one is in attendance and the very reasonably priced fruit is paid for on the honor system.

(Hawaii State Archives)

SPORTS AND RECREATION

Maui won't let you down when you want to go outside and play. More than just a giant sandbox for big kids, its beaches and surf are warm and inviting, and there are all sorts of water sports from scuba diving to parasailing. You can fish, hunt, camp, or indulge yourself in golf or tennis to your heart's content. The hiking is marvelous and the horseback riding along beaches and on Haleakala is some of the most exciting in the world. The information offered in this chapter is merely an overview to let you know what's available. Specific areas are covered in the travel sections. Have fun!

SWIMMING AND BEACHES

Since your island is blessed with 150 miles of coastline, over 32 of which is wonderful beach, your biggest problem is to choose which one you'll grace with your presence. The following should help you choose just where you'd like to romp about.

Southwest Maui beaches
The most and best beaches for swimming and sunbathing are on the south coast of West Maui, strung along 18 glorious miles from Kapalua to Olowalu. For an all-purpose beach you can't beat **Kapalua Beach** (Fleming Beach) on Maui's western tip. It has everything: safe surf (except in winter), great swimming, snorkeling, and body surfing in a first-class, family-oriented area. Then comes the Kaanapali beaches along Rt. 30, bordered by the hotels and condos. All are open to the public and "rights of way" skirt hotel grounds. **Black Rock** at the Sheraton is the best for snorkeling. Just east and west of Lahaina are **Lahaina Beach,** convenient but not private; **Launiupoko and Puamana Waysides** with only fair swimming, but great views and grassy beaches. **Olowalu** has very good swimming beaches across from the General Store, and **Papalaua Wayside** offers seclusion on a narrow beach fringed by *kiawe* trees that surround tiny patches of white sand.

Kihei and Wailea beaches
The 10 miles stretching from the west end of Kihei to Wailea are dotted with beaches that range from poor to excellent. **Kihei Beach**

extends for miles from Maalaea to Kihei. Excellent for walking and enjoying the view, but little else. **Kamaole Beach Parks I, II and III** are at the east end of Kihei. Top-notch beaches, they have it all—swimming, snorkeling and safety. **Keawakapu** is more of the same. Then come the great little beaches of Wailea that get more secluded as you head east: **Mokapu, Ulua, Wailea, Polo.** All are surrounded by the picture-perfect hotels of Wailea and all have public access. **Makena Beach,** down an unpaved road east from Wailea, is very special. It's one of the island's best beaches. At one time, alternative people made Makena a haven and it still attracts free-spirited souls. There's nude bathing here in secluded coves, unofficial camping, and freedom. It gets the highest compliment when locals, and those staying at hotels and condos around Maui, come here to enjoy themselves.

Wailuku and Kahului

Poor ugly ducklings! There are shallow, unattractive beaches in both towns and no one spends any time there. However, **Kanaha Beach** between Kahului and the airport isn't bad at all. **Baldwin Beach Park** has the reputation of hostile locals protecting their turf, but the beach is good and you won't be hassled if you "live and let live." **Hookipa Beach** just west of Paia isn't good for the average swimmer but it is the "sailboarding capital" of Hawaii, and you should visit here just to see the exciting, colorful spectacle of people skipping over the ocean with bright sails.

Hana beaches

Everything about Hana is heavenly, including its beaches. There's **Red Sand Beach,** almost too pretty to be real. **Wainapanapa** is surrounded by the state park and good for swimming and snorkeling, even providing a legendary cave whose waters turn blood red. **Hana Bay** is well protected and safe for swimming. Farther along at **Oheo Stream** (Seven Sacred Pools) you'll find the paradise you've been searching for—gorgeous freshwater pools at the base of wispy waterfalls and fronted by a tremendous sea of pounding surf only a few yards away.

Freshwater swimming

The best place for swimming is in various stream pools on the road to Hana. One of the very best is **Twin Falls,** up a short trail from Hoolawa Bridge. **Helio's Grave** (marked) is another good swimming spot between Hana and Oheo Stream, which are excellent themselves, especially the upper pools. Also, you can take a refreshing dip at Iao Valley stream when you visit Iao Needle.

SNORKELING AND SCUBA

Maui is as beautiful from under the waves as it is above. There is world-class snorkeling and diving at many coral reefs and beds surrounding the island. You'll find the best, coincidentally, just where the best beaches are: mainly from Kihei to Makena, up around Napili Bay and especially from Olowalu to Lahaina. Backside Maui is great (but mostly for experts), and for a total thrill, try diving Molokini, the submerged volcano, just peeking above the waves and designated a Marine Life Conservation district.

Great underwater spots

These are some of the best on Maui, but there are plenty more (see "Sights" in individual chapters). Use the same caution when scuba diving or snorkeling as when swimming. Be mindful of currents. It's generally safer to enter the water in the center of a bay than at the sides where rips are more likely to occur. The following sites are suitable for beginners to intermediates: on Maui's western tip **Honolua Bay,** a Marine Life Conservation District; nearby **Mokuleia Bay,** known as "Slaughterhouse," but gentle; in Kaanapali you'll enjoy **Black Rock** at the Sheraton Hotel; at **Olowalu,** very gentle with plenty to see; also try **Kamaole Parks II** and **III** in Kihei and **Ulua,** and **Polo** and **Wailea** beaches in Wailea. Under no circumstances should you miss taking a boat out to Molokini. It's worth every penny!

For **scuba divers,** there are underwater caves at **Nahuna Point** ("Five Graves") between Wailea and Makena, great diving at Molokini, magnificent caves out at the **Lanai**

Cathedrals and a sunken Navy sub, the USS *Bluegill,* to explore. Advanced divers *only* should attempt the backside of West Maui, The Seven Sacred Pools and beyond Pu'uiki Island in Hana Bay.

Equipment

Sometimes condos and hotels have snorkeling equipment free for their guests, but if you have to rent it, don't do it from a hotel or condo, but go to a dive shop where it's much cheaper. Expect to spend $7 a day for mask, fins, and snorkel. Scuba divers can rent gear for about $30 from most shops. In Lahaina rent from: **American Dive Maui,** 628 Front, tel. 661-4885; **Central Pacific Divers,** 780 Front, tel. 661-8718; **Hawaii Reef Divers,** 129 Lahainaluna, tel. 667-7647; **Scuba Schools,** 1000 Limahana, tel. 661-8036. In Kihei: an excellent all-around shop is **The Dive Shop,** 1975 S. Kihei Rd., tel. 879-5172; **Maui Dive Shop,** Azeka Pl., tel. 879-3388; **Maui Sailing Center,** at the Kealia Beach Center, tel. 879-6260. You might also consider renting an underwater camera. Expect to spend $12-$15, including film.

Scuba certification

A number of Maui companies take you from your first dive to PADI, NAUI, or NASDS certification. Prices range from $40 for a quickie refresher dive up to around $200 for a 4-5 day certification course. Courses or arrangements can be made with any of the dive shops listed above.

Snorkel and scuba excursions

Many boats will take you out snorkeling or diving. Prices range from $30 (half day, 4 hours) to $60 (full day, 8 hours), check "Getting Around/Ocean Tours" for many of the boats that do it all, from deep-sea fishing to moonlight cruises. Any of the "activities centers" can arrange these excursions for no extra charge, check "Getting Around/Sightseeing Tours" for names and numbers. For an excellent scuba/snorkel excursion, try **The Dive Shop** in Kihei at tel. 879-5172, where you might be lucky enough to go with Capt. Dave Ventura on the *Maui Diamond.* **Snorkeling Hawaii** in downtown Lahaina,

tel. 661-8156, has reasonable rates ($16, half day) including equipment, instruction and hotel pickup. **Sea Safari Travel,** 2770 Highland Ave., Manhattan Beach CA 90266, even offers a seven-night package for scuba divers to Maui.

World-class instructor

With a name like **Chuck Thorne,** what else can you expect but a world-class athlete of some kind?! Well, Chuck is a diver who lives on Maui. He's written *The Diver's Guide to Maui,* the definitive book on all the best dive/snorkel spots on Maui. Chuck has a one-man operation, so unfortunately, he must limit his leadership and instruction to advanced divers only. People have been known to cancel flights home to dive with Chuck, and he receives the highest accolades from other watermen. You can buy his book at many outlets or write: Maui Dive Guide, P.O. Box 1461, Kahului HI 96732. You can contact Chuck through **The Dive Shop** tel. 879-5172, or at 879-7068.

MORE WATER SPORTS

For great **bodysurfing** try: Ulua, Wailea, Polo or Makena Beaches, the N end of Kamaole Beach Park I in Kihei, Napili Bay, and Baldwin Park. For **surfing** try: Lower Paia Park, Napili Bay, Baldwin Park, Maalaea and Hookipa Beach. For surfing lessons: **Nancy Emerson,** Maui's surfing champion in Lahaina at tel. 244-3728, $40 private, $25 group.

Sailboarding

This is one of the world's newest sports, and unlike surfing which tends to be male-dominated, women, too, are excellent at surfboarding. Hookipa Beach, just east of Paia, is the "sailboarding capital of the world," and the **O'Neill International Championship** is held here every year in March and April. To rent boards and to take instructions, try: **Maui Sailing Center** at Kealia Beach Center, N. Kihei Rd., tel. 879-5935. You can rent here for $15 an hour or $60 a day. Lessons are extra; **Sailboards Maui,** 247 Kaahumanu Ave., Kahului, tel. 877-6882. $25

sailboards at Kealia Beach

half day, $35 full. Remember—start with a big board and a small sail! Take lessons to save time and energy.

Jet skis
To try this exciting sport, contact: **Kaanapali Jet Ski**, at Whalers' Village, tel. 667-7851; **Jamin Jet Skis**, in Kihei at 242-4339.

Parasailing
To rise above it all call **Lahaina Para Sail**, 628 Front St., tel. 661-4887.

Waterskiing
Again, the **Maui Sailing Center**, or **Rainbow Custom Water Sports**, where you can also arrange just about anything dealing with water, at tel. 661-3980.

Sailing
The most popular day sails are from Maui to Molokai or Lanai (fully discussed in "Getting Around-Ocean Tours"). Your basic half-day snorkel and swim sail will be $35. For serious sailors, some top-notch boats in Lahaina Harbor are open for lengthy charters. Try: **Alihilani Yacht Charters**, at Lahaina Harbor; **Mareva**, tel. 667-7013; **Scotch Mist**, tel. 661-0368.

HORSEBACK RIDING

Those who love sightseeing from the back of a horse are in for a big treat on Maui. Stables dot the island, so you have a choice of terrain for your trail ride: a slow canter along the beaches of West Maui, a breathtaking ride through Haleakala Crater, or a backwoods ride out at the Seven Sacred Pools. Unfortunately, none of this comes cheap. In comparison, a bale of alfalfa, which goes for under $5 on the mainland, fetches $18-$22 on Maui. If you plan to do some serious riding, it's advisable to bring jeans (jogging suit bottoms will do) and a pair of boots, or at least jogging shoes.

The Rainbow Ranch
One of the best stables on Maui, it's run by Rick, a Canadian cowboy, who arrived here about 10 years ago. You'll have your choice of rides: beginners ride daily at 9:00 a.m., $15, gentle horses; beach ride (very popular) daily, 4:00 p.m., $40, experienced riders; beach and mountain, through pineapple fields, extended ride, experienced riders, $55; picnic rides, b.y.o., 10:30 a.m. to 2:00 p.m., $40; BBQ, 10:30 a.m. to 2:00 p.m., great food, $55. The Rainbow Ranch is also starting a mini rodeo, and Rick has a few pair of rubber boots that he'll lend for free to those lacking proper footwear. No dress code, but no thongs please. **Rainbow Ranch**, P.O. Box 712, Lahaina 96761, tel. 669-4991, located at mile marker 29 along Rt. 30 toward Kapalua.

Oheo Riding Stables
These stables, out near the Seven Pools (Hana), are the best riding bargain on the island. Greg, the local-born owner, will take you up to the pools and waterfalls of Kipahulu Valley for $10 per hour (average

ride, two hours). He knows the best spots, and his sure-footed horses are specially mountain trained. Just past the Oheo Gulch Campground, tel. 248-7722.

Moomuku Stables
Recently opened, these stables provide unique beach rides and overnight camping at La Perouse Bay. Just past Polo Beach in Wailea on the road to Makena. You can't go wrong with these local cowpokes who have an old-fashioned love and respect for the land, tel. 879-0244.

Haleakala and environs
A few upcountry companies offer trail rides through the crater or over the mountain. Wear *warm* clothes! Here are some of the best: **Haleakala Outfitters & Guides** offers an all-day ride (9:30 a.m. to 3:30 p.m.) featuring a journey across the face of Haleakala Crater, $125. Full-day trip includes picnic lunch. Write c/o Maui Island Tours, P.O. Box 247, Kahului 96732, tel. 877-5581. **Charley's Trailride and Pack Trips** takes you overnight camping in Haleakala, arranging for

cabins and supplying all meals. Run by Charles Aki, c/o Kaupo Store, Hana 96713, tel. 248-8209. **Pony Express Tours** offers rides through Haleakala with very experienced guides, who give a full narration of the area. Lunch provided. Full day $110, partial $75. Write Pony Express, P.O. Box 507, Makawao 96768, tel. 667-2202. **Thompson Riding Stables** guides you over the slopes of Haleakala on one of Maui's oldest cattle ranches. Write Thompson Stables, Thompson Rd., Kula 96790, tel. 878-1910.

Adventures on Horseback
Offers a three-day, two-night horseback camping trip. Everything provided, $1500 for two. Also, waterfall rides from Hana, $85, tel. 242-7445.

Kau Lio Stables
Just near Lahaina, they offer two-hour rides leaving at 8:30 and 11:30 a.m. and at 2:30 p.m., $33 including snack. They're located on private land, so they'll pick you up in Kaanapali. Write P.O. Box 16056, Kaanapali Beach, 96761, tel. 667-7869.

GOLF COURSES OF MAUI

	Course	Holes	Par	Yards	Week day	Week end	Cart
1.	Kapalua Golf Club Bay	18	71	6,145	35.00	35.00	Incl.
	Kapalua Golf Club Villa	18	73	6,194	25.00	Guests	Incl.
	Kapalua HI 96791					only	M
2.	Makena Golf C.	18	72	6,798	18.00	18.00	8.00
	Kikei HI 96753						
3.	Maui Country Club Front	9	37	3,148	7.00	6.00	6.00
	Maui Country Club Back	9	37	3,247	7.00	6.00	
	Paia HI 96779				Mon. only for visitors		
4.	Pukalani C.C.	9	36	3,000	4.00	4.00	6.00
	Pukalani, 96788	9	36	3,200	7.00	7.00	12.00
5.	Royal Kaanapali North	18	72	7,179	23.00	23.00	10.00
	Kaanapali HI 96761						M
6.	Royal Kaanapali South	18	72	6,758	23.00	23.00	10.00
	Kaanapali HI 96761						M
7.	Waiehu Municipal G.C.	18	72	6,367	10.00	15.00	10.40
	Waiehu HI 96793						
8.	Wailea Golf						
	Blue Course	18	72	6,327	28.00	28.00	Incl.
	Orange Course	18	72	6,405	28.00	28.00	M
	Wailea HI 96753						

TENNIS AND GOLF

Maui specializes in both these sports. The two high-class resort areas of Kaanapali and Wailea are built around golf courses, with tennis courts available all over the island.

HUNTING

Most people don't think of Hawaii as a place to hunt, but actually it's quite good. Seven species of introduced game animals are regularly hunted, and 16 species of game birds. Not all species of game animals are open on all islands, but every island offers hunting.

General hunting rules

Hunting licenses are mandatory to hunt on public, private, or military land anywhere in Hawaii. They're good for one year beginning July 1. Hunting licenses cost $7.50 resident, $15 non-resident, senior citizens free. Licenses are available from sporting goods stores and from the various offices of The Division of Forestry and Wildlife (see below). This government organization also sets and enforces the rules, so contact them with any questions. Generally hunting hours are from

TENNIS COURTS OF MAUI

COUNTY COURTS

Under jurisdiction of the Dept. of Parks & Recreation, 200 High St., Wailuku, Maui 96793.
Phone: 244-7750
Courts listed are in or near visitor areas. There are 3 additional locations around the island.
*Courts on state land, under state jurisdiction.

Name & Location of Courts		No. of Courts	Lighted
Hana	Hana Ball Park	2	Yes
Kahului	Kahului Community Center	2	Yes
Kihei	Kalama Park	2	Yes
Kihei	*Fronting Maui Pacific Shores	2	No
Lahaina	Lahaina Civic Center	2	Yes
Lahaina	Malu-ulu-olele Park	4	Yes
Makawao	Eddie Tam Memorial Center	2	Yes
Pukalani	Pukalani Community Center	2	Yes
Wailuku	Maui Community College/Ph. 244-9181 Courts available after school hours	4	No
Wailuku	Wailuku Community Center	7	Yes
Wailuku	Wailuku War Memorial	4	Yes
HOTEL & PRIVATE COURTS—OPEN TO PUBLIC			
Lahaina	Maui Marriott Resort	5	No
Kihei	Maui Sunset	2	No
Kaanapali	Maui Surf	3	No
Napili Bay	Napili Kai Beach Club	2	No
Kaanapali	Royal Lahaina Hotel	11	6
Kaanapali	Sheraton Maui Hotel	3	Yes
Kapalua	Tennis Garden	10	No
Wailea	Wailea Tennis Center	14	3

a half-hour before to a half-hour after sunset. At times, there are "checking stations," where the hunter must check in before and after hunting.

Rifles must have greater than a 1,200-foot-pound muzzle velocity. Shotguns larger than .20 gauge are allowed, as are muzzleloaders with a .45 caliber bore or larger. Bows require a minimum draw of 45 pounds for straight bows and 30 pounds for compounds. Arrows must be broadheads. Dogs are permitted only with some birds and game, and smaller caliber rifles and shotguns are permitted with their use, along with spears and knives. Hunters must wear orange safety cloth on front and back no smaller than a 12-inch square. Certain big game species are hunted only by lottery selection; contact the Division of Forestry and Wildlife two months in advance. Guide service is not mandatory, but is advised if you're unfamiliar with hunting in Hawaii. You can hunt on private land only with permission, and you need to possess a valid hunting license. Guns and ammunition brought into Hawaii have to be registered with the Chief of Police of the corresponding county within 48 hours of arrival.

Information

Hunting rules and regulations are always subject to change. Also, environmental considerations often change bag limits and seasons. Make sure to check with The Division of Forestry and Wildlife for the most current information. Request "Rules Regulating Game Bird Hunting, Field Trails and Commercial Shooting Preserves," "Rules Regulating Game Mammal Hunting," and "Hunting in Hawaii." Direct inquiries to: Dept. of Land and Natural Resources, Division of Forestry and Wildlife Office, 1151 Punchbowl St., Honolulu 96813, tel. 548-2861; on Maui, 54 S. High St., P.O. Box 1015, Wailuku, 96793, tel. 244-4352.

Game animals

All game animals have been introduced into Hawaii. Some are adapting admirably and becoming well entrenched, while the existence of others is still precarious. **Axis deer** originated in India and were brought to Lanai and Molokai, where they're doing well. The small herd on Maui is holding its own. Their unique flavor makes them one of the best wild meats, and they're hunted on Molokai and Lanai in March and April, by public lottery. **Feral pigs** are escaped domestic pigs that have gone wild and are found on all islands except Lanai. The stock is a mixture of original Polynesian pigs and all that came later. As they are hunted with dogs and usually killed with a spear or long knife, pig hunting is not recommended for the timid or tenderhearted. These beasts' four-inch tusks and fighting spirit make them tough and

feral pig

dangerous. **Feral goats** come in a variety of colors. Found on all islands except Lanai, they have been known to cause erosion and are considered a pest in some areas, especially on Haleakala. Openly hunted on all the islands, their meat when properly done is considered delicious.

gray francolin

Game birds

A number of game birds are found on most of the islands. Bag limits and hunting seasons vary, so check with the Division of Forestry and Wildlife for details. **Ring-necked pheasants** are one of the best game birds, and found on all the islands. **Green pheasants** are found on Maui. **Francolins,** gray and black, from India and the Sudan, are similar to partridges. They are hunted with dogs and make great roasted birds. There are also **chukar** from Tibet, found on the slopes of all islands; a number of **quail,** including the **Japanese and California** varieties; **doves;** and the **wild Rio Grande turkey.**

GONE FISHING

Surrounding Maui are some of the most exciting and productive "blue waters" in all the oceans and seas of the world. Here you can find the "sport fishing fleet," made up of skippers and crews who are experienced professional anglers. You can also fish from jetties, piers, rocks, and from shore. If rod and reel don't strike your fancy, try the old-fashioned "throw net," or take along a spear when you go snorkeling or scuba diving. There's nighttime torch fishing that requires special skills and equipment, and freshwater fishing in public areas. Streams and irrigation ditches yield introduced trout, bass and catfish. While you're at it, you might want to try crabbing for Kona and Samoan crabs, or working low-tide areas after sundown hunting squid (really octopus), a long-time island delicacy.

Deep-sea fishing

Most game fishing boats work the blue waters on the calmer leeward sides of the islands. Some skippers, carrying anglers who are accustomed to the sea, will also work the much rougher windward coasts and island channels where the fish bite just as well. Trolling is the preferred method of deep-sea fishing; this is done usually in waters of between 1000-2000 fathoms (a fathom is 6 feet). The skipper will either "area fish," which means running in a crisscrossing pattern over a known productive area, or "ledge fish," which involves trolling over submerged ledges where the game fish are known to feed. The most advanced marine technology, available on many boats, sends sonar bleeps searching for fish. On deck, the crew and anglers scan the horizon in the age-old Hawaiian tradition. They're searching for seabirds clustered in an area, feeding on the very baitfish which are pursued to the surface by the huge and aggressive game fish. There is some "still fishing," or bottomfishing, with hand lines, that yields some tremendous fish.

The game fish

The most thrilling game fish in Hawaiian waters is marlin. These are generically known as "billfish" or *a'u* to the locals. The king of them is the blue marlin, with record catches well over 1000 pounds. There's also striped marlin and sailfish, which often go over 200 pounds. The best times for marlin are during spring, summer and fall. The fishing tapers off in January and picks up again by late February. "Blues" can be caught year-round, but oddly enough, when they stop biting it seems as though the striped marlin pick up. Second to the marlin are tuna. The *ahi,* (yellowfin tuna) are caught in Hawaiian waters of depths of 100-1000 fathoms. They can weigh 300 pounds, but between 25 and 100 pounds is common. There's also *aku,* skipjack tuna, and the delicious *ono,* which average between 20 and 40 pounds.

Mahi mahi is another strong, fighting, deep-water game fish abundant in Hawaii. These delicious eating fish can weigh up to 70 pounds. Shorefishing and baitcasting yield *papio,* a jack tuna. *Akule,* a scad (locally called *halalu*), is a smallish schooling fish that comes close to shore and is great to catch on light tackle. *Ulua* are shore fish and can be found in tidepools. They're excellent eating, average two to three pounds, and are taken at night or with spears. *O'io* are bonefish that come close to shore to spawn. They're caught baitcasting and bottomfishing with cut bait. They're bony, but they're a favorite for fish cakes and *poki. Awa* is a schooling fish that loves brackish water. It can get up to three feet long, and is a good fighter. A favorite for "throw netters," it's even raised commercially in fish ponds. Besides these, there are plenty of goatfish, mullet, mackerel, snapper, various sharks, and even salmon.

Deep-sea fishing boats

The waters around Maui are extremely bountiful. Deep-sea fishing on a **share basis** is approximately $50 half day (4 hours) and $80 full day. On a **private basis,** expect $250 half

day, $400 full day. Some of the best boats include: *Maui Diamond,* tel. 879-5172; *Reel Hooker,* tel. 572-0202; *Blue Max,* a real beauty, tel. 244-3259 or 878-6585; in Lahaina you can't go wrong with the *Judy Ann.* tel. 667-6672; *Aerial Sportfishing,* tel. 667-9089.

uhu, *parrot fish*

CAMPING AND HIKING

A major aspect of the "Maui experience" is found in the simple beauty of nature and the outdoors. Visitors come to Maui to luxuriate at resorts and dine in fine restaurants, but everyone heads for the sand and surf, and most are captivated by the lush mountainous interior. What better way to savor this natural beauty than by hiking slowly through it or pitching a tent in the middle of it? Maui offers a full range of hiking and camping, and what's more, most of it is easily accessible and free. Camping facilities are located near many choice beaches and amid the most scenic areas of the island. They range in amenities from full housekeeping cabins to primitive "hike in" sites. Some restrictions to hiking apply because much of the land is privately owned, so you may require advance permission to enter. But plenty of public access trails along the coast and deep into the interior would fill the itineraries of even the most intrepid trekkers. If you enjoy the great outdoors on the mainland, you'll be thrilled by these "mini-continents," where in one day you can go from the frosty summits of alpine wonderlands down into baking cactus-covered deserts and emerge through jungle foliage onto a sun-soaked sub-tropical shore.

Note
Descriptions of individual State Parks, County Beach Parks, and Haleakala National Park, along with directions on how to get there, are given under "Sights" in the respective travel chapters.

HALEAKALA NATIONAL PARK

Camping at Haleakala National Park is free. Permits are not needed to camp at Hosmer Grove, just a short drive from Park Head-quarters, or at Oheo Stream Campground (formerly Seven Sacred Pools) near Kipahulu, along the coastal road 10 miles south of Hana. Camping is on a first-come, first-served basis, and there's an official three-day stay limit, but it's a loose count, especially at Oheo which is almost always empty. The case is much different at the campsites located inside Haleakala crater proper. On the floor of the crater are two primitive tent-ing campsites, one at Paliku on the east side and the other at Holua on the north rim. For these you'll need a wilderness permit available from Park Headquarters. Because of ecological considerations, only 25 campers per night can stay at each site, and a three-night, four-day maximum stay is strictly enforced, with tenting allowed at any one site for only two nights. However, because of the strenuous hike involved, campsites are open most of the time. You must be totally self-sufficient, and equipped for cold weather camping to be comfortable at these two sites.

Also, Paliku, Holua, and another site at Kapalaoa on the south rim offer cabins. Fully self-contained with stoves, water, and near-by pit toilets, they can handle a maximum of 12 campers each. Cots are provided, but you must have your own warm bedding. The same maximum-stay limits apply as in the campgrounds. Staying at these cabins is at a premium—they're popular with visitors and residents alike. They're geared toward the group with rates at $2 per person, but there is a $6 minimum for a single. To have a chance at getting a cabin you must make reserva-tions, so write well in advance for complete information to: Haleakala National Park, Box 537, Makawao, HI 96768, tel. 572-9306. For general information write: National Park Service, 300 Ala Moana Blvd., Honolulu HI 96850, tel. 546-7584.

STATE PARKS

There are 10 State Parks on Maui managed by the Department of Land and Natural Resources, through their Division of State Parks. These facilities include everything from historical sites to wildland parks ac-

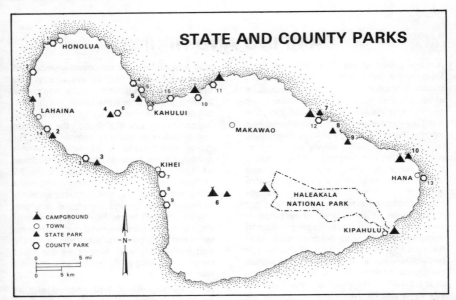

STATE AND COUNTY PARKS

HONOLUA
LAHAINA
KAHULUI
MAKAWAO
KIHEI
HANA
HALEAKALA NATIONAL PARK
KIPAHULU

▲ CAMPGROUND
○ TOWN
▲ STATE PARK
◇ COUNTY PARK

0   5 mi
0   5 km

−N−

cessible only by trail. Some are only for looking at, some are restricted to day use and three of them have overnight camping. Poli Poli and Wainapanapa offer free tenting, or self-contained cabins are available on a sliding fee; reservations highly necessary. At the other, Kaumahina, tent camping is free. Permits are required at all, and RVs technically are not allowed.

Park rules

Tent camping permits are free and good for a maximum stay of five nights at any one park. A permit to the same person for the same park is again available only after 30 days have elapsed. Campgrounds are open every day. You can arrive after 2:00 p.m. and you should check out by 11:00 a.m. The minimum age for park permits is 18, and anyone under that age must be accompanied by an adult. Alcoholic beverages are prohibited, as are nude sunbathing and swimming. Plants and wildlife are protected, but reasonable amounts of fruits and seeds may be gathered for personal consumption. Fires on cook stoves or in designated pits only. Dogs and other pets must be under control at all times and are not

permitted to run around unleashed. Hunting and freshwater fishing is allowed in season and only with a license, but ocean fishing is permitted, except when disallowed by posting. Permits are required for certain trails, so check at the State Parks office.

Cabins and shelters

Housekeeping cabins are available as indicated on the accompanying chart. As with camping, permits are required with the same five-day maximum stay. Reservations are absolutely necessary, especially at Wainapanapa, and a 50 percent deposit at time of confirmation is required. There's a three-day cancellation requirement for refunds, and payment is to be made in cash, money order, certified check, or personal check, only if the latter is received 30 days before arrival so that cashing procedures are possible. The balance is due on date of arrival. Cabins are on a sliding scale of $10 single, $14 double and about $5 for each person thereafter. These are completely furnished down to the utensils, with heaters for cold weather and private baths.

STATE PARKS

CODE NUMBER	PARK NAME	RESTROOMS	OVERLOOKS	PICNIC TABLES	OUTDOOR STOVES	DRINKING WATER	SWIMMING	SHELTERS	TENT CAMPING	CABINS	SHOWERS
1.	Wahikuli State Wayside	•		•	•	•	•	•			•
2.	Launiupoko State Wayside	•		•	•	•					•
3.	Ukumehame State Wayside			•			•				
4.	Iao Valley	•	•			•	•	•			
5.	Halekii-Pihana Heiau		•								
6.	Polipoli Spring Recreation Area	•		•	•	•			•	1	
7.	Kaumahina State Wayside	•	•	•	•	•			•		
8.	Keanae-Wailua Lookout		•								
9.	Puaa Kaa State Wayside	•		•	•	•	•				
10.	Waianapanapa	•		•	•	•	•	•		12	•

COUNTY PARKS

CODE NUMBER	PARK NAME	RESTROOMS	OVERLOOKS	PICNIC TABLES	OUTDOOR STOVES	DRINKING WATER	SWIMMING	SHELTERS	TENT CAMPING	CABINS	SHOWERS
1.	D.T. Fleming						•				•
2.	Honokowai	•		•		•					•
3.	Ukumehame	•		•	•	•					•
4.	Waihee	•		•	•	•					•
5.	Waiehu	•			•	•		•			•
6.	Kepaniwai	•	•	•	•	•					•
7.	Maipoina Oe Iau	•		•	•	•	•				•
8.	Kalama	•		•	•	•	•				•
9.	Kamaole	•		•	•	•					•
10.	H.A. Baldwin	•	•	•			•	•	•		•
11.	Hookipa	•		•	•	•		•	•		•
12.	Honomanu Bay								•		
13.	Hana	•		•	•		•				•
14.	Paunau	•		•							•
15.	Kanaha Beach	•		•	•	•					•

Permit-issuing office

Permits can be reserved two months in advance by writing a letter including your name, address, phone number, number of persons in your party, type of permit requested, and duration of your stay. They can be picked up on arrival with proof of identification. Office hours are 8:00 a.m. to 4:15 p.m., Mon. through Friday. Usually, tent camping permits are no problem to secure on the day you arrive, but reserving insures you a space and alleviates anxiety. The permits are available from the Maui (Molokai also) Division of State Parks, 54 High St., Wailuku, 96793, tel. 244-4354; or write, Box 1049 Wailuku HI 96793.

COUNTY PARKS

There are 15 County Parks scattered primarily along Maui's coastline, and because of their locations, they're generally referred to as **beach parks**. Most are for day use only,

A refreshing cold water shower removes sand and salt.

where visitors fish, swim, snorkel, surf, picnic, and sunbathe, but three have overnight camping. The rules governing use of these parks are just about the same as those for State Parks. The main difference is that along with a use permit, County Beach Parks charge a fee for overnight use. Again, the differences between individual parks are too numerous to mention, but the majority have a central pavilion for cooking, restrooms and cold water showers, individual fire pits and picnic tables, with electricity usually only at the central pavilion. RVs are allowed to park in appropriate spaces.

Fees and permits

The fees are quite reasonable at $1 per night per person, children $ .50. One safety point to consider is that beach parks are open to the general public and most are used with regularity. This means that quite a few people pass through, and your chances of encountering a hassle or running into a rip-off are slightly higher in beach parks. To get a permit and pay your fees for use of a County

Beach Park, either write in advance, or visit the following issuing office, open 9:00 a.m. to 5:00 p.m., Mon. through Friday. County Parks Department, War Memorial Gym, Baldwin High School, Rm 102, Route 32, Wailuku HI 96793, tel. 244-5514.

HIKING

The hiking on Maui is excellent. Most times you have the trails to yourself, and the wide possibility of hikes ranges from a family saunter to a strenuous trek. The trails are mostly on public lands with some crossing private property. With the latter, the more established routes cause no problem, but for others you'll need special permission.

Haleakala hikes

The most spectacular hikes on Maui are through Haleakala Crater's 30 miles of trail. **Halemauu Trail** is 10 miles long, beginning three miles up the mountain from Park Headquarters. It quickly winds down a switchback descending 1,400 feet to the crater floor. It passes Holua Cabin and goes six more miles to Paliku Cabin, offering expansive views of Koolau Gap along the way. A spur leads to Sliding Sands Trail with a short walk to the Visitors Center. This trail passes Silversword Loop and the Bottomless Pit, two attractions in the crater. **Sliding Sands Trail** might be considered the main trail, beginning from the Visitor Center at the summit and leading 10 miles over the crater floor to Paliku Cabin. It passes Kapaloa Cabin enroute and offers the best walk through the crater, with up-close views of cinder cones, lava flows, and unique vegetation. **Kaupo Gap Trail** begins at Paliku Cabin and descends rapidly through the Kaupo Gap, depositing you in the semi-ghost town of Kaupo. Below 4,000 feet the lava is rough and the vegetation thick. You pass through the private lands of the Kaupo Ranch along well-marked trails. Without a "pickup" arranged at the end, this is a tough one because the hitching is scanty.

West Maui Trails

The most frequented trails on West Maui are at Iao Needle. From the parking area you can follow the **Tableland Trail** for two miles, giving you beautiful panoramas of Iao Valley as you steadily climb to the tableland above, or you can descend to the valley floor and follow Iao Stream for a series of small but secluded swimming holes. **Waihee Ridge Trail** is a three-mile trek leading up the windward slopes of the West Maui Mountains. Follow Rt. 34 around the backside of Maluhia Rd. and turn up it to the Boy Scout Camp. From here the trail rises swiftly to 2,560 feet. The views of Waihee Gorge are spectacular. **Kahakuloa Valley Trail** begins from this tiny forgotten fishing village on Maui's backside along Rt. 34. Start from the schoolhouse, passing burial caves and old terraced agricultural sites. Fruit trees line the way to trails ending two miles above the town.

Kula and Upcountry Trails

Most of these trails form a network through and around Poli Poli State Park. **Redwood Trail**, 1.7 miles, passes through a magnificent stand of redwoods, past the ranger station and down to an old CCC camp where there's a rough old shelter. **Tie Trail**, one-half mile, joins Redwood Trail with **Plum Trail**, so named because of its numerous plum trees, which bear during the summer. **Skyline Trail**, 6.5 miles, starts atop Haleakala at 9,750 feet, passing through the southwest rift and eventually joining the **Haleakala Ridge Trail**, 1.6 miles, at the 6,500-foot level, then descends through a series of switchbacks. You can join with the Plum Trail or continue to the shelter at the end. Both the Skyline and Ridge trails offer superb vistas of Maui. Others throughout the area include: **Poli Poli**, .6 mile, passing through the famous forests of the area; **Boundary Trail**, 4 miles, leading from the Kula Forest Reserve to the ranger's cabin, passing numerous gulches still bearing native trees and shrubs; **Waiohuli Trail** descends the mountain to join Boundary Trail and overlooks Keokea and Kihei with a shelter at the end; **Waiakoa Trail**, 7 miles, begins at the Kula Forest Reserve Access Road. It ascends Haleakala to the 7,800-foot level and then descends through a series of switchbacks. Covering rugged territory and passing a natural cave shelter, it eventually meets up with **Waiakoa**

Loop Trail, 3 miles. All of these trails offer intimate views of native, introduced forests, and breathtaking views of the Maui coastline far below.

Coastal trails

Along Maui's southernmost tip the **King's Highway Coastal Trail**, 5.5 miles, leads from La Perouse Bay through the rugged and desolate lava flow of 1790, the time of Maui's last volcanic eruption. Kihei Rd. leading to the trail gets extremely rugged past La Perouse and should not be attempted by car, but is easy on foot. It leads over smooth stepping stones that were at one time trudged by royal tax collectors. The trail heads inland and passes many ancient Hawaiian stone walls and stone foundation building sites. Spur trails lead down to the sea, including an overview of Cape Hanamanioa and its Coast Guard lighthouse. The trail eventually ends at private land. **Hana Wainapanapa Coastal Trail**, 3 miles, is at the opposite side of East Maui. You start from Wainapanapa State Park or from a gravel road near Hana Bay and again you follow the flat, laid stones of the "King's Highway." The trail is well maintained but fairly rugged due to lava and cinders. You pass natural arches, a string of *heiau*, blowholes and caves. The vegetation is lush and long fingers of black lava stretch out into cobalt blue waters.

Hiking tour

This special Maui tour is a one-man show operated by an extraordinary man. It's called **Hike Maui**, and as its name implies, it offers walking tours to Maui's best scenic areas accompanied by Ken Schmitt, a professional nature guide. Ken has dedicated years to hiking Maui and has accumulated an unbelievable amount of knowledge about this awesome island. He's proficient in Maui archaeology, botany, geology, anthropology, zoology, history, oceanography, and ancient Hawaiian cosmology. Moreover, he is a man of dynamic and gracious spirit who has tuned in to the soul of Maui. He hikes every day and is superbly fit, but will tailor his hikes for anyone, though good physical conditioning is essential. Ken's hikes are actually workshops in Maui's natural history. As you walk along, Ken imparts his knowledge but he never seems to intrude on the beauty of the site itself.

Ken Schmitt

His hikes require a minimum of two people and a maximum of six. He offers RT transportation from your hotel, gourmet breakfasts, lunches, and snacks with an emphasis on natural health foods. All special equipment, including snorkel and camping gear for overnighters, is provided. His hikes take in sights from Hana to West Maui and to the summit of Haleakala, and range from the moderate to the hardy ability level. Half-day hikes last about 5 hours and all-day hikes go for at least 12 hours. The rates vary from $45 (about half for children) to $85. Overnighters are on a sliding 'scale, by number of people and number of days, but start at $190. A day with Ken Schmitt is a classic outdoor experience. Don't miss it! Ken has an office at the Passport Ocean Safari Shop, Kealia Beach Center, 101 N. Kihei Rd., Kihei, tel. 879-5270. Mailing address is **Hike Maui**, P.O. Box 10506, Lahaina, Maui HI 96761.

EQUIPMENT INFORMATION AND SAFETY

Camping and hiking equipment

Like everything else you take to Maui, your camping and hiking equipment should be lightweight and durable. Camping equipment size and weight should not cause a problem with baggage requirements on airlines: if it does, it's a tip-off that you're hauling too much. One odd luggage consideration you might make is to bring along a small **styrofoam cooler** packed with equipment. Exchange these for food items when you get to Hawaii; if you intend to car camp successfully and keep food prices down, you'll definitely need a cooler. You can also buy one on arrival for only a few dollars. You'll need a lightweight **tent**, preferably with a rainfly, and a sewn-in floor. This will save you from getting wet and miserable, and will keep out mosquitoes, cockroaches, ants, and the few stinging insects on Maui. In Haleakala Crater, where you can expect cold and wind, a tent is a must; in fact you won't be allowed to camp without one.

Sleeping bags are a good idea, although you can get along at sea level with only a blanket. Down-filled bags are necessary for Haleakala — you'll freeze without one. **Camp stoves** are needed because there's very little wood in some volcanic areas, it's often wet in the deep forest, and open fires are often prohibited. If you'll be car camping, take along a multi-burner stove, and for trekking, a backpacker's stove will be necessary. The grills found only at some campgrounds are popular with many families that go often to the beach parks for an open-air dinner. You can buy a very inexpensive charcoal grill at many variety stores throughout Maui. It's a great idea to take along a **lantern**. This will give added safety for car campers. Definitely take a **flashlight**, replacement batteries, and a few small **candles**. A complete **first aid kit** can be the difference between life and death, and is worth the extra bulk. Hikers, especially those leaving the coastal areas, should take rain gear, a plastic ground cloth, utility knife, compass, safety whistle, mess kit, water purification tablets, canteen, nylon twine, and waterproof matches. You can find plenty of stores that sell, and a few stores that rent, camping equipment. A good one is **Outdoor Sports** in Makawao. For others, see the Yellow Pages under "Camping Equipment."

Safety

There are two things on Maui that you must keep your eye on to remain safe: humans and nature. The general rule is, the farther you get from towns, the safer you'll be from human-induced hassles. If possible, don't hike or camp alone, especially if you're a woman. Don't leave your valuables in your tent, and always carry your money, papers, and camera with you. (See "Theft" below.) Don't tempt the locals by being overly friendly or unfriendly, and make yourself scarce if they're drinking. While hiking, remember that many trails are well maintained, but trailhead markers are often missing. The trails themselves can be muddy, which may make them treacherously slippery and knee-deep. Always bring food because you cannot, in most cases, forage from the land. Water in most streams is biologically polluted and will give you bad stomach problems if you drink it without purifying it first, either through boiling or with tablets. For your part, please don't use the streams as a toilet.

Precautions

Always tell a ranger or official of your hiking intentions. Supply an itinerary and your expected route, then stick to it. Twilight is short in the islands, and night sets in rapidly. In June, sunrise and sunset are around 6:00 a.m. and 7:00 p.m.; in Dec., these occur at 7:00 a.m. and 6:00 p.m. If you become lost at night, stay put, light a fire if possible, and stay as dry as you can. Hawaii is made of volcanic rock which is brittle and crumbly. Never attempt to climb steep *pali* (cliffs). Every year people are stranded and fatalities have occurred on the *pali*. If lost, walk on ridges and avoid the gulches which have more obstacles and make it harder for rescuers to spot you. Be careful of elevation sickness, especially on Haleakala. The best cure is to head down as soon and as quickly as possible.

Heat can cause you to lose water and salt. If you become woozy or weak, rest, take salt, and drink water as you need it. Remember, it takes much more water to restore a dehydrated person; take small frequent sips. Be mindful of flash floods. Small creeks can turn into raging torrents with upland rains. Never camp in a dry creek bed. Fog is only encountered at the 1,500 to 5,000-foot level, but be careful of disorientation. Generally, stay within your limits, be careful, and enjoy yourself.

Guide books

For a well-written and detailed hiking guide complete with maps, check out *Hiking Maui* by Robert Smith, published by Wilderness Press, 2440 Bancroft Way, Berkeley CA 94704. Another book by the same company is *Hawaiian Camping* by Shirley Rizzuto. Geared toward family camping, it's adequate for basic information and listing necessary addresses, but at times it's limited in scope.

Helpful departments and organizations

The following will be helpful in providing trail maps, accessibility information, hunting and fishing regulations, and general forest rules. Write to The Dept. of Land and Natural Resources, Division of Forestry and Wildlife, 1151 Punchbowl, St., Honolulu HI 96813, tel. 548-2861. Their "Maui Recreation Map" is excellent and free. The following organizations can provide general information on wildlife, conservation and organized hiking trips although they are not based on Maui: Hawaiian Trail and Mountain Club, P.O. Box 2238, Honolulu HI 96804; Hawaiian Audubon Society, Box 22832, Honolulu HI 96822; Sierra Club, 1212 University Ave., Honolulu HI 96826, tel. 946-8494.

Topographical and nautical charts

For in-depth topographical maps, write U.S. Geological Survey, Federal Center, Denver CO 80225. In Hawaii, a wide range of topographical maps can be purchased at Trans-Pacific Instrument Co., 1406 Colburn St., Honolulu HI 96817, tel. 841-7538. For nautical charts, write National Ocean Survey, Riverdale MD 20240.

HEALTH AND CONDUCT

In a recent survey published by the *Science Digest,* Hawaii was cited as the healthiest state in the Union to live in. Indeed, Hawaiian citizens live longer than people do anywhere else in America: men to 74 years and women to 78. Lifestyle, heredity, and diet help with these figures, but Hawaii is still an oasis in the middle of the ocean, and germs just have a tougher time getting there. There are no cases of malaria, cholera, or yellow fever. Because of a strict quarantine law, rabies is also nonexistent. On the other hand, tooth decay, perhaps because of a wide use of sugar and enzymes present in certain tropical fruits, is 30 percent above the national average. With the perfect weather, a multitude of fresh air activities, soothing negative ionization from the sea, and a generally relaxed and carefree lifestyle, everyone feels better there. Hawaii is just what the doctor ordered: a beautiful natural health spa. That's one of the main drawing cards. The food and water are perfectly safe, and the air quality is the best in the country.

Handling the sun

Don't become a victim of your own exuberance. People can't wait to strip down and lie on the sand like a beached whale, but the tropical sun will burn you to a cinder if you're silly. The burning rays come through easier in Hawaii because of the sun's angle, and you don't feel them as much because there's always a cool breeze. The worst part of the day is from 11:00 a.m. until 3:00 p.m. You'll just have to force yourself to go slowly. Don't worry; you'll be able to flaunt your best souvenir, your golden Hawaiian tan, to your green-with-envy friends when you get home. It's better than showing them a boiled lobster body with peeling skin! If your skin is snowflake white, 15 minutes per side on the first day is plenty. Increase by 15-minute intervals every day, which will allow you a full hour per side by the fourth day. Have faith; this is enough to give you a deep golden uniform tan.

Haole rot

A peculiar condition caused by the sun is referred to locally as *haole* rot, so called because it supposedly affects only white people, but you'll notice some dark-skinned people with the same condition. Basically, the skin becomes mottled with white spots that refuse to tan. You get a blotchy effect, mostly on the shoulders and back. Dermatologists have a fancy name for it, and they'll give you a fancy prescription with a not-so-fancy price tag to cure it. It's common knowledge throughout the islands that Selsun Blue Shampoo has some ingredient that stops the white mottling effect. Just wash your hair with it and then make sure to rub the lather over the affected areas, and it should clear up.

Cockroaches and bugs

Everyone, in varying degrees, has an aversion to vermin and creepy crawlers. Hawaii isn't infested with a wide variety, but it does have its share. Mosquitoes were unknown in the islands until their larvae stowed away in the water barrels of the *Wellington* in 1826 and were introduced at Lahaina. They bred in the tropical climate and rapidly spread to all the islands. They are a particular nuisance in the rainforests. Be prepared, and bring a natural repellent like citronella oil, available in most health stores on the islands, or a commercial product available in all groceries or drug stores. Campers will be happy to have mosquito coils to burn at night as well. Cockroaches are very democratic insects. They hassle all strata of society equally. They breed well in Hawaii and most hotels are at war with them, trying desperately to keep them from being spotted by guests. One comforting thought is that in Hawaii they aren't a sign of filth or dirty housekeeping. They love the climate like everyone else, and it's a real problem keeping them under control.

WATER SAFETY

Hawaii has one very sad claim to fame: more people drown here than anywhere else in the world. Moreover, there are dozens of yearly victims of broken necks, backs, and scuba and snorkeling accidents. These statements shouldn't keep you out of the sea, because it is indeed beautiful, benevolent in most cases, and a main reason to go to Hawaii. But if you're foolish, it'll bounce you like a basketball and suck you away for good. The best remedy is to avoid situations you can't handle. Don't let anyone dare you into a situation that makes you uncomfortable. "Macho men" who know nothing about the power of the sea will be tumbled into a Cabbage Patch doll in short order. Ask lifeguards or beach attendants about conditions, and follow their advice. If local people refuse to go in, there's a good reason. Even experts get in trouble in Hawaiian waters. Some beaches, such as Waikiki, are as gentle as a lamb and you would have to tie an anchor around your neck to drown there. Others, especially on the north coasts during the winter months, are frothing giants.

While beachcombing, or especially when walking out on rocks, never turn your back to the sea. Be aware of undertows (the waves drawing back into the sea). They can knock you off your feet. Before entering the water, study it for rocks, breakers, reefs, and riptides. Riptides are powerful currents, like rivers in the sea, that can drag you out. Mostly they peter out not too far from shore, and you can often see their choppy waters on the surface. If caught in a "rip," don't fight to swim directly against it, you'll lose and only exhaust yourself. Swim diagonally across it, while going along with it, and try to stay parallel to the shore. Don't waste all your lung power yelling, and rest by floating.

When body surfing, never ride straight in; come to shore at a 45-degree angle. Remember, waves come in sets. Little ones can be followed by giants, so watch the action awhile instead of plunging right in. Standard procedure is to duck under a breaking wave. You can even survive thunderous oceans using this technique. Don't try to swim through a heavy froth and never turn your back and let it smash you. Don't swim alone if possible, and obey all warning signs. Hawaiians want to entertain you and don't put up signs just to waste money. The last rule is, "If in doubt, stay out."

Yikes!

Sharks live in all the oceans of the world. Most mind their own business and stay away from shore. Hawaiian sharks are well fed—on fish—and don't usually bother with unsavory humans. If you encounter a shark, don't panic! Never thrash around because this will trigger his attack instinct. If one comes close, scream loudly. Portuguese men-o-war put out long floating tentacles that sting if they touch you. Don't wash it off with fresh water, this will only aggravate it. Hot salt water will take away the sting, as will alcohol, the drinking or rubbing kind, after shave, and meat tenderizer (MSG), which can be found in any supermarket or Chinese restaurant. Coral can give you a nasty cut, and it's known for causing infections because it's a living organism. Wash the wound immediately and apply an antiseptic. Keep it clean and covered, and watch for infection.

Poisonous sea urchins, such as the lacquer-black *wana,* can be beautiful creatures. They are found in shallow tide pools and can only hurt you if you step on them. Their spines will break off, enter your foot and burn like blazes. There are cures. Vinegar and wine poured on the wound will stop the burning. If not available, the Hawaiian method is urine. It might be ignominious to have someone pee on your foot, but it'll put the fire out. The spines will disintegrate in a few days, and there are generally no long-term effects. Hawaiian reefs also have their share of moray eels. These creatures are ferocious in appearance, but will never initiate an attack. You'll have to poke around in their holes while snorkeling or scuba diving to get them to attack. Sometimes this is inadvertent on the diver's part, so be careful where you stick your hand while underwater.

Kahuna *concocted an amazing pharmacopia from plants, roots and herbs (photo by Fritz Kraft).*

HAWAIIAN FOLK MEDICINE AND CURES

Hawaiian folk medicine is well developed, and its cures for common ailments have been used effectively for centuries. Hawaiian *kahuna* were highly regarded for their medicinal skills, and native Hawaiians were by far some of the healthiest people in the world until the coming of the Europeans. Many folk remedies and cures are used to this day and, what's more, they work. Often the most common plants and fruits that you'll encounter provide the best remedies. When roots and seeds and special exotic plants are used, the preparation of the medicine is as painstakingly done as in a modern pharmacy. These prescriptions are exact and take an expert to prepare. They should never be made or administered by an amateur.

Common curative plants

Arrowroot, for diarrhea, is a powerful narcotic used in rituals and medicines. The pepper plant, *piper methisticum,* is chewed and the juice is spat into a container for fermenting. Used as a medicine in urinary tract infections, rheumatism, and asthma, it also induces sleep and cures headaches. A poultice for wounds is made from the skins of ripe bananas. Peelings have a powerful antibiotic quality and contain vitamins A, B, and C, phosphorous, calcium, and iron. The nectar from the plant was fed to babies as a vitamin juice. Breadfruit sap is used for healing cuts and as a moisturizing lotion. Coconut is used to make moisturizing oil, and the juice was chewed, spat into the hand and used as a shampoo. Guava is a source of vitamins A, B, and C. Hibiscus has been used as a laxative. *Kukui* nut oil is a gargle for sore throats, laxative, and the flowers are used to cure diarrhea. *Noni* reduces tumors, diabetes, high blood pressure, and the juice is good for diarrhea. Sugarcane sweetens many concoctions, and the juice of toasted cane was a tonic for sick babies. Sweet potato is used as a tonic during pregnancy, and juiced as a gargle for phlegm. Tamarind is a natural laxative, and contains the most acid and sugar of any fruit on Earth. Taro has been used for lung infections, thrush, and as suppositories. Yams are good for coughs, vomiting, constipation, and appendicitis.

HELP FOR THE HANDICAPPED

A handicapped or physically disabled person can have a wonderful time on Maui; all that's needed is a little pre-planning. The following is general advice that should help with your planning.

Commission on the Handicapped

This commission is designed with the expressed purpose of aiding handicapped people. It is a source of invaluable information and distributes self-help booklets free of charge. Any handicapped person heading to Hawaii should write first or visit its offices on arrival. For a "Handicapped Travelers Guide" to each of the four islands, write or visit the head office at: Commission on the Handicapped, Old Federal Bldg., 335 Merchant St., No. 215, Honolulu HI 96813, tel. (808) 548-7606; on Maui, 54 High St., Wailuku, Maui HI 96793, tel. 244-4441.

General information

The key for a smooth trip is to make as many arrangements ahead of time as possible. Here are some tips concerning transportation and accommodations. Tell the companies concerned of the nature of your handicap in advance so they can make arrangements to accommodate you. Bring your medical records and notify medical establishments of your arrival if you'll be needing their services. Travel with a friend or make arrangements for an aid on arrival (see below). Bring your own wheelchair if possible and let airlines know if it is battery powered; boarding interisland carriers requires steps. No problem. They'll board you early on special lifts, but they must know that you're coming. Many hotels and restaurants accommodate disabled persons, but always call ahead just to make sure.

Maui services

On arrival at Kahului Airport, you'll find parking spaces directly in front of the main terminal. The restaurant here has steps, so food will be brought to you in the cocktail lounge. No special emergency medical services.

Visitor information at tel. 877-6431. There is no centralized medical service, but **Maui Memorial Hospital** in Wailuku will refer, tel. 244-9056. Getting around can be tough because there is no public transportation on Maui, and no tours or companies to accommodate non-ambulatory, handicapped persons. However, both **Hertz** and **Avis** rent cars with hand controls. Health care is provided by **Maui Center for Independent Living** at tel. 242-4966. Medical equipment is available at **Crafts Drugs**, tel. 877-0111; **Hawaiian Rentals**, 877-7684; **Maui Rents,** 877-5827. Special recreation activities referrals are made by **Easter Seal Society**, tel. 242-9323, or by the Commission on the Handicapped, tel. 244-4441.

ILLEGAL DRUGS

The use and availability of illegal, controlled, and recreational drugs is about the same in Hawaii as it is throughout the rest of America. Cocaine constitutes the fastest growing use of a recreational drug, and it's available on the streets of the main cities, especially Honolulu. Although most dealers are small-time, the drug is brought in by organized crime. The underworld here is mostly populated by men of Asian descent, and the Japanese *yakuza* is said recently to be displaying a heightened involvement in Hawaiian organized crime. Cocaine trafficking fans out from Honolulu. However, the main drug available and commonly used in Hawaii is marijuana, which is locally called *pakalolo*. There are also three varieties of psychoactive mushrooms that contain the hallucinogen psilocybin. They grow wild, but are considered illegal controlled substances.

magic mushrooms

Pakalolo growing

About 10 years ago, mostly *haole* hippies from the mainland began growing pot in the more remote sections of the islands, such as Puna on Hawaii and around Hana on Maui. They discovered what legitimate planters had known for 200 years: plant a broomstick in Hawaii, treat it right, and it'll grow. *Pakalolo*, after all, is only a weed, and it grows in Hawaii like wildfire. The locals quickly got into the act when they realized that they, too, could grow a "money tree." As a matter of fact, they began resenting the *haole* usurpers, and a quiet and sometimes dangerous feud has been going on ever since. Much is made of the viciousness of the backcountry "growers" of Hawaii. There are

tales of booby traps and armed patrols guarding their plants in the hills, but mostly it's a cat and mouse game between the authorities and the growers. If you, as a tourist, are tramping about in the forest and happen upon someone's "patch," don't touch anything. Just back off and you'll be OK. Pot has the largest monetary turnover of any crop in the islands, and as such, is now considered a major source of agricultural revenue.

Buying *pakalolo*

There are all kinds of local names for pot in Hawaii, the most potent being "Kona Gold," "Puna Butter," and "Maui Wowie." Actually, these names are all becoming passe. At one time the best *pakalolo* came from plants grown from Thai and Colombian seeds. Today, the growing is much more sophisticated. The most potent grass is *sinsemilla* (Latin for "without seeds"), the flowering heads of female plants that have not been allowed to be fertilized by males. They waste no energy growing seeds and all of the potent THC stays in the flowers. The next step up is raising plants from "clones." These are *sinsemilla* plants grown in hothouses from proven super-good "mother plants," and then transplanted outside where they all grow large, resiny colas. Today, the generic term for the best pot is "buds."

Prices vary, but if the pot has seeds it's only Colombian or some lesser strain and should sell for about $50 an ounce. If it's Thai Stick or seedless "buds," it will be about $200 an ounce, and the potency will be very high. You can normally buy anything from a quarter ounce ($50) on up. The best time to buy is around Christmas or just before, when the main harvest is in. As you get closer to the summer, *pakalolo* gets a little more scarce and prices tend to rise. You can ask a likely person for pot, but mostly dealers will approach you. Their normal technique is to stroll by, and in a barely audible whisper say, "Buds?"

Hawaiian *pakalolo* is sold slightly differently than on the mainland. The dealers all seem to package it in those heat-sealed "Seal-a-Meal" plastic bags instead of the good old "baggie," and this makes it hard to check out your purchase. Mostly deals are on the up and up, but you can always get ripped off with counterfeit drugs. If the dealer refuses to let you smell it, or better yet, smoke a bit, don't bother. Smoking pot while in Hawaii is usually cool, but trying to bring it home is a hassle. All passengers leaving Hawaii are open to a thorough "agricultural inspection," and you can bet they're not only looking for illegal papayas. In 1984 there was an uproar involving a particular post office on the Big Island. It turned out that a staggering 80 percent of the outgoing packages contained *pakalolo*. The authorities are getting wise.

Magic mushrooms are also available in the islands. There are poisonous mushrooms around, so you're much better off letting the experts pick them and sell them to you. If you insist on finding your own, the best time to search is just after a rain shower. Go to a cow pasture and inspect the "cow pies" (manure droppings), where the mushrooms will be growing. If you crush them, the stems will turn a purplish color in your hands.

THEFT AND HASSLES

From the minute you sit behind the wheel of your rental car, you'll be warned about not leaving valuables unattended and locking your car up tighter than a drum. Signs warning about theft at most major tourist attractions help to fuel your paranoia. Many hotel rooms offer coin-operated safes, so you can lock your valuables away and be able to relax while getting sunburned. Stories abound about purse snatchings and surly locals who are just itching to give you a hard time. Well, they're all true to a degree, but Hawaii's reputation is much worse than the reality. In Hawaii you'll have to observe two golden laws: if you look for trouble, you'll find it; and, a fool and his camera are soon parted.

Theft
The majority of theft in Hawaii is of the "sneak thief" variety. If you leave your hotel door unlocked, a camera sitting on the seat of your rental car, or valuables on your beach towel, you'll be inviting a very obliging thief

to pad away with your stuff. You'll have to learn to take precautions, but they won't need to be anything like those employed in rougher traveling areas such as South America or Southeast Asia; just normal American precautions.

If you must walk alone at night, stay on the main streets in well-lit areas. Always lock your hotel door and windows and place all valuable jewelry in the hotel safe. When you leave your hotel for the beach, there is absolutely no reason to carry all your traveler's cheques, credit cards, or a big wad of money. Just take what you'll need for drinks and lunch. If you're uptight about leaving any money in your beach bag, just stick it in your bathing suit or bikini. American money is just as negotiable if it is damp. Don't leave your camera or portable stereo on the beach unattended. Ask a person nearby to watch them for you while you go for a dip. Most people won't mind at all, and you can repay the favor.

While sightseeing in your shiny new rental car, which immediately brands you as a tourist, again, don't take more than what you'll need for the day. Why people leave a camera sitting on the seat of their car is a mystery! Many people lock valuables away in the trunk, but remember most good car thieves can "jimmy" it as quickly as you can open it with your key. If you must, for some reason, leave your camera or valuables in your car, lock them in the trunk or consider putting them under the hood. Thieves usually don't look there and on most modern cars, you can only pop the hood with a lever on the inside of the car. It's not failsafe, but it's worth a try.

Campers face special problems because their entire scene is open to thievery. Most campgrounds don't have any real security, but who, after all, wants to fence an old tent or a used sleeping bag? Many tents have zippers that can be secured with a small padlock. If you want to go trekking and are afraid to leave your gear in the campgrounds, take a large green garbage bag with you. Transport your belongings down the trail and then walk off through some thick brush. Put your gear in the garbage bag and bury it under leaves and other light camouflage. That's about as safe as you can be. You can also use a variation on this technique instead of leaving your valuables in your rental car.

Hassles
Another self-perpetuating myth about Hawaii is that "the natives are restless." An undeniable animosity exists between locals, especially those with some Hawaiian blood, and *haoles*. Fortunately, this prejudice is directed mostly at the "group" and not at the "individual." The locals are resentful against those *haoles* who came, took their land, and relegated them to second-class citizenship. They realize that this is not the average tourist and they can tell what you are at a glance. Tourists usually are treated with understanding and are given a type of immunity. Besides, Hawaiians are still among the most friendly, giving and understanding people on earth.

Haoles who live in Hawaii might tell you stories of their children having trouble at school. They could even mention an unhappy situation at some schools called "beat-up-a-*haole*" day, and you might hear that if you're a *haole* it's not a matter of "if" you'll be beaten up, but "when." Truthfully, most of this depends upon your attitude and your sensitivity. The locals feel infringed upon, so don't fuel these feelings. If you're at a beach park and there is a group of local people in one area, don't crowd them. If you go into a local bar and you're the only one of your ethnic group in sight, you shouldn't have to be told to leave. Much of the hassle involves drinking. Booze brings out the worst prejudice on all sides. If you're invited to a beach party, and the local guys start getting drunk, make this your exit call. Don't wait until it's too late.

Most trouble seems to be directed towards white men. White women are mostly immune from being beaten up, but they have to beware of the violence of sexual abuse and rape. Although plenty of local women marry white men, it's not a good idea to try to pick up a local girl. If you're known in the area and have been properly introduced, that's another story. Also, girls out for the night in bars or discos can be approached if they're not in the company of local guys. If you are with your bikini-clad girlfriend, and a bunch of local guys are, say, drinking beer at a beach park, don't go over and try to be friendly and ask, "What's up?" You, and especially your girlfriend, just might find out. Maintain your own dignity and self-respect by treating others with dignity and respect. Most times you'll reap what you sow.

FACTS, FIGURES AND PRACTICALITIES

MAUI INFORMATION

Emergency
To summon the police, fire department, or ambulance to any part of Maui, dial 911. This help number is available throughout the island. **Helpline,** the islands crisis center, is 244-7407. **Maui Memorial Hospital,** Kaahumanu Ave., Kahului, tel. 244-9056. **Pharmacies:** Kahului, 877-0041; Kihei, 879-1951; Lahaina, 661-3119; Pukalani, 572-8244.

Information
The State operates a **Visitors' Kiosk** at Kahului Airport. Open seven days, 6:00 a.m. to 9:00 p.m., tel. 877-6413, plenty of practical brochures. **Hawaii Visitors Bureau,** 26 N. Puunene Ave., Kahului, tel. 877-7822. Open Mon. to Fri., 8:00 a.m. to 4:30 p.m. **Chamber of Commerce,** Kahului Shopping Center, tel. 877-0425. **Consumer Complaints,** tel. 244-7756. **Time,** 242-0212.

Reading material
For bookstores try: **The Book Cache** in Kahului at the Kaahumanu Mall, tel. 877-6836, and in Kaanapali at the Whalers Village, tel. 661-3259; **Waldenbooks,** Maui Mall, Kahului, tel. 877-0181; **Upstart Crow,** at The Wharf, Front St., Lahaina, tel.

667-9544. **Libraries,** main branch at 251 High St., Wailuku, tel. 244-3945, other branches in Kahului, Lahaina, Makawao and Hana. Hodge-podge of hours through the week, usually closed Fri. or Saturday.

Free tourist literature is well done and loaded with tips, discounts, maps, happenings, etc. Found everywhere, in hotels, restaurants, and street stands. They include: **This Week Maui,** every Friday; **Guide to Maui** on Thursdays; **Maui Beach Press,** newspaper format and in-depth articles, every Friday; **Maui Gold,** one for each season; **Drive Guide,** excellent maps and tips, given out free by all car rental agencies, bi-monthly; **The Bulletin,** a TV guide with feature articles and local events; **Maui News,** local newspaper, 25 cents, Mon. to Friday.

Parks and Recreation
State Parks in Wailuku, tel. 244-4345; County Parks in Wailuku, tel. 244-5514; Haleakala Natl. Park H.Q., tel. 527-7749.

Weather and whales
For all Maui weather, tel. 877-5111; for recreational areas, tel. 877-5124; for Haleakala, tel. 572-7749; for marine weather, tel. 877-3477; for whale sighting and reports in season, tel. 661-8527.

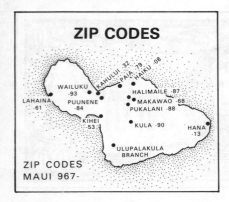

ZIP CODES

WAILUKU
-93

KAHULUI -32
PAIA -79
HAIKU -08

HALIMAILE -87
MAKAWAO -68
PUKALANI -88

LAHAINA
-61

PUUNENE
-84

KIHEI
-53

KULA -90

HANA
-13

ULUPALAKULA
BRANCH

ZIP CODES
MAUI 967-

Post offices
In Wailuku, tel. 244-4815; in Kahului, tel. 871-4710; in Kihei, tel. 879-2403; in Lahaina, tel. 667-6611. Other branch offices are scattered around the island.

Maui facts
Maui is the second youngest and second largest Hawaiian island after Hawaii. Its nickname is The Valley Island. Its color is pink and its flower is the *lokelani,* a small rose.

HAWAII VISITORS BUREAU OFFICES

Hawaii offices
The main HVB administration office is at Waikiki Business Plaza, 2270 Kalakaua Ave. Suite 801, Honolulu HI 96815, tel. 923-1811. On **Maui,** 25 N. Puunene Ave., Kahului HI 96732, tel. 244-9141. On **Kauai,** 3016 Umi St., Lihue HI 96799, tel. 245-3971. Hawaii has two branches: Hilo Plaza, 180 Kinoole St. Suite 104, Hilo HI 96720, tel. 961-5797, and 75-5719 W. Alii Dr., Kailua-Kona HI 96740, tel. 329-7787.

North America offices
New York, 441 Lexington Ave. Room 1407, New York NY 10017, tel. (212) 986-9203. **Washington D.C.,** 1511 K St. N.W., Suite 415, Washington DC 20005, tel. (202) 393-6752. **Chicago,** 180 N. Michigan Ave.

Suite 1031, Chicago IL 60601, tel. (312) 236-0632. **Los Angeles,** Central Plaza, 3440 Wilshire Blvd. Room 502, Los Angeles CA 90010, tel. (213) 385-5301. **San Francisco,** Brooks Bros. Bldg., 209 Post St. Room 615, San Francisco CA 94108, tel. (415) 392-8173.

Canada
4915 Cedar Crescent, Delta, B.C., Canada V4M 1J9.

United Kingdom
c/o Hewland Brook Hart Ltd., 15 Albemarle St., London W1X 4QL, England.

Australia
c/o Walshes World, 92 Pitt St., Sydney, N.S.W. 2000.

Asian offices
Japan, 630 Shin Kokusai Bldg., 4-1 Marunouchi 3-chome, Chiyoda-ku, Tokyo 100; **Indonesia,** c/o Odner Hotels, Kartika Plaza Hotel, Jl. M.H. Thamrin No. 10, Jakarta; **Hong Kong,** c/o Pacific Leisure, Suite 904, Tung Ming Bldg., 40 Des Voeux Rd., Central Hong Kong; **Philippines,** c/o Philippine Leisure Inc., Peninsula Hotel Arcade, Ayala Ave., Metro Manila; **Korea,** c/o Pacific Leisure, 1&2 Hong-Ik Bldg., 198-1 Kwanhoon-Dong, Chongno-ku, Seoul 110; **Singapore,** c/o Pacific Leisure, #03-01 UOL Bldg., 96 Somerset Rd., Singapore 0923; **Thailand,** c/o Pacific Leisure, 542/1 Ploenchit Rd., Bangkok; other offices are found through Pacific Leisure in **Kuala Lumpur, Penang,** and **Taipei.**

OTHER PRACTICALITIES

Telephone: Area code 808
Like everywhere else in the U.S., it's cheapest to make long-distance calls on weekday evenings. Rates go down at 5:00 p.m. and again at 11:00 p.m. until 8:00 a.m. the next morning. From Fri. at 5:00 p.m. until Mon. morning at 8:00 a.m., rates are also cheapest. Local calls from public telephones (anywhere on the same island is a local call) cost 20 cents. Calling between islands is a toll call, and the price depends on when and from

MEASUREMENTS

Distance, weights, and measures

Hawaii like all of the U.S., employs the "English method" of measuring weights and distances. Basically, dry weights are in ounces and pounds; liquid measures are in ounces, quarts and gallons; and distances are measured in inches, feet, yards and miles. The metric system, based on units of 10, is known but is not in general use. The following conversion charts should be helpful.

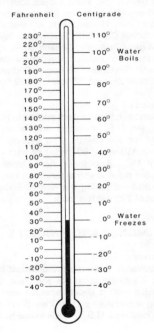

1 inch = 2.54 centimeters (cm)
1 foot = .3048 meters (m)
l mile = 1.6093 kilometers (km)
1 km = .6214 miles
1 nautical mile = 1.852 km
1 fathom = 1.8288 m
1 chain = 20.1168 m
1 furlong = 201.168 m
1 acre = .4047 hectares (ha)
1 sq km = 100 ha
1 sq mile = 2.59 sq km
1 ounce = 28.35 grams
1 pound = .4536 kilograms (kg)
1 short ton = .90718 metric ton
1 short ton = 2000 pounds
1 long ton = 1.016 metric tons
1 long ton = 2240 pounds
1 metric ton = 1000 kg
1 quart = .94635 liters
1 U.S. gallon = 3.7854 liters
1 Imperial gallon = 4.5459 liters

To compute Centigrade temperatures, subtract 32 from Fahrenheit and divide by 1.8. To go the other way, multiply Centigrade by 1.8 and add 32.

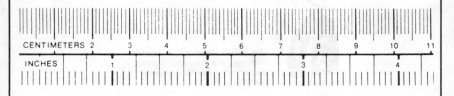

where you call and for how long you speak. Emergency calls are always free. The area code for the entire state of Hawaii is 808. For directory assistance: local, 1-411; interisland, 1-555-1212; mainland, 1-(area code) 555-1212; toll free, 1(800) 555-1212.

Time zones

There is no "daylight savings time" observed in Hawaii. When "daylight savings time" is not observed on the mainland, Hawaii is two hours behind the West Coast, four hours behind the Midwest, and five hours behind the East Coast. Hawaii, being just east of the International Date Line, is almost a full day behind most Asian and Oceanic cities. Hours behind these countries and cities are: Japan, 19 hours; Singapore, 18 hours; Sydney, 20 hours; New Zealand 22 hours; Fiji 22 hours.

Electricity

The same electrical current applies in Hawaii as on the U.S. mainland and is uniform throughout the islands. The system functions on 110 volts, 60 cycles of alternating current (AC). Appliances from Japan will work, but there is some danger of burnout, while those requiring the normal European current of 220 will not work.

MONEY AND FINANCES

Currency

U.S. currency is among the drabbest in the world. It's all the same size and color; those unfamiliar with it should spend some time getting acquainted so that they don't make costly mistakes. U.S. coinage in use is: $ .01,

$ .05, $ .10, $ .25, $ .50, and $1 (uncommon); paper currency is $1.00, $2.00 (uncommon), $5.00, $10.00, $20.00, $50.00, $100.00. Bills larger than $100.00 are not in common usage.

Banks

Full-service banks tend to open slightly earlier than mainland banks, at 8:30 a.m. Mon. through Friday. Closing is at 3:00 p.m., except for late hours on Fri. when most banks remain open until 6:00 p.m. Of most value to travelers, banks sell and cash traveler's cheques, give cash advances on credit cards, and exchange and sell foreign currency.

Traveler's cheques

TCs are accepted throughout Hawaii at hotels, restaurants, car rental agencies, and in most stores and shops. However, to be readily acceptable they should be in American currency. Some larger hotels that often deal with Japanese and Canadians will accept their currency. Banks accept foreign currency TCs, but it'll mean an extra trip and inconvenience.

Credit cards

More and more business is transacted in Hawaii using credit cards. Almost every form of accommodation, shop, restaurant and amusement accepts them. For renting a car they're almost a must. With "credit card insurance" readily available, they're as safe as TCs and sometimes even more convenient. Don't rely on them completely because there are some establishments that won't accept them, or perhaps won't accept the kind that you carry.

The "HVB Warrior" is posted alongside the roadway, marking sites of cultural and historical importance.

CENTRAL MAUI:
THE ISTHMUS

KAHULUI

It is generally believed that Kahului means "The Winning," but perhaps it should be "The Survivor." Kahului suffered attack by Kamehameha I in the 1790s, when he landed his war canoes here in preparation for battle at Iao Valley. In 1900 it was purposely burned to thwart the Plague, then rebuilt. Combined with Wailuku, the county seat just down the road, this area is home to 22,000 Mauians, over one-third of the island population. Here's where the people live. It's a practical, homey town, the only deep-water port from which Maui's sugar and pineapples are shipped. Although Kahului was an established sugar town by 1880, it's really only grown up in the last 20 years. In the 1960s, Hawaiian Commercial and Sugar Co. began building low-cost housing for its workers which became a model development for the whole of the U.S. Most people land at the air-

port, blast through for Lahaina or Kihei, and never give Kahului a second look. It's in no way a resort community, but it has the best general purpose shopping on the island, a few noteworthy sites, and a convenient location to the airport.

SIGHTS

Kanaha Pond Wildlife Sanctuary
This one time royal fishpond is 1½ miles SW of the airport at the junctions of SR Rt. 36 and 37. It's on the migratory route of various ducks and Canadian geese, but most importantly it is home to the endangered Hawaiian stilt *(Ae'o),* and the Hawaiian coot *('alae ke'oke'o).* The stilt is a 16-inch-tall, slender bird with a black back, white belly and stick-like pink legs. The coot is a gray-black duck-

Hawaiian coot

like bird, which builds large floating nests. An observation shelter is maintained along Rt. 396 (just off Rt. 36). Kanaha Pond is always open and free of charge. Bring binoculars.

Maui Community College
Just across the street from the Kaahumanu Shopping Center on Rt. 32, this is a good place to check out the many bulletin boards

Hawaiian stilt

for various activities, items for sale and cheaper long-term housing. The **Student Center** is conspicuous as you drive in, and is a good place to get most information. The library is adequate. For those interested in a hot shower, go to the gymnasium and act like you belong. Try not to bring your backpacks, but lockers are available.

Maui Zoo and Botanical Gardens
These grounds are more aptly described as a children's park. Plenty of young families enjoy themselves in this fenced-in area. The zoo houses various colorful birds such as cockatoos, peacocks and macaws, as well as monkeys, baboons, and a giant tortoise that looks like a slow-moving boulder. The chickens, ducks, and swans are run-of-the-mill, but the ostriches, over seven feet tall, are excellent specimens. With pygmy goats and plenty of sheep, the atmosphere is like a kiddies' petting zoo. It's open daily 9:00 a.m. to 4:00 p.m., free.

Turn at the red light onto Kanaloa Ave. off Rt. 32 about midway between Kahului and Wailuku. At this turn is **Wailuku War Memorial**. Here, too, is a gymnasium and free hot showers.

H. C. & S. Sugar Mill
Tours are given at the mill every Tues. and Thurs. during harvest. Follow Puunene Rd. (Rt. 350) off Kaahumanu Ave. to Puunene Town, and look for the mill on your left.

Kanaha Beach Park
This is the only beach worth visiting in the area. Good for a swim and a picnic. Follow Rt. 36 towards the airport. Turn left on Keolani Pl. and left again on Kaa Street.

ACCOMMODATIONS

Kahului features motels instead of hotels since most people are short-term visitors, heading to or from the airport. These accommodations are all bunched together across from the Kahului Shopping Center on the harbor side of Kaahumanu Ave. (Rt. 32). The best are the **Maui Beach Hotel**, tel. 877-0051, and just across a parking lot, its sister hotel, **The Maui Palms**, tel. 877-0071. Both are owned by Hawaiian Pacific Resorts, an excellent hotel group. The Maui Beach has a pool on the second floor, and its daily buffet is good value. The central courtyard, tastefully landscaped, is off the main foyer,

Maui Beach Hotel

which has a Polynesian flavor. The Red Dragon Room provides the only disco (weekends mostly) on this part of the island. For reservations, call (800) 367-5004; interisland (800) 272-5275. The two other hotels, within 100 yards, are the **Maui Hukilau**, tel. 877-3311 and **Maui Seaside**, tel. 877-3311. Both are part of the Sand and Seaside Hotels, an island-owned chain. For reservations, call (800) 367-7000. Except for the Maui Palms, which is about $10 cheaper, all of the above hotels are in the same price range and begin at $35, single.

FOOD

The Kahului area has some elegant dining spots as well as an assortment of inexpensive yet good eating establishments. Here are some of the best.

Inexpensive

Ma Chan's is a terrific little "no atmosphere" restaurant in the Kaahumanu Shopping Center (Kaahumanu Ave.) offering Hawaiian, American and Asian food — breakfast, lunch or dinner. Order the specials, such as the shrimp dinner, and for under $4 you get soup, salad, grilled shrimp, rice and garnish. No credit cards, friendly island waitresses, and good quality; tel. 877-7818.

Hats is located in the Maui Mall (Kaahumanu Ave., tel. 877-6475 (also in Paia). This small no-frills restaurant serves up excellent platters from a variety of cuisines for under $4. Open daily 8:00 a.m. to 9:00 p.m. Especially good breakfast for only $2 including eggs, home fries, breakfast meats, juice and coffee.

At counter seating in the back of **Toda Drugs**, locals go to enjoy daily specials of Hawaiian and other ethnic foods. Better than you'd think! Daily special under $4. In the Kahului Mall, open daily 8:30 a.m. to 4:00 p.m., tel. 877-4550.

Back-easterners will love **Philadelphia Lou's**, an authentic hoagie (submarine) sandwich shop. A little expensive at $5 per sandwich, but those babies are loaded and really man-sized. Two people could feed off one. In the Kahului Mall on the Lono Ave. side. Open weekdays 7:00 a.m. to 11 p.m., weekends until 2:00 a.m., Sun. till 11:00 p.m., tel. 871-8626. Free ice for coolers with picnic purchase.

Others worth trying include **Shirley's** and **Dairy Queen**, next door to each other across Lono Ave. from Philadelphia Lou's. Both serve good and inexpensive plate lunches and sandwiches, and Shirley's is open early mornings. **Aloha Restaurant** on Puunene Ave. near the Kahului Mall is open daily serving Hawaiian food at cheap prices. Tel. 877-6318.

Finally, for those who need their weekly fix of something fried and wrapped in styrofoam, Kahului's main streets are dotted with McDonald's (Puunene Ave.), Pizza Hut (Kamehameha Ave.), Burger King (Kaahumanu Ave.), and Kentucky Fried Chicken (Wakea St.).

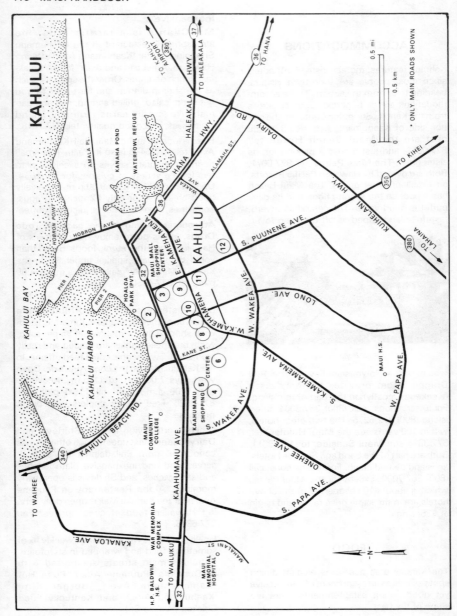

Moderate

The **Maui Beach Hotel** serves good food in the second floor dining room. You can fill up here at their lunch buffet from 11:30 a.m to 2:00 p.m., $6.50 ($5.50 salad bar only), or come for dinner from 5:30 to 8:30 p.m. (except Mon.) for their "Ten Course Chinese Dinner," offered for a very reasonable $9.95 ($5.25 children under 11). Prime rib and seafood dinners are also served. Breakfast (from 7:00 a.m.) features fresh-baked goods from $5.75. For reservations, tel. 877-0051.

Maui Palms Hotel specializes in an authentic "Japanese Imperial Buffet Dinner," every day except Sun. from 5:30 to 8:30 p.m. $9.95. On Sundays an exemplary Hawaiian buffet is offered (same time, price). All-you-can-eat salad bar daily for lunch 11:00 a.m to 1:00 p.m., $6. Excellent sampling of these two island cuisines, tel. 877-0071.

At **Ming Yuen,** for under $7 you can dine on sumptuous Chinese treats such as oysters with ginger and scallions. The hot and sour soup ($4.50) is almost a meal in itself. Inexpensive lunch from 11:00 a.m to 2:00 p.m., dinner 5:00 to 9:00 p.m. Behind the Maui Mall at 162 Alamaha St., off E. Kamehameha Avenue. Cantonese and Szechuan specialties. Reservations suggested, tel. 871-7787.

Vi's Restaurant is located at the Maui Hukilau Hotel. Breakfast from 7:00 to 9:45 a.m., dinner 6:00 to 8:45 p.m. Over 20 dinners under $6. Breakfast "special" is adequate but not special, tel. 877-3311.

KAHULUI

1. Maui Palms Hotel
2. Maui Hukilau Hotel
3. bank
4. movie theater
5. bank
6. Foodland
7. laundromat
8. library
9. movie theater
10. bank
11. post office
12. fairgrounds

In the Kaahumanau Mall try: **Guacamole's,** a Mexican restaurant with a cozy atmosphere featuring wall tapestries. A bit costly for Mexican starting at $6: **Apple Annie's** is good for their daily lunch and dinner specials under $4, but overpriced on other items on menu. **The Pizza Factory** down the road in the Maui Mall is owned by Apple Annie's and serves up decent pizza, but not at bargain prices. Little Annie might have a worm in her apples! **Olga's Wayang** in the Kaahumanu Mall serves vegetarian and Indonesian food, tel. 871-4605. **Barrio Fiesta Restaurant** in the Maui Mall specializes in Filipino delicacies, opens at 7:00 a.m., tel. 871-7938.

Expensive

The Chart House, located on Kahului Bay at 500 N. Puunene Ave. (also in Lahaina), is a steak and seafood house that's not really *that* expensive. This is a favorite with businessmen and travelers in transit to or from the airport. The quality is good and the atmosphere is soothing. Open for dinner from 5:30 to 10:00 p.m., daily, tel. 877-2476.

Island Fish House is the only really elegant restaurant in Kahului. Located in the Kahului Bldg. at 333 Lono Ave., they specialize in serving island fish prepared seven different ways. Open for lunch with slightly cheaper prices. Expect to spend $15 and up per person for dinner, tel. 877-7225.

Liqour

Maui Wine and Liquor at 333 Dairy Rd (out near the airport) is an excellent liquor store. They have an enormous wine selection, over 80 different types of imported beer, and even delivery service, tel. 871-7006. **Idini's** in the Kaahumanu Mall has a good selection of wine and beer and a top-notch deli offering picnic packages, tel. 877-3978. For a quick stop at a basic bottle shop try **Party Pantry** on Dairy Rd. or at the Maui Beach Hotel.

ENTERTAINMENT

Red Dragon Disco at the Maui Beach Hotel is the only disco and dance spot on this side of the island. Open Fri. to Sat. from 10:00

p.m. to 2:00 a.m. Reasonable dress code and cover charge.

Pizza Factory in the Maui Mall offers live music on Tues. and Wed. evenings. This large warehouse-looking building has fair acoustics, and is also the home of "Rudolph, the Red-Nosed Moose."

Maui Palms Hotel hosts the "Sakuras" every weekend. They specialize in "oldies," and their large repetoire includes "top 40," country and even Hawaiian and Japanese ballads. Good for listening and dancing!

Village Cinema, tel. 877-6622, is at the Kaahumanu Mall, and **The Maui Theater,** tel. 877-3560, is at the Kahului Mall. In addition, legitimate theater is offered by the **Maui Community Theater,** tel. 877-6712, at the Kahului Fairgrounds. Major productions occur four times a year.

SERVICES AND INFORMATION

Shopping
Because of the three malls right in a row along Kaahumanu Ave., Kahului has the best all-around shopping on the island. Here you can find absolutely everything you might need (see "Shopping" in the Introduction). Don't miss the **flea market** at the fairgrounds on Puunene St. every Saturday. You can also shop almost the minute you arrive or just before you leave at three touristy but good shops along Airport Road. At the **Little Airport Shopping Center** at the first stop sign from the airport is **Factory Tees and Things** and **Airport Flower and Fruit.** Almost next door is the **Pink and Black Coral Factory.** When Airport Rd. turns into Dairy Rd., you'll find **Floral Hawaii.** Both floral and fruit shops can provide you with produce that's pre-inspected and admissible to the mainland. They also have a large *lei* selection which can be packed to go. The T-shirt stores offer original Maui designs and custom shirts, and The Coral Factory makes distinctive Maui jewelry on the premises.

Banks
There are two **Banks of Hawaii,** tel. 871-8220, on Puunene Street. **Bank of Maui,** tel. 871-6284, is at Kahului Mall. **City Bank,** tel. 871-7761, is at Kaaahumanu Mall. And find **First Hawaiian Bank,** tel. 877-2311, at 20 W. Kaahumanu Avenue.

Post offices
The Kahului P.O. is on Puunene Ave. (Rt. 350) just across the street from the Fairgrounds; tel. 871-4710.

Library
Located at 90 School St., it has irregular hours. tel. 877-5048.

Laundromats
The Washhouse is open daily from 5:00 a.m. to 10:00 p.m. at 74 Lono Ave., tel. 877-6435. Clean and has a moneychanger. **W & F Washerette** features video games to while away the time, 125 S. Wakea, tel. 877-0353.

WAILUKU

Often, historical towns maintain a certain aura long after their time of importance has passed. Wailuku is one of these. Today Maui's county seat, you feel that it also used to be important. Wailuku earned its name, which means "Bloody Waters," from a ferocious battle fought by Kamehameha I against Maui warriors just up the road in Iao Valley. The slaughter was so intense that over four miles of the local stream literally ran red with blood. Last century the missionaries settled in Wailuku, and their architectural influences, such as a white-steepled church and the courthouse at the top of the main street, give an impression of a New England town.

Wailuku is actually a pretty town, especially in the back streets. Built on the rolling foothills of the West Maui Mountains, this adds some character — unlike the often flat layout of many other Hawaiian towns. You can "do" Wailuku in only an hour, though most people don't even give it this much time. They just pass through on their way to Iao Needle, where everyone goes, or to Happy Valley and on to Kahakuloa, around the backside, where the car companies hope that no one goes. You *can* see Wailuku's sights from the window of your car, but don't short-change yourself this way. Definitely visit the **Bailey House,** now called **Hale Hoikeike,** and while you're out, walk the grounds of **Kaahumanu Church.** Market Street, just off Main, has a clutch of intriguing shops that you can peek into while you're at it.

SIGHTS

Kaahumanu Church

It's fitting that Maui's oldest existing stone church is named after the resolute but loving Queen Kaahumanu. This rock-willed woman is the "Saint Peter" of Hawaii, upon whom Christianity in the islands was built. She was *the* most important early convert, often at-

Kaahumanu Church

tending services in Kahului's humble grass hut chapel. In 1832 an adobe church was built on the same spot and named in her honor. Rain and time washed it away, to be replaced by the island's first stone structure in 1837. In 1876 the church was reduced to about half its original size, and what remained is the white-and-green structure we know today. Oddly enough, the steeple was repaired in 1984 by the Skyline Engineers who hail from Massachusetts, the same place from which the missionaries came 150 years earlier! You can see the church sitting there on High St., (Rt. 30), but it's usually closed during the week. Sunday services are at 9 a.m., when the Hawaiian congregation sings the Lord's praise in their native language. An excellent cultural and religious event to attend!

Hale Hoikeike

This is the old **Bailey House** which was built from 1833-1850, with various rooms added throughout the years. In the 1840s it housed the "Wailuku Female Seminary," of which Edward Bailey was principal until it closed in 1849. Bailey then went on to manage the Wailuku Sugar Company. More importantly, for posterity, he became a prolific landscape painter, and provided a pictorial portrayal of various areas around the island. Most of his paintings record the period from 1866 through 1896. These paintings are now displayed in the "annex," known as the Bailey Gallery. This one-time seminary dining room was his actual studio. In July 1957 this old missionary homestead formally became the **Maui Historical Society Museum** at which time it acquired its new name of Hale Hoikeike, "House of Display." It closed in 1973, then was refurbished and reopened in July, 1975.

You'll be amazed at the two-foot-thick walls the missionaries taught the Hawaiians to build, using goat hair as the binding agent. Years of whitewashing make them resemble new-fallen snow. The rooms inside are given to various themes. **The Hawaiian Room** houses excellent examples of the often practical artifacts of pre-contact Hawaii; especial-

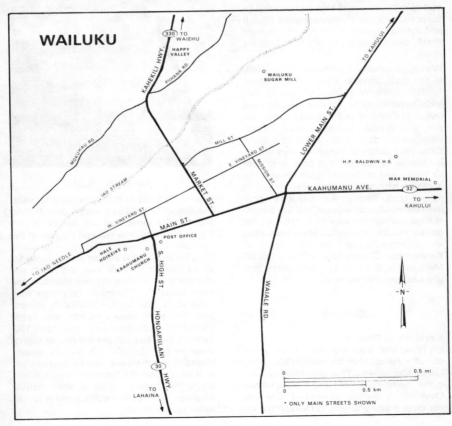

WAILUKU

the heart of Hale Hoikeike

the people who once lived here. The stonework on the floor is well laid and the fireplace is totally homey.

Go outside! The *lanai* runs across the entire front and down the side. Around back is the canoe shed, housing accurate replicas of Hawaiian-sewn sennit outrigger canoes, as well as Duke Kahanamoku's redwood surfboard. On the grounds you'll also see exhibits of sugar cane, sugar pots, *kunane* boards and various Hawaiian artifacts. Hale Hoikeike is open daily 9:00 a.m. to 3:30 p.m., on Main St. (Hwy. 32) on your left, just as you begin heading for Iao Valley. Admission is well worth $2 (students $ .50). Usually self-guided, tour guides available free if arrangements are made in advance. The bookstore/gift shop has a terrific selection of souvenirs and Hawaiiana at better-than-average prices.

Kepaniwai Park

As you head up Rt. 32 to Iao Valley, you're in for a real treat. Two miles after leaving

ly notice the fine displays of *tapa* cloth. Hawaiian *tapa,* now a lost art, was considered Polynesia's finest and most advanced. Upstairs is the bedroom. It's quite large and dominated by a canopied bed. There's a dresser with a jewelry box and fine lace gloves. Also, notice the display of Hawaiian *papales* (hats). Traders brought them, and the intrigued Hawaiians soon rendered their own versions in a wide variety of local materials. Peek beind the wooden gate in the rear of the bedroom: swords, dolls, walking canes, toys and muskets— now only a jumble, one day they'll be a display. Upstairs at the front of the house is the old office. Here you'll find roll-top desks, ledgers, and excellent examples of old-time wicker furniture, prototypes of examples you still see today. Downstairs you'll discover the sitting room and kitchen, heart of the house: the "feelings" are strongest here. There are excellent examples of Hawaiian adzes, old silverware and plenty of photos. The lintel over the doorway is as stout as the spirits of

a Japanese Pagoda at Kepaniwai

Wailuku, you come across Kepaniwai Park and Heritage Gardens. Here the architect, Richard C. Tongg, envisioned and created a park dedicated to all of Hawaii's people. See the Portuguese villa and garden complete with an outdoor oven, a thatch-roofed Hawaiian grass shack, a New England "salt box," a Chinese pagoda, a Japanese tea house with authentic garden, and a bamboo house, the little "sugar shack" that songs and dreams are made of. Admission is free and there are pavillions with picnic tables. This now-tranquil spot is where the Maui warriors fell to the invincible Kamehameha and his merciless patron war-god, Ku. *Kepaniwai* means "damming of the waters"—literally with corpses. Kepaniwai is now a monument to man's higher nature: harmony and beauty.

John F. Kennedy profile

Up the road toward Iao Valley you come to a scenic area long known as *Pali Ele'ele,* or Black Gorge. This stream-eroded, amphitheater canyon has attracted attention for centuries. Amazingly, after President Kennedy was assassinated, people noticed his likeness portrayed by a series of large boulders; mention of a profile had never been noted or recorded there before. A pipe stuck in the ground serves as a rudimentary telescope. Squint through it, and there he is, with eyes closed in deep repose. The likeness is uncanny, and easily seen, unlike most of these formations where you have to stretch your imagination to the breaking point.

Iao Valley State Park

This valley has been a sacred spot and a place of pilgrimage since ancient times. Before Westerners arrived, the people of Maui, who came here to pay homage to the "Eternal Creator," named this valley *Iao,* "Supreme Light." In the center of this velvety green valley is a pillar of stone rising over 1,200 feet (actual height above sea level is 2,250 feet), that was at one time a natural altar. Now commonly called "The Needle," it's a tough basaltic core that remained after water swirled away the weaker stone surrounding it. Iao Valley is actually the remnant of the volcanic caldera of the West Maui Mountains, whose grooved walls have been smoothed and enlarged by the restlessness of mountain streams. Robert Louis Stevenson had to stretch poetic license to create a word for Iao when he called it "viridescent."

The road here ends in a parking lot, where signs point you to a myriad of paths that criss-cross the valley. The paths are tame and well maintained, some even paved, with plenty of vantage points for photographers. If you take the lower path to the river below, you'll find a good-sized and popular swimming hole; but remember, these are the West Maui Mountains, and it can rain at any time! You can escape the crowds even in this heavily touristed area by following the path toward "The Needle" until you come to the

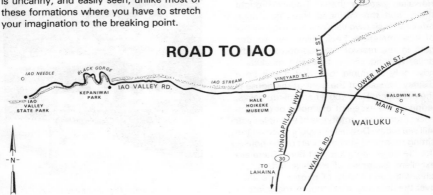

ROAD TO IAO

the Needle

pavillion at the top. As you head back, take the paved path that bears to the right. It soon becomes dirt, skirting the river and the tourists magically disappear. Here are a number of pint-sized pools where you can take a refreshing dip. Iao is for day use only. On your way back to Wailuku you might take a five-minute side excursion up to Wailuku Heights. Look for the road on your right. There's little here besides a housing development, but the view of the bay below is tops!

PRACTICALITIES

Accommodations

Visitors to Wailuku mostly stay elsewhere on Maui since the only place to lodge in town is one specialized and very humble hotel. The **Hotel Riverview**, tel. 244-4786, at 310 Market St. (in Happy Valley across from Yori's Restaurant), costs about $12 per night ($60-80 weekly). Until very recently, it was a "flop house" for locals who were down on their luck. Now, it's an upbeat, clean hotel that is a *mecca* for avid sailboarders from around the world. The owner, an American named Keenan, is a top-notch sailboarder himself, and provides all the info you'll need on equipment, conditions, and the best windsurfing beaches in the area. The Riverview is basic accommodation, but if you care more about wind and surf conditions than what your bedroom looks like, this is the place for you.

Food

The establishments listed below are all in the bargain or reasonable range. The decor in most is basic and homey, with the emphasis placed on the food.

Hale Lava is a little cafe/lodge serving Japanese and American food. For under $4, you can get a full meal. Located at 740 Lower Main (Rt. 340, Kahului Beach Rd.), tel. 244-0871. Opens at 6:00 a.m., closed Monday.

Archie's Place is a favorite with locals and serves full meals for $4. Specialty is Japanese. Located at 1440 Lower Main (Kahului Beach Rd.) tel. 244-9401. Open daily 10:30 a.m. to 2:00 p.m., 5:00 to 8:00 p.m., closed Sunday.

Paradise Cafe offers vegetarian and Mexican food. Breakfast special might be veggie-cheese omelette with hash browns for $3.75. Located at 16 Market St., tel. 244-5747.

Sang Thai is a small restaurant painted black and white at 123 N. Market, tel. 244-3817. Excellent Thai food with an emphasis on vegetarian cuisine. Open Mon. to Sat., 11:00 a.m. to 3:00 p.m., 5:00 to 10:00 p.m. Almost next door to Sang Thai at 133 N. Market is **Fujiya's**, tel. 244-0216, offering a full range of Japanese food and *sushi*. Open 11:00 a.m. to 5:00 p.m. The miso soup and tempura are inexpensive and quite good.

Yori's is more than a restaurant, it's an experience. It's located at 309 N. Market in a little red building that says Happy Valley Tavern on the roof. It specializes in Hawaiian food and *luau*. The specialty is squid in coconut milk. Inside, festooning the walls from floor to ceiling, are photos of patrons and friends. You can eat for $5. Open 11:00 a.m. to 9:30 p.m., closed Mon., tel. 244-3121. Also, just across the street is **Kameta's Sushi** if you're in the mood for these delectibles.

Down To Earth sells natural and health foods and has an excellent snack bar — basically a little window around back with a few tables available. $2.75 for a tofu burger with cheese and mock bacon. Really filling! Located at 1910 Vineyard, tel. 242-6821. Open daily 8:00 a.m. to 6:00 p.m., til 5:00 Sat., til 4:00 Sunday.

The best place to people watch and whet your whistle in Wailuku is at **Vineyard Tavern**, 2171 Vineyard, tel. 244-9597.

Shopping
Most shopping in this area is done in Kahului at the three big malls. But for an interesting diversion (all shops on Market St.) try: **Maui Wholesale Gold**, selling gold, jewelry and eel-skin items; **Treasure Imports**, selling just about the same type of articles; **Fantasea** for designer women's apparel; **Junktique**, a discovery shop which sells junk, Maui style; **Maui Fishing Supply**, with all

you need to land the big ones.

Services
Bank of Hawaii, 2105 Main, tel. 871-8200; First Interstate, 2005 Main, tel. 244-3951. The post office is at High St., tel. 244-4815.

The library is at 251 High St., tel. 244-3945, closed Saturday. For laundry, Happy Valley Wash-o-matic, 300 Block of N. Market.

For conventional health care, go to Maui Memorial Hospital, Rt. 32, tel. 244-9056; for alternative health care try the New Life Health Center at 90 Central Ave, tel. 244-9313. Here are a group of naturopaths, chiropractors and massage therapists. Dr. Jonathan Loube, M.D., is one of the naturopaths who charges a donation, based on what you can pay.

Camping permits at County Parks are available at War Memorial Gym, Room 102, Baldwin H.S., Rt. 32, tel. 244-5514. Cost $1 adult, $0.50 children, per person, per night. State Parks permits can be had at State Bldg., High St., tel. 244-4354. See "General Introduction-Accommodation-Camping" for more details.

KAHAKULOA - WEST MAUI'S BACKSIDE

To get around to the backside of West Maui you can head northeast from Kaanapali, but the majority of those few who defy the car companies and brave the bad road strike out northwest from Wailuku. Before you start this rugged 18-mile stretch, make sure you have adequate gas, water and food. It'll take you a full three hours to go from Wailuku to Kapalua. Start heading north on Market St., down toward the area of Wailuku called **Happy Valley** (good restaurants — see "Food," above). At the end of Market St. (Rt. 330) you'll find **T.K. Supermarket**, your best place to buy supplies (open 7 days). At mile 2, Rt. 330 turns into Rt. 340, which you'll follow toward Kahakuloa Bay and all the way around. In a few minutes, just when you come to the bridge over Iao Stream, will be Kuhio Place on your left. Turn here to **Halekii and Pihana Heiaus**. Although uninspiring, this area is historical and totally unvisited.

Back on Rt. 340 you come shortly to **Waihee** (Slippery Water). There's a little store here, but even if it's open it's probably under-stocked. On the right, a sign points you to **Waiehu Golf Course**. Mostly local people golf here, and the fees during the week are $10 ($15 weekends). The fairways, strung along the sea, are beautiful to play. **Dani's** is an adequate little restaurant at the golf course. Also here are two county beach parks: **Waiehu** and **Waihe'e**. They're secluded and frequented mostly by local people. Although for day use only, they'd probably be OK for an unofficial overnight stay. For Waiehu go left just before the golf course parking lot along the fence; for Waihe'e go left instead of right at the intersection leading to the golf course.

At mile 7 the pavement begins to deteriorate. The road hugs the coastline and gains eleva-

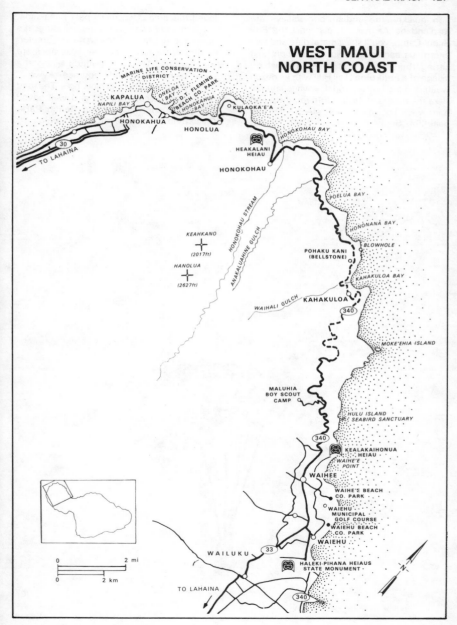

WEST MAUI NORTH COAST

MARINE LIFE CONSERVATION DISTRICT

ONELOA BAY

D. T. FLEMING BEACH CO. PARK

KAPALUA

NAPILI BAY 3

HONOKAHUA BAY

HONOKAHUA

KULAOKA'E'A

HONOLUA

HONOKOHAU BAY

HEAKALANI HEIAU

30

TO LAHAINA

HONOKOHAU

POELUA BAY

HONOKOHAU STREAM

HONONANA BAY

KEAHKANO
(2017ft)

ANAKALUAHINE GULCH

BLOWHOLE

POHAKU KANI (BELLSTONE)

HANOLUA
(2627ft)

KAHAKULOA BAY

WAIHALI GULCH

KAHAKULOA

340

MOKE'EHIA ISLAND

MALUHIA BOY SCOUT CAMP

HULU ISLAND SEABIRD SANCTUARY

340

KEALAKAIHONUA HEIAU

WAIHE'E POINT

WAIHEE

WAIHE'S BEACH CO. PARK

WAIEHU MUNICIPAL GOLF COURSE

WAIEHU BEACH CO. PARK

WAIEHU

WAILUKU

33

HALEKI-PIHANA HEIAUS STATE MONUMENT

TO LAHAINA

340

0 ____ 2 mi

0 ____ 2 km

N

tion quickly; the undisturbed valleys are resplendent. At mile 11, just past the Boy Scout Camp, you'll see a metal gate and two enormous carved *tiki*. No explanation, just sitting there. You next enter the fishing village of **Kahakuloa** (Tall Hill) with its dozen weather-worn houses and tiny white church. Here the road is at its absolute roughest and narrowest! The valley is very steep-sided and beautiful. Supposedly, great Maui himself loved this area. Two miles past Kahakuloa, you come to *Pohaku Kani,* the bell stone. It's about six feet tall and the same in diameter. Graffiti despoils it. Here the seascapes are tremendous. The surf pounds along the coast below and sends spumes skyward, roaring through a natural blow hole. The road once again becomes wide and well paved and you're soon at **Fleming Beach Park**. Civilization comes again too quickly.

tree fern

WEST MAUI

LAHAINA

INTRODUCTION

Lahaina ("Merciless Sun") is and always has been the premier town on Maui. It's the most energized town on the island as well, and you can feel it from the first moment you walk down Front Street. Maui's famed warrior-king Kahekili lived here and ruled until Kamehameha, with the help of new-found cannon power, subdued his son in Iao Valley at the turn at the 19th century. When Kamehameha I consolidated the Island Kingdom, he chose Lahaina as his seat of power. It served as such until Kamehameha III moved to Honolulu in the 1840s. Lahaina is where the modern world of the West and the old world of Hawaii collided, for better or worse. The *ali'i* of Hawaii loved to be entertained here; the **royal surf spot**, which was mentioned numerous times as an area of revelry in old missionary diaries, is just south

of the Small Boat Harbor. Kamehameha I built in Lahaina the islands' first Western structure in 1801, known as the **Brick Palace**; a small ruin still remains. Queens Keopuolani and Kaahumanu, the two most powerful wives of the Great Kamehameha's harem of over twenty, were local Maui women who remained after their husband's death and helped to usher in the new order.

The whalers came preying for "sperms and humpbacks" in 1819 and set old Lahaina Town a-reelin'. Island girls, naked and willing, swam out to meet the ships, trading their favors for baubles from the modern world. Grog shops flourished, and drunken sailors with their brown-skinned doxies owned the debauched town. The missionaries, invited by Queen Keopuolani, came praying for souls in 1823. Led by the Reverend Stuart and Richards, they tried to harpoon moral chaos. In short order, there was a curfew, a *kapu* placed on the ships by wise but ineffectual old governor Hoapili, a jail and a fort to discourage the strong-armed tactics of unruly captains. The pagan Hawaiians transformed like willing children to the new order, but the Christian sailors damned the meddling missionaries. They even whistled a few cannonballs into the Lahaina homestead of Rev. Richards, hoping to send him speedily to his eternal reward. Time, a new breed of sailor, and the slow death of the whaling industry eased the tension.

WEST MAUI SOUTH COAST

Meanwhile, the missionaries built the first school and printing press west of the Rockies at **Lahaianaluna**, just in the mountains above the town, along with downtown's **Wainee Church**, the first stone church on the island. Lahaina's glory days slipped by and it became a sleepy "sugar town" dominated by the Pioneer Sugar Mill that has operated since the 1860s. In 1901, the **Pioneer Inn** was built to accommodate inter-island ferry passengers, but no one *came* to Lahaina. In the 1960s, AMFAC had a brilliant idea. They turned Kaanapali, a magnificent stretch of beach just west, into one of the most beautifully planned and executed resorts in the world. The Pioneer Sugar Mill had long used the area as a refuse heap, but now the ugly duckling became a swan, and Lahaina flushed with new life. With superb far-sightedness, the **Lahaina Restoration Society** was begun in those years and almost the entire town was made a **National Historical Landmark**. Lahaina, subdued but never tamed, throbs with its special energy once again.

SIGHTS

In short, strolling around Lahaina is the best of both worlds. It's busy, but it's bite-sized. It's engrossing enough, but you can "see" it in half a day. The main attractions are mainly downtown within a few blocks of each other. Lahaina technically stretches, long and narrow, along the coast for about four miles, but you'll only be interested in the central core, a mere mile or so. All along Front St., the main drag, and the side streets running off it are innumerable shops, restaurants, and hideaways where you can browse, recoup your energy, or just wistfully watch the sun set. Go slow and savor, and you'll feel the dynamism of Lahaina past and present all around you. Enjoy!

Parking
Traffic congestion is a problem that needs to be addressed. Stay away from town from 4:30 to 5:30 p.m. when traffic is heaviest. There're only two traffic lights in town, one

block apart, and they're not synchronized! The other thing to know to make your visit carefree is where to stash your car. The parking lot on the corner of Wainee and Dickenson Sts. charges only $1.50 all day. There's another large lot on Prison St., just up from Front, and two smallish lots along Luakini Street. The Lahaina Shopping Center has three-hour parking. Most of the meters in town are a mere one hour, and the most efficient people on Maui are the "meter patrol!" Your car will wind up in the pound if you're not careful! You can also park for a short time in the Burger King lot on Front Street. The best place to find a spot is down at the end of Front St. past the Kamehameha School and along Shaw. You'll have to walk a few minutes, but it's worth it. For those staying in Napili or Kaanapali, leave your car at your hotel and take the Blue Shoreline Bus for the day. See "Getting Around" for details in the main Introduction.

The Banyan Tree
The best place to start your tour of Lahaina is at this magnificent tree at the corner of Hotel and Front. For one, you can't miss it as it spreads its shading boughs over almost an entire acre. Use the benches to sit and reconnoiter while the sun, for which Lahaina is infamous, is kept at bay. Children love it, and it seems to bring out the "Tarzan" in everyone. Old-timers sit here chatting, and you might be lucky enough to hear Ben Victorino, a tour guide who comes here frequently, entertain people with his ukelele and endless repertoire of Hawaiian tunes. The tree was planted in April 1873 by sheriff Bill Smith in commemoration of the Congregationalist Missions' Golden Anniversary. One hundred years later, a ceremony was held and over 500 people could be accommodated under this natural canopy. Just left of the Banyan, down the lane toward the harbor, was a canal and the Government Market. All kinds of commodities, manufactured and human, were sold here during the whaling days, and it was given the apt name of "Rotten Row."

The Courthouse
Behind the Banyan on Wharf Street is The Courthouse. Built in the 1850s from coral blocks recycled from Kamehameha III's ill-fated palace, *Hale Piula* (House of Iron), it also served as the police station, complete with a jail in the basement. Today, the jail is home to the **Lahaina Art Foundation**, where paintings and artifacts are kept behind bars, waiting for patrons to liberate them. Adjacent is **The Fort**, built in the 1830s to show the sailors that they couldn't run amuck in Lahaina. It was more for show than for force, though. When it was torn down, the blocks were hauled over to Prison St. to build the real jail, **Hale Pa'ahao**. A corner battlement of the fort was restored, but that's it, because restoring the entire structure means mutilating the Banyan.

Hawaiian tunes filter through the shade of The Banyan.

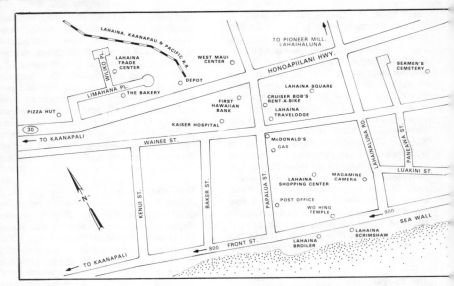

Small Boat Harbor

Walking along the harbor stimulates the imagination and the senses. The boats waiting at anchor sway in confused syncopation. Houser ropes groan and there's a feeling of anticipation and adventure in the air. Here you can board for all kinds of sea-going ex-

cursions. In the days of whaling there was no harbor. The boats tied up one to the other in the "roads," at times forming an impromptu floating bridge. The whalers came ashore in their chase boats; with the winds always up, departure could be made at a moment's notice. The activity here is still totally dominated by the sea.

The Carthaginian II

The masts and square rigging of this replica of the enterprising freighters that braved the Pacific tower over Lahaina Harbor. You'll be drawn to it... go! It's the only truly square-rigged ship left afloat on the seas. It replaced the *Carthiginian I,* when that ship went aground in 1972 while being hauled to Honolulu for repairs. The Lahaina Restoration Foundation found this steel-hulled ship in Denmark; built in Germany in 1920 as a two-masted schooner, it tramped around the Baltic under converted diesel power. The society shipped it 12,000 miles to Lahaina where it underwent extensive conversion until it became the beautiful replica that you see today. The sails are yet to be made for lack of funds.

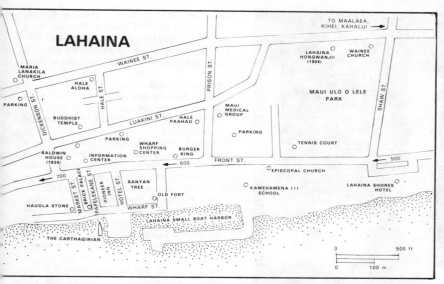

LAHAINA

the Carthaginian II

The Carthaginian is a floating museum dedicated to whaling and to whales. Richard Widmark, the actor, narrates a superb film documenting the life of humpbacks. Belowdecks is the museum containing artifacts and implements from the whaling days. There's even a whaling boat which was found intact in Alaska in the 1970s. The light belowdecks is subdued, and while you sit in the little "captains' chairs" the humpbacks chant their peaceful hymns in the background. Flip Nicklin's sensitive photos

adorn the bulkheads. It's open daily 9:30 a.m. to 4:30 p.m., but arrive by 3:45 to see all the exhibits and videos. Admission $2.

Pioneer Inn

This vintage inn, situated at the corner of Hotel and Wharf Streets, is just exactly where it belongs. Stand on its veranda with the "honky tonk" piano playing in the open bar behind you and gaze at the *Carthaginian*. Presto—it's magic! You'll see. It was even a favorite spot for Errol Flynn when he was in Lahaina filming "Devil at Four O'Clock." The green and white Inn was only built in 1901 to accommodate inter-island ferry passengers, but its style seems much older. If ironwork had been used on the veranda, you'd say it was New Orleans. A new wing was built behind it in 1965 and the two form a courtyard. Make sure to read the hilarious rules governing behavior that are posted in the main lobby. The Inn is still functional. The rooms in the old wing are colorfully seedy—spotlessly clean, but with character and atmosphere. The wooden stairway, painted red, leads upstairs to an uneven hallway lined with a threadbare

This "old salt" guards the grog shop at the Pioneer Inn.

carpet. The interior smells like the sea. There's no luxury here, but you might consider one night just for the experience. (See "Accommodations," below, for details). Downstairs the **Snug Harbor Restaurant** serves dinners, and you can't find a better place to watch life go by with a beautiful sunset backdrop than in the **Old Whaler's Grog Shop.**

The Brick Palace
This rude structure was commissioned by Kamehameha I in 1801 and slapped together by two forgotten Australian ex-convicts. It was the first Western structure in Hawaii, but unfortunately the sub-standard materials have disintegrated, for the most part. Kamehameha never lived in it, but it was occupied and used as a storehouse until the 1850s. Now, only an archaeological excavation, covered in plexiglass, remains of this site. Just to the right of the Brick Palace, as you face the harbor, is **Hauola Stone,** marked by an HVB Warrior. Formed like a chair, it was believed by the Hawaiians to have curative powers if you sat on it and let the ocean bathe you. Best view at low tide.

Baldwin Home
One of the best attractions in Lahaina is the Baldwin Home on the corner of Front and Dickenson. It was occupied by the Doctor/ Reverend Dwight Baldwin, his wife Charlotte, and their eight children. He was a trained teacher, as well as the first doctor/dentist in Hawaii. The building served as a dispensary, meeting room, and boarding home for anyone in need from the 1830s to 1868. The two-foot-thick walls are of cut lava, and the mortar was of crushed coral, over which plaster was applied. As you enter, notice how low the doorway is, and that the doors inside are "Christian doors"—with a cross forming the upper panels and with an open Bible at the bottom. The Steinway piano that dominates the entrance was built in 1859. In the bedroom to the right, along with all of the period furniture, is a wooden commode, a prototype of the portable toilet. Also notice the lack of closets; all items were kept in chests. Upstairs was a large dormitory where guests slept.

The doctor's fees are posted and are hilarious. Payment was by "size" of sickness: very big $50, diagnosis $3, refusal to pay $10! The Rev. Baldwin was 41 when he arrived in Hawaii from New England and his wife was 25. She was supposedly sickly (8 children!) and he had heart trouble, so they moved to Honolulu in 1868 to receive better health care. The home became a community center housing the library and meeting rooms. Today, The Baldwin Home is a showcase museum of the Lahaina Restoration Society. It's open daily 9:30 a.m. to 5:00 p.m., admission $2, kids free accompanied by a parent.

Masters' Reading Room
Originally a missionaries' store room, the Masters' Reading Room was converted to an Officers' Club in 1834. Located next door to the Baldwin Home, these two venerable buildings constitute the oldest Western

structures on Maui, and fittingly, this uniquely constructed coral stone building is home to the Lahaina Restoration Foundation. The building is not really open to the public, but you can visit to pick up maps, brochures and information about Lahaina.

The **Lahaina Restoration Foundation,** begun in 1962, is headed by Jim Luckey, an historian in his own right who knows a great deal about Lahaina and the whaling era. The main purpose of the Foundation is to preserve the flavor and authenticity of Lahaina without stifling progress — especially tourism. The Foundation is privately funded and has managed to purchase many of the important historical sites in Lahaina. They own the two buildings mentioned, the restored Wo Hing Temple, the land under the U.S. Seamen's Hospital, and the plantation house next door, which they'll own outright in 18 years. The 42 people on the Board of Directors come from all socio-economic backgrounds. You don't get on the board by how much money you give, but by how much effort and time you are willing to invest in the Foundation; the members are extremely dedicated. Merchants approach the Foundation with new ideas for business and ask how they can best comply with the building codes. The townspeople know that their future is best served if they preserve the feeling of old Lahaina rather than rush headlong into frenzied growth. The historic village of Williamsburg, Virginia, is often sited as Lahaina's model, except that Lahaina wishes to remain a "real" living, working town.

Hale Pa'ahao
Mid-block on Prison Street, literally means "stuck-in-irons house." It was constructed by prisoners in the 1850s from blocks of stone salvaged from the old defunct Fort. It had a catwalk for an armed guard, and cells complete with shackles for hardened criminals, but most were drunks who yahooed around town on the Sabbath, wildly spurring their horses. The guardhouse and cells were rebuilt in 1959, and the structure is maintained by the Restoration Foundation. The cells, curiously, are made of wood, which shows the inmates weren't that interested in busting out. It's open Mon. to Fri., from 9:00 a.m. to 3:00 p.m. Admission free.

Maluuluolele Park
This nondescript area at the corner of Shaw and Front was at one time the most important spot in Lahaina. Here was a small pond with a diminutive island in the center. The pond, Mokuhinia, was home to a *moo,* a lizard spirit. The tiny island, Mokuula, was the home of the Maui chiefs, and the Kamehamehas, when they were in residence. It became

The influence of New England architecture is obvious in the Baldwin Home.

a royal mausoleum, but later all the remains were taken away and the pond was filled and the ground leveled. King Kamehameha III and his sister Princess Nahienaena were raised together in Lahaina. They fell in love, but the new ways caused turmoil and tragedy. Instead of marrying and producing royal children, a favored practice only twenty years earlier, they were wrenched apart by the new religion. He, for a time, numbed himself with alcohol, while she died woefully from a broken heart. She was buried here, and for many years Kamehameha III could be found at her grave quietly sitting and meditating.

Wainee Church and Cemetery
The church itself is not impressive, but its history is. This is the spot where the first Christian services were held in 1823. A church was built here in 1832 which could hold 3,000 people, but it was razed by a freak hurricane in 1858. Rebuilt, it survived until 1894, when it was deliberately burned by an angry mob, upset with the abolition of the monarchy in Hawaii and its annexation by the U.S. Another church was built, but it, too, was hit not only by a hurricane but by fire as well. The present structure was built in 1953. In the cemetery is a large part of Maui's history: buried here are Hawaiian royalty. Lying near each other are Queen Keopuolani, her star-crossed daughter, Princess Nahienaena, and old Governor Hoapili, their Royal Tomb marked by two large headstones surrounded by a wrought iron fence. Other graves hold missionaries such as William Richards, and many infants and children.

Churches and temples
You may wish to stop for a moment at Lahaina's churches and temples dotted around town. They are reminders of the mixture of faiths and peoples that populated this village and added their particular style of energy. **The Episcopal Cemetery** on Wainee Street shows the English influence in the islands. Many of the royal family, including King Kalakaua, became Anglicans, and this cemetery holds the remains of many early Maui families, and of Walter Murray

Gibson, the notorious settler, politician and firebrand of the 1880s. Just behind is **Hale Aloha,** "House of Love," a small structure built by Maui residents in thanksgiving for being saved from a terrible smallpox epidemic that ravaged Oahu but bypassed Maui in 1858. The structure was restored in 1974. Also on Wainee is **Maria Lanakila Church,** the site of the first Roman Catholic Mass in Lahaina, celebrated in 1841. The present structure dates from 1928. Next to the church's cemetery is the **Seaman's Cemetery** where many infirm from the ships that came to Lahaina were buried. Most stones were obliterated by time and only a few remain. Herman Melville came here to pay his last respects to a cousin buried in this yard. **Hongwanji Temple** is also on Wainee, between Prison and Shaw. It's a Buddhist temple with the largest congregation in Lahaina and dates from 1910, with the structure being raised in 1927.

The **Wo Hing Temple** is on Front Street, and is the Lahaina Restoration Foundation's newest reconstruction. It was opened to the public in 1984, and shows the Chinese influence in Lahaina. It's open 9:00 a.m. to 9:00 p.m., small admission. **Holy Innocents Episcopal Church,** built in 1927, is also on Front Street, near Kamehameha III school. Known for its "Hawaiian Madonna," its altar is resplendent with fruits, plants and birds of the islands. The **Lahaina Jodo Mission** is at the opposite end of Front Street, near Mala

The restored Wohing temple houses the Thomas Edison Museum, featuring early footage of Hawaii filmed by the great inventor himself.

The Buddha of the Jodo Mission is a facsimile of the Daibutsu *(Giant Buddha) of Kamakura, Japan.*

Wharf on Ala Moana Street. Here the giant bronze Buddha, the largest outside of Asia, was dedicated in 1968 in commemoration of the centennial of the Japanese arrival. The grounds are impeccable and serenely quiet. You may stroll around, but the buildings are closed to the public. If you climb the steps to peek into the temple, kindly remove your shoes.

U.S. Seamen's Hospital

This notorious hospital was reconstructed by the Lahaina Restoration Foundation in 1982. Here is where sick seamen were cared for under the auspices of the U.S. State Department. Allegations during the late 1850s claimed that the care here extended past the grave! Unscrupulous medicos supposedly charged the U.S. government for care of seamen who had long since died. Located at Front and Baker, heading toward Kaanaplai, near the Jodo Mission.

Lahainaluna

Head up the mountain behind Lahaina on Lahainaluna Road for approximately two miles. On your left you'll pass the **Pioneer Sugar Mill**, in operation since 1860. Once at Lahainaluna ("Above Lahaina") you'll find the oldest school west of the Rockies, opened by the Congregationalist Missionaries in 1831. Children from all over the islands, and many from California, came here to school, if their parents could afford to send them away to boarding school. Today, the school is West Maui's public high school, but many children still come here to board. The first students were not only given a top-notch academic education, but a practical one as well. They not only built the school buildings, many were also apprentices in the famous **Hale Pai** (Printing House) that turned out Hawaii's first newspaper and made Lahaina famous as a printing center.

One look at Hale Pa'i and you think of New England. It's a white stucco building with blue trim and a wood-shake roof. It was restored in 1982 and is open Mon. to Sat., 9:00 a.m. to 4:00 p.m., admission $2. (If you visit the Baldwin Home, admission to Hale Pa'i is included.) If you visit the campus when school is in session, you may go the Hale Pa'i, but if you want to walk around, please sign in at the Vice-principal's office. Lahainaluna H.S. is still dedicated to the preservation of Hawaiian culture. Every year, in April, they celebrate the anniversary of one of their most famous students, David Malo. Considered Hawaii's first scholar, he authored the definitive *Hawaiian Antiquities.* His final wish was to be buried "high above the tide of foreign invasion" and his grave is close to the giant "L" atop Mount Ball, behind Lahainaluna. On the way back down to Lahaina, you get a wide, impressive panorama of the port and the sea.

Hale Pai, *the oldest printing house west of the Rocky Mountains*

Heading east

Five miles east of Lahaina along the coastal road (Rt. 30) is the little village of Olowalu. Today, little more than a general store and a French restaurant are here. This was the place of the Olowalu Massacre perpetrated by Capt. Metcalfe. Its results were far-reaching, greatly influencing Hawaiian history. Two seamen, Young and Davis, were connected with this incident, and with their help Kamehameha I subdued all of Hawaii. Behind the store are petroglyphs. Follow the dirt track behind the store for about one-half mile; make sure you pass a water tower within the first few hundred yards because there are three similar roads here. You'll come to the remains of a wooden stairway going up a hill. There once was an HVB Warrior here, but he might be gone. Claw your way up the hill to the petroglyphs, which are believed to be 300 years old. If you continue east on Rt. 30, you'll pass **Papawai** and **McGregor Point**, both noted for their vistas and as excellent locations to spot migrating whales, in season. The road sign merely says "Scenic Lookout."

BEACHES

The best beaches around Lahaina are just west of town in Kaanapali, or just east toward Olowalu. A couple of adequate places to spread your towel are right in Lahaina, but they're not quite on a par with the beaches just a few miles away.

Maluulu o Lele Park

"The Breadfruit Shelter of Lele" is in town and basically parallels Front Street. It's crowded at times and there's plenty of "wash up" on this beach. It's cleaner and quieter at the east end down by Lahaina Shores, a one-time favorite with the *ali'i*. There are restrooms, the swimming is fair, and the snorkeling acceptable past the reef. **Lahaina Beach** is at the west end of town near Mala Wharf. Follow Front to Puunoa Place and turn down to the beach. This is a good place for families with tots because the water is clear, safe, and shallow.

Puamana Beach County Park

About two miles before you enter Lahaina

from the east along Rt. 30, you'll see signs for this Beach Park. A narrow strip between the road and the sea, the swimming and snorkeling are only fair. The setting, however, is quite nice with picnic tables shaded by ironwood trees. The views are terrific and this is a great spot to eat your plate lunch only minutes from town. **Launiupoko State Park** a mile farther east has restrooms and showers, but no beach. This is more of a pit stop than anything else.

Wahikuli State Park
Along Rt. 30 between Lahaina and Kaanapali. It's a favorite with local people and excellent for a picnic and swim. Restrooms and tennis courts are just across the street. The park is very clean and well maintained.

ACCOMMODATIONS

Lodging in Lahaina is limited, surprisingly inexpensive, and an experience... of sorts. Most visitors head for Kaanapali, because Lahaina tends to be hot and hot to trot, especially at night. But you can find good bargains here, and if you want to be in the thick of the "action," you're in the right spot.

Pioneer Inn
The oldest hotel on Maui still accommodating guests. At 658 Wharf St., Lahaina,

HI 96764, tel. 661-3636. Absolutely no luxury whatsoever, but a double scoop of atmosphere. Here's the place to come if you want to save money, and be the star of your own movie with the Pioneer Inn as the stage set. Enter the tiny lobby full of memorabilia, follow the creaking stairway up to a wooden hallway painted green on green. This is the old wing. Screen doors cover inner doors to clean but basic rooms which have ceiling fans and open out onto the building-long *lanai,* overlooking the harbor. $18/$21, shared bath, private bath (showers) a few dollars extra. Music and the sounds of life from the bar below late in the evening at no extra charge. The "new wing," basic modern, circa 1966, is attached. Starting at $36, it's no bargain. It offers a private *lanai,* bath, a/c, and overlooks the central courtyard. Pool. The old section is fun; the new section is only adequate.

Lahainaluna Hotel
You can't really have a town without a "down-at-the-heels" hotel, and this is Lahaina's. It is, however, clean and safe. What better place for an adventurous traveler to stay than a hotel that cuts costs by suggesting you bring your own beach towel, and offers no maid service for stays less than three days? $30 for preferred rooms with a/c, TV (b&w), private shower and view of mountains or harbor, $27.50 with no view. There

the Pioneer Inn

are even unadvertised rooms "in the back" that go for cheaper, usually for residents or for a long-term stay. The Lahainaluna Hotel is at 127 Lahainaluna Rd., Lahaina HI 96761, tel. 661-0577. There are only 18 rooms and they do sell out.

Maui Islander
Located a few blocks away from the hubbub, at 660 Wainee St., Lahaina 96761, tel. 667-9766, (800) 367-5226. A very adequate hotel offering rooms with kitchenettes, studios and suites up to three bedrooms for seven guests or more. All a/c with TV, pool and tennis courts. Homey atmosphere with daily planned activities. Basic hotel rooms start at $42, studios $55, $6 extra per person.

Lahaina Shores
This six-story condo was built before the Lahaina building code limited the height of new construction. Located at the east end of town, at 475 Front St., Lahaina 96761, tel. 661-4835, (800) 367-2972. The tallest structure in town, it's become a landmark for incoming craft. It offers a swimming pool and spa and is located on the only beach in town. From a distance, the southern mansion facade is striking: up close, though, it becomes painted cement blocks and false colonnades. The rooms, however, are a good value for the money. The basic contains a full bathroom, powder room, large color TV, and equipped kitchen. They're all light and airy, and the backside views of the harbor or frontside of the mountains are the best in town. Studios begin at $60, suites $85, $6 for additional guests.

Lahaina Roads
This condo/apartment is located at the far west end of town at 1403 Front St., Lahaina 96761, tel. 661-3166. There is a three-night minimum stay with a one-week minimum during peak season. All units have fully equipped kitchens, a/c, TV and maid service on request. One-bedroom units start at $55, $6 additional guests. No credit cards honored. Discounts are offered for more than one-week stays.

Puamana
One-bedroom units (fully equipped) begin at $60. Special car rental rates are offered. This condo is located one mile SE of town. Write O. Box 515, Lahaiana 96767, tel. 667-2551, (800) 367-5630. Check in at Manager's Office in Lahaina at 910 Honoapiilani, #11.

Travelodge
Your one-time basic motel became an office building as of August, 1985.

FOOD

Lahaina's menu of restaurants is gigantic, all palates and pocketbooks can easily be satisfied: there's fast food, sandwiches, sushi, happy hours, and elegant cosmopolitan restaurants. Because Lahaina is a dynamic tourist spot, restaurants and eateries come and go with regularity. The following is not an exhaustive list of Lahaina's food spots—it couldn't be. But there is plenty listed here to feed everyone at breakfast, lunch, and dinner. Bon appetit!

Inexpensive
Lahaina Natural Foods: Located at 1295 Front Street, west end almost out of town toward Kaanapali. Open seven days, 8:00 a.m to 8:00 p.m., Sun. 6:00 p.m., tel. 667-2251. They have an excellent deli and feature fresh-baked goods. Take out picnic lunches and tables on the premises at the **Waterfront Cafe.** Great sandwiches and you can't beat the smoothies for 99 cents.

Naokee's, Too: If you're looking for atmosphere, drive on by this place. Also at Lahaina's west end at 1307 Front St, tel. 667-7513. They feature "regular" island food like chicken, pork and beef, with rice, macaroni salad and corn. Plate lunches $4, specialty one-lb. steak $6.95. Basic but good.

Taco, Burrito and Tostada: This little hole-in-the-wall doesn't even have a real name. Everything is less than $4, but they seem like a place that'll disappear quicker than a Mexican flea. It's located in the 700-800 block of Front St., in about the middle of the sea wall.

Expresso Cafe: Located at 693 Front, tel. 661-4710. The kind of place that locals keep secret. Its motto is "yours, mine and auras." It's a tiny little place where you can have an excellent coffee, or sandwich on whole wheat or pita bread. Good pastries. More for a snack, a quick breakfast or to people watch.

The Fish Fry: Located at the Lahaina Shopping Center, tel. 667-9243. Their name almost says it all, but they also have filling plate lunches for under $4, sandwiches for under $2, and a wide range of omelettes for under $3. Limited seating, good value. Open daily.

Sushi: There is a tiny "no name" sushi bar and plate lunch place on Prison St. just after you turn toward the mountains off Front Street. Look for it across the street from the "bus parking" lot. Very reasonable prices.

The Bakery: Your sweet tooth will begin to sing the moment you walk into this bakery/sandwich shop. Located at 911 Limahana, near the "Sugar Cane Train Depot" off Honoapiilani Rd. (Hwy. 30) as you head toward Kaanapali. You can't beat their stuffed croissants for under $1, or their sandwiches for under $2! Coffee is a mere 40 cents, and their pastries, breads and pasta are goooood! Open daily 7:00 a.m. to 5:00 p.m., until 12:00 noon on Sun., tel. 667-9062. The **Cafe Allegro,** located next door, has decent and inexpensive Italian-style food, and pizza.

Togo's: At the Lahaina Shores Village, 505 Front., tel. 667-6917. Sun. to Thurs. from 9:30 a.m. to 12:00 midnight; Fri. and Sat. closes earlier. Basically your good old sub shop. Selling "stubbies, regulars and giants" from $3-$15.

Fast food: Fanatics can get their fix at: **Burger King,** Front St., near the Banyan Tree; **McDonald's,** at the Lahaina Shopping Center; **Skipper's,** for deep-fried seafood at The Wharf Shopping Center; **Kentucky Fried Chicken** at the Lahaina Shopping Center; **Pizza Hut** at 127 Hinau Street.

Moderate

Hamburger Mary's: At the southeast end of town at 608 Front St., tel. 667-6989. This is a Maui branch of the same restaurant located in San Francisco. Walk along the gravelled walkway to the entrance and beer garden around back. Soup and salad for $7 will definitely fill you up. Tremendous sandwiches up to $6.75. Famous, enormous (2 people?) hamburgers for $5.50. The best deal is breakfast, served all day, with an assortment of omelettes for under $3. Popular with gay people of both sexes, literally and figuratively. Open daily 7:00 a.m. to 11:00 p.m.

Banyan Inn: Perhaps the least expensive "full service" restaurant in Lahaina. Located at 640 Front, across from the Banyan Tree, tel. 661-4489. Open daily for lunch and dinner, featuring live Hawaiian music on the weekends. This is where local people "eat out." Not very elegant, but not tacky either, especially at night, outlined by torchlight. You can get a full dinner for around $10, and the fresh-baked pie is an excellent dessert. Home cooking, Hawaiian-style.

Harbor Front Restaurant: Located on the second floor, at The Wharf Shopping Center on Front Street, tel. 667-78212. Their logo reads, "established a long time ago." Lunch up to $6, $5 sandwiches, $15 dinners. A display case at the entrance holds the fresh catch-of-the-day. The interior is surprisingly well-done with many hanging plants in distinctive planters, high-backed wicker chairs, with white tables and bright orange table settings.

Blackbeard's: Also at The Wharf, tel. 667-9535. Lunch from 11:00 a.m. to 4:00 p.m., dinner from 5:00 to 10:00. They have an excellent happy hour and feature live music nightly. Good selection of imported beers. Try the Hawaiian fruit boat for $3.95, or buy a submarine at $ .50 an inch.

Tortilla Flats: On the lower level of The Wharf Shopping Center, tel. 667-9581. Daily 11:30 a.m. to 10:00 p.m. Mexican food at very reasonable prices, and huge margaritas! Unfortunately, it varies in the quality of cooking depending on the day's chef, according to workers at The Wharf who are in the know.

Greenthumb's: Overlooking the harbor at 839 Front, tel. 667-6126. Daily 10 a.m. to 10 p.m. Plenty of salads to choose from and vegetarians are not forgotten. You can fill up for under $6. These guys are new and are trying hard (and succeeding) to build a good reputation. For a light meal, you can't go wrong. Take out, too.

The Oceanhouse: At 831 Front St., tel. 661-3359. Daily lunch 11:00 a.m. to 2:30 p.m., dinner 5:00 p.m. to 10:00 p.m. Happy hour with free munchies and beer 85 cents, well drinks $1. Known for its extensive salad bar. Lunch is available for under $5. Dinner begins at $8. There's an "early bird special" with a good discount from 5:00 to 6:00 p.m. Nice atmosphere and terrific sunset view.

Moose McGuillicudy's: On the upper level of **Mariner's Alley** at 844 Front., tel. 667-7758. Daily 7:30 a.m. until the wee hours. They have a large-screen TV, overstuffed chairs and a great view overlooking Front Street. Plenty of specials including an "early-bird " breakfast for only $1.99, a "beggar's banquet" for $2.29. Mid-day and evening happy hours offer truly inexpensive drinks, featuring margaritas in 11 flavors and highballs for 90 cents. Every night has a different featured event: Monday, dance; Tuesday, tequila; Wednesday, live music, etc. The big Moose is OK.

Marco's Italian Restaurant: Also at Mariner's Alley just downstairs from Moose, tel. 661-8877. Daily breakfast 9:00 to 11:00 a.m., dinner from 5:00 p.m. The breakfasts tend to be continental with coffee and pastry. Dinners are well priced at less than $10. Calzone is only $6, lasagna $8.50. Good Italian salads for $4.50.

Lahaina Broiler: At the west end of town in the 800 block of Front St., under the enormous monkey pod tree, tel. 661-3111. You can't get closer to the sea than this almost open-air restaurant. Great sunsets, better-than-average island cooking for a good price.

The Keg: Name changed from the well-known **Blue Max**, located at 730 Front St., tel. 661-3137. Comfortable decor of old couches, coffee tables, etc. Like old aunty's parlor. Also a terrific view of "the roads." Happy hour, and good lunch specials. At night it becomes a disco/restaurant. At one time any celebrity passing through, such as Elton John, stopped in for a drink and a jam.

Whale's Tail: Just next door to **The Wharf Shopping Plaza**, second level at 666 Front St., tel. 661-3676. Daily lunch, 11:30 a.m. to 2:30 p.m., dinner from 5:00 p.m. They usually offer a musician playing guitar, or sometimes an entire band. Teriyaki and Oriental steak for $7.95, seafood entrees from $10. Children's menu.

Harpooner's Lanai: At the Pioneer Inn, tel. 661-3636. Daily breakfast from 7:00 a.m., lunch from 11:30 a.m. Basic but good foods including pancakes and Portuguese bean soup. Most dishes and sandwiches under $5. Also, **South Seas** on the harborside of the Pioneer Inn. Seafood and cook-your-own, all for under $10. Children's menu. Daily dinner only, tel. 661-3636.

Ma's Dimsum: At Lahaina Square, tel. 667-9378. Daily except Sun., from 11:00 a.m. to 5:00 p.m. Chinese "take out" featuring a wide variety of dimsum. All kinds of plate lunches available for picnicking.

Fujiyama: At Lahaina Square, tel. 667-7207. Open Mon. to Fri., from 11:00 a.m. to 1:30 p.m. and from 5:00 to 9:00 p.m. Teppenyaki dinners at your table for under $15. A full sushi bar. Most Japanese favorites like tempura and sukiyaki.

Organ Grinder: At 811 Front St., tel. 661-4593. A family-run business giving you your money's worth. Terrific sandwiches that'll fill you up. Open for breakfast, too.

Kimo's: At 845 Front St., tel. 661-4811. Great harbor and sunset view on the lower level. Popular, but no reservations taken. They offer seafood from $8 and are known for their "catch-of-the-day," usually the best offering on the menu. The downstairs bar has top-notch well drinks featuring brand name liquor. A limited menu for children.

Bettino's: Located at 505 Front, Lahaina Shores Village, tel. 661-8810. Daily from 7:00 a.m. Off the beaten track and a favorite with locals. Italian offerings like fettuccine from $6.95. Also, steaks and seafood. Renowned for their enormous salads. Worth the trip, and when others are overcrowded you can usually find a good table here. The **Whaler's Pub** just next door has good drinks and an exemplary view. Friendly atmosphere and no trouble finding a great table.

Blackie's Bar: On Rt. 30 about one-half mile out of town toward Kaanapali. Look for the orange roof. Daily 10:00 a.m. to 10:00 p.m., tel. 667-7979. An institution, sort of, selling Mexican food and hot dogs! Known for its jazz on Fri. and Sat. evenings from 5:00 to 8:00 p.m.

Chart House: At the far west end of Lahaina at 1450 Front St., tel. 661-0937. Daily dinner 5:00 to 9:30 p.m. No reservations, and a wait is common. They have another, less crowded, restaurant in Kahului. Good selection of seafood and beef. Reasonably priced with a decent salad bar.

Expensive
When you feel like putting a major dent in your budget, and satisfying your desire for some gourmet food, you should be pleased with one of the following:

Alex's Hole-in-the-Wall: Contrary to the name, this little restaurant, down an alleyway at 834 Front, will put a little hole in your wallet. The food is Italian with delights like veal parmagiana for $17.95, and chicken cacciatore for $12.95. The pasta is locally made and fresh. Open daily except Sun. from 6:00 to 10:00 p.m., tel. 661-3197.

Longhi's: Located at 888 Front St., tel. 667-2288. Daily from 7:30 a.m. to 10:00 p.m. Longhi owns the joint and he's a character. He feels that his place has "healing vibes" and that man's basic food is air. He's got an old dog, Freddy, who might still be alive (you can't tell by looking at him). If you don't like eating where a dog eats, then hit the road. The waiters come around and recite the menu to you. Pay attention. Prawns amaretto and shrimp Longhi are a good choice. Save room for the fabulous desserts that circulate

on a tray, and from which you may choose. There's always a line, no reservations, and it's hard not to have a fine meal. Breakfast is terrific, too.

Gerard's: At the Lahaina Market Place, corner of Lahainaluna Rd., tel. 661-8939. Daily lunch and dinner, Sunday dinner only. Menu changes daily. Oh so French! The owner is the chef, so "care" goes into the food.

La Bretagne: At the east end town at 562 C Front St., in a vintage historical house, tel. 661-8966, daily, dinner only. Reservations. French? But of course, mon cherie! $20 and up. Elegant dining with exemplary desserts.

Chez Paul: Located five miles east of Lahaina in Olowalu. This French (what else?) restaurant is secluded, romantic and very popular. The wine list is tops, the desserts fantastic and the food, magnifique! Prices start at $20. On Rt. 30, tel. 661-3843. Daily from 5:30 p.m. Credit cards? For sure—no one carries that much cash!

ENTERTAINMENT

Lahaina is one of those places where the real entertainment is the town itself. The best thing to do here is to stroll along Front St. and people-watch. As you walk along, it feels like a block party with the action going on all around you. Some people duck into one of the many establishments along the south side of Front St. for a breather, a drink or just to watch the sunset. It's all free, enjoyable, and safe.

Night spots
All of the evening entertainment in Lahaina is in restaurants and lounges (see "Food" for details). The following should provide you with a few laughs: jazz at **Blackie's** every Fri. and Sat. evening; Hawaiian music at the **Banyan Inn** on weekends; jam sessions and popular combos at the **Whale's Tale** and **Blackbeard's** nightly; disco at **Moose McGuillicuddy's** nightly; jam sessions at **The Keg,** formerly the Blue Max. Many of the other restaurants and lounges offer live performances on any given night.

Drugs

Like everywhere in Hawaii, the main street drug is *pakalolo*. If you're "looking," cruise Front St., especially around the sea wall, and make friendly eye contact with the local guys. Listen for that distinctive "joint sucking" sound or for a whispered, "Buds?" It's usually vacuum-packed in Seal-a-Meal plastic bags, but if the guy won't let you smell it, or better yet taste it, try again. Usually all deals are straight, although inflated, business transactions.

Hookers

Lahaina had more than its share last century, and thankfully they haven't had a great resurgence, like Waikiki. In the words of one long-time resident, "There's no prostitution in Lahaina. People come as couples. For single people, there's so much free stuff around that the pros would go hungry."

SHOPPING

Once learned, everybody loves to do the "Lahaina Stroll." It's easy. Just act cool, nonchalant, and give it your best strut as you walk the gauntlet of Front Street's exclusive shops and exotic boutiques. The fun is just in being here. If you begin in the evening, go to the east end of town and park down by Prison Street; much easier to find a spot and you walk westward catching the sunset. On Prison, check out **Dan's Exotic Greenhouse,** specializing in birds, and *fukobonsai*. These miniatures were originated by David Fukomoto. They're mailable (except to Australia and Japan), and when you get them home, just plop them in water and presto... a great little plant. From $10-$20. On Front, start with **Silks Lahaina.** The manager, Jill Jones, explains that the designs are all originals by Gay Pope, a local, done in a unique dying process that adds beauty and longevity. Slacks $100, tops from $60, silk accessories under $20. **The Wharf** is three floors of eateries and shops. Check out **Ecology House,** selling T-shirts with seal and whale motifs; **The Woodpecker,** featuring ukeleles, flutes and hand-painted Ts; and

The Royal Art Gallery, with distinctive paintings of island dream scenes of superimposed faces in the clouds. Make sure to visit the **Lahaina Art Foundation** in the old jail basement of the Court House. **Greenpeace** is a "must stop," especially during whale season. Profits on items sold here go to ecological causes. **The Scentuous Shop** will make you swoon with its assortment of heady perfumes and oils that make great gifts. Don't miss the **Lahaina Scrimshaw Factory.** The staff here is not only knowledgeable on this old art, but also willing to chat. Pieces in all price ranges. **Jade and Jewels** is a treasure chest laden with

Dan and friends

rubies, emeralds and carvings from India and China. **Whale of a Shirt** sells Ts for under $10, **Apparels by Pauline** are reasonably priced, and **Alexia** features natural clothing with supernatural price tags. Check out the

Lahaina Courthouse, home of the Lahaina Art Foundation

aerotechnics at **High as a Kite**, the assortment of shoes at **Peg Leg's**, and the outdoor gear and good prices at **Vagabond**.

For art work, try **Lahaina Gallery** on Lahainaluna, **Village Gallery** on Front, and **Nagamine Camera** for your photo needs. **Lahaina Shopping Center** has a clutch of practical shops along with Cliff McQueen's **Wizard of Ahs** where you can eat organic yogurt in a tennis pro shop. **Skin Deep Tattooing** on Lahainaluna offers you a permanent memento, features "new-age primal, tribal tattooing," with female artists for shy ladies. The **Waterfront Gallery and Gifts** will tickle big kids with their fine ships, models and imported sheepskins. Across from **Lahaina One Hour Photo** you find tucked away **Tropical Boutique** with *batiks* from Java, and **Pacific Visions** where cut glass and etched crystals will dazzle your senses.

SERVICES AND INFORMATION

Banks
In Lahaina during normal banking hours try:

Bank of Hawaii in the Lahaina Shopping Center, tel. 661-8781; **First Interstate** at 135 Papalaua St., tel. 667-9714; **First Hawaiian** Papalaua St., tel. 661-3655.

Post office
The post office is in the Lahaina Shopping Center off Papalaua St., tel. 667-6611; **Mail Home Maui** is a post office contract station located at The Wharf Shopping Plaza, 658 Front St., tel. 667-6620. They're open seven days from 10:00 a.m. to 5:00 p.m. Along with the normal stamps, etc., they specialize in sending packages home. They've got mailing boxes, tape and packaging materials. They also sell souvenir packs of coffee, nuts, candies and teas which might serve as a last-minute purchase, but are expensive.

Emergency
For fire, police or ambulance, dial 911 throughout the Lahaina area.

Medical treatment
A concentration of all types of specialists is found at **Lahaina Medical Group**, located at Lahaina Square, tel. 667-2534. Alter-

natively, the **Lahaina Health Center,** located at the west end of town at 1287 Front St., tel. 667-6268, offers accupunture, chiropractic, therapeutic massage, and podiatry. Most practitioners charge approximately $30 for their services. Pharmacies in Lahaina include: **Craft's** at the Lahaina Shopping Center, tel. 661-3119, and **Valley Isle** at 130 Prison, tel. 661-4747.

Laundromat
Try **Maui Dry Cleaning,** Lahaina Shopping Center, tel. 667-2659.

Information
The following groups and organizations should prove helpful: **Lahaina Restoration** **Foundation,** P.O. Box 338, Lauaina, Maui HI 96761, tel. 661-3262, or in the "Masters' Reading Room" along Front Street. They are a storehouse of information about historical Maui, and make sure to pick up their brochure, "Lahaina, A Walking Tour of Historic and Cultural Sites"; **Library** at 680 Wharf St., tel. 661-0566; open Mon. through Thursday. Stop in at **Upstart Crow and Co.** in the upper level of The Wharf Mall along Front Street. They have an excellent book selection as well as a gourmet coffee and sandwich shop if you get tired browsing. The **Kelsey Gallery** at 129 Lahainaluna Rd. also deals in a limited supply of books; also see "Information" in the main Introduction for newspapers, radio stations and general information sources.

KAANAPALI

Five lush valleys, nourished by streams from the West Maui Mountains, stretch luxuriously for 10 miles from Kaanapali west to Kapalua. All along the connecting **Honoapiilani Highway** (Rt. 30), the dazzle and glimmer of beaches is offset by black volcanic rock. Two sensitively planned and beautifully executed resorts are at each end of this drive. Kaanapali Resort is 500 acres of fun and relaxation at the E end. It houses six luxury hotels, six beautifully appointed condos, a shopping mall and outdoor museum, 36 holes of world-class golf, tennis courts galore and epicurean dining in a chef's salad of cuisines. Two of the hotels, the **Hyatt Regency** and **Sheraton-Maui**, are inspired architectural showcases that blend harmoniously with Maui's most beautiful seashore surroundings. At the western end is another gem, **The Kapalua Resort,** 750 of Maui's most beautifully sculpted acres with its own showcase, **The Kapalua Bay Hotel**. Here, too, is prime golfing, **Fleming Beach,** perhaps the best on the island, exclusive shopping, horseback riding and tennis aplenty.

Kaanapali, with its four miles of glorious beach, is actually Maui's westernmost point. In general, it begins where Lahaina ends, and continues west along Rt. 30 until a mile or so before the village of Honokawai. Adjacent at the west end are the villages of Honokawai and Kahana that service the condos tucked away here and there along the coast and mountainsides. Both are practical stops where you can buy food, gas, and all necessary supplies to keep your vacation rolling. The accommodations are not as grand, but the beaches and vistas are. Along this entire southwestern shore, Maui flashes its most captivating pearly-white smile. The sights all along this coast are either natural or man-made, but not historical. This is where you come to gaze from mountain to sea and bathe yourself in natural beauty. Then, after a day of surf and sunshine, you repair to one of the gorgeous hotels or restaurants for a drink or dining, or just to promenade around the grounds.

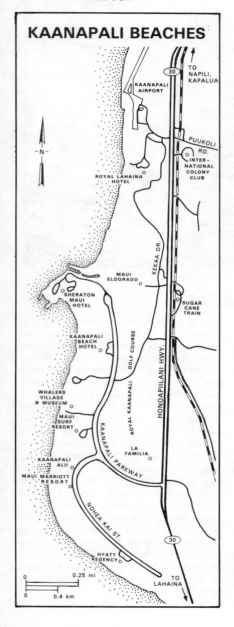

KAANAPALI BEACHES

TO
NAPILI,
KAPALUA

KAANAPALI
AIRPORT

PUUKOLI
RD.

INTER-
NATIONAL
COLONY
CLUB

-N-

ROYAL LAHAINA
HOTEL

KEKAA DR.

MAUI
ELDORADO

SHERATON
MAUI
HOTEL

SUGAR
CANE
TRAIN

KAANAPALI
BEACH
HOTEL

GOLF COURSE

WHALERS
VILLAGE
& MUSEUM

HONOAPIILANI HWY.

ROYAL KAANAPALI

MAUI
SURF
RESORT

LA
FAMILIA

KAANAPALI
ALII

MAUI MARRIOTT
RESORT

KAANAPALI PARKWAY

NOHEA KAI ST.

30

HYATT
REGENCY

0   0.25 mi
0   0.4 km

TO
LAHAINA

History

Southwestern Maui was a mixture of scrub and precious *lo'i* land, reserved for taro, the highest life-sustaining plant given by the gods. The farms stretched to Kapalua skirting the numerous bays all along the way. The area was important enough for a "royal highway" to be built by chief Piilani, and it still bears his name. Westerners used the lands surrounding Kaanapali to grow sugarcane, and **The Lahaina, Kaanapali and Pacific Railroad,** known today as the "Sugarcane Train," chugged to Kaanapali Beach to unburden itself onto barges that carried the cane to waiting ships. Kaanapali, until the 1960s, was a blemished beauty where the Pioneer Sugar Mill dumped its rubbish. Then AMFAC, one of the "Big Five," decided to put the land to better use. In creating Hawaii's first planned resort, they outdid themselves. Robert Trent Jones was hired to mold the golf course along this spectacular coast, while the Hyatt Regency and its grounds became an architectural marvel. The Sheraton-Maui was built atop, and integrated with, *Puu Kekaa* (Black Rock). This area is a wave-eroded cinder cone, and the Sheraton architects used its sea cliffs as part of the walls of the resort. Here, on a deep underwater shelf, daring divers descend to harvest Maui's famous black coral trees. The Hawaiians believed that *Puu Kekaa* was a very holy place where the spirits of the dead left this earth and migrated into the spirit world. Kahekili, Maui's most famous 18th C. chief, often came here to leap into the sea below. This old time daredevil was fond of the heart-stopping activity, and made famous "Kahekili's Leap," an even more treacherous seacliff on nearby Lanai. Today, the Sheraton puts on a sunset show where this "leap" is re-enacted.

Unfortunately, developers picked up on AM-FAC's great idea and built condos up the road starting in Honokawai. Interested in profit, not beauty, they earned that area the dubious title of "condo ghetto." Fortunately, the Maui Land and Pineapple Co. owned the land surrounding the idyllic Kapalua Bay, and Col-

When the cane fields are burning should everyone add two strokes to their handicap?

in Cameron, one of the heirs to this holding, had visions of developing 750 acres of the plantation's 20,000 into the extraordinary **Kapalua Bay Resort**. He teamed up with Rockresort Management, headed by Laurence Rockefeller, and the complex was opened in 1979.

Transportation
The **Blue Shoreline Bus** runs all along the southwest coast from Kapalua to Lahaina and points east. Kaanapali is serviced by the **Kaanapali Jitney.** The Sugarcane Train offers a day of fun for the entire family. For details see "Getting Around," "public transportation" in the General Introduction. **Kaanapali Airport** is a small strip located at the western end of Kaanapali. It is owned by AMFAC Company, which plans to build a resort on the land. It was closed to inter-island flights in January, 1986.

Kaanapali extras
Two situations in and around Kaanapali mar its outstanding beauty—you might refer to them as "Kaanapali Perfume." There are still plenty of sugarcane fields in the area, and when they're being burned off, the smoke is heavy in the air. Also, the sewage treatment plant is inadequate, and even the constantly blowing trade winds are insufficient to push this stench out to sea.

BEACHES

The four-mile stretch of pristine sand at Kaanaali is what people come to expect from Maui, and they are never disappointed.

Hanakaoo Beach
This is an uninterrupted stretch of sand running from the Hyatt Regency to the Sheraton. Although these are some of the most exclusive hotels on the island, public access to the beach is guaranteed in the state's Constitution. There are "rights of way," but parking your car is definitely a hassle. A good idea is to park at **Wahikuli State Park** and walk westward along the beach. You can park (10 cars) in the Hyatt's lower lot and enter along a right of way. There's access between the Hyatt and the Marriott (no parking) and between the Marriott and the Kaanapali Alii, which also has limited parking. There is parking near the Sheraton (11 cars) and at the Whaler's Shopping Center, but you must pass through the gauntlet of shops.

Black Rock
One of the most easily accessible and visually engaging snorkeling spots on Maui is located at the Sheraton's Black Rock. "No Parking"

Anyone can have fun snorkeling at Black Rock.

signs are everywhere, but you can find a spot. Follow the main road past the Sheraton until it climbs the hill around back. You'll take your chances parking in the lot just near the "Discovery Room" sign, because parking tickets are given here sporadically. Turn around instead and head back down the hill. Park on the right, where you'll see many cars. The sign says "No Parking," but usually you aren't ticketed here. Walk back up the hill and through the hotel grounds until you come to a white metal fence. Follow the fence down toward the sea. You'll come to a spur of rock jutting out and that's it. The entire area is like an underwater marine park. Enter at the beach area and snorkel west around the rock, staying close to the cinder cone. There are schools of reef fish, rays and even a lonely turtle.

Sports

For a full listing of the sporting facilities and possibilities in the Kaanapali area, contact the

Aloha Activity Center in the Whalers Village, tel. 661-3815. **Golf** at the Royal Kaanapali North/South costs $27 plus $11 for a mandatory cart. Both courses are a par 72, tel. 661-3691. For **tennis**, the most famous is the Royal Lahaina Tennis Ranch with 11 courts, tennis clinics and tournaments. The Sheraton has three courts, the Hyatt five, The Whaler three courts, one each at the Kaanapali Royal and Kaanapali Plantation and three at the Maui Surf. For **water sports**, catamarans are available twice a day from Kaanapali Beach. Contact any major hotel activities desk in the resort area, or **Kaanapali Jet Ski** at the Whalers Village, tel. 667-7851.

ACCOMMODATIONS

The Kaanapali Resort offers accommodations ranging from "moderate deluxe" to "luxury." There are no budget accommodations here, but just west toward Honokawai are plenty of reasonably-priced condos. As usual, they're more of a bargain the longer you stay, especially if you can share costs with a few people by renting a larger unit. And as always, you'll save money on food costs. The following should give you an idea of what's available.

Hyatt Regency

Located at Kaanapali's eastern extremity, at 200 Nohea Kai Drive, Lahaina, 96761. Reservations are made at (800) 228-9000, or on Maui at 667-7474. The least expensive room in this truly luxury hotel is $135 a day; they go as high as $1400 for the Presidential Suite. Of course, like many Hyatts, you don't have to stay there to appreciate its beauty. If you visit, expensive valet parking is only in front of the hotel. Around back is a lot, but most spaces are numbered by the room with only a few for visitors. During the day, if a numbered one is empty, you can take your chances.

The moment you enter the main lobby the magic begins. A multi-tiered architectural extravaganza open to the sky, birds fly freely, and magnificent potted plants and full-sized palm trees create the atmosphere of a tel. (800) 325-3535, or on Maui 661-0031. The prices are not as astronomical as the Hyatt's, with a basic room at $95, up to $225 for an oceanside suite. The snorkeling around Black Rock is the best in the area. There are two pools, and the view from the upper-level **Berkentine Bar** is worth the price of a drink. A catamaran is available to guests, and you can rent snorkeling equipment at a poolside kiosk, but the prices are triple of what you can get from a dive shop.

Royal Lahaina

This massive 727-room complex is the most extensive in Kaanapali, as well as being one of the first. The **Maui Hilton** is completely enveloped by it. Reservations can be made at (800) 227-4700, in California at (800) 622-0838, on Maui at 661-3611. Prices for standard rooms start at $85, cottages go for $105-150, and suites are up to $450. There are no less than seven restaurants and six swimming pools on the well-maintained grounds. It's also home to the **Royal Lahaina Tennis Ranch**, boasting ten courts and a stadium.

Other hotels

For Kaanapali, the following hotels might be considered a bargain. The **Kaanapali Beach** offers standard rooms from $70, has a distinctive whale-shaped pool and tennis privileges at the Royal Lahaina, tel. (800) 227-4700, on Maui 661-0011. The **Maui Surf**, tel. (800) 367-5360, on Maui 661-4411, has standard rooms for $79. This hotel features free scuba lessons in their pool. **The Maui Marriott** is actually a luxury hotel. Standard rooms begin at $95 and go up to $800 for a suite. However, they offer a 50 percent reduction coupon from April 15 to December 15, found in the free tourist magazines. You cannot make reservations through a travel agent, or the (800) 228-9290 number to use it. You must call the hotel at (808) 667-1200 to redeem the coupon on a space available basis.

Condos

Generally much less expensive than the hotels, most begin at $70 per night. They all offer full kitchens, some maid service, swim-

one of the many art pieces gracing the impeccable grounds of the Hyatt

modern Polynesian palace. Nooks and crannies abound where you can lounge in kingly wicker thrones. The walls are adorned with first-class art works and tapestries, while glass showcases hold priceless ceramics. Peacocks strut their regal stuff amid impeccable Japanese gardens, and ducks and swans are floating alabaster on a symmetry of landscaped ponds. Around the swimming pool, the guests luxuriate on huge pink hotel towels. The pool's architecture is inspired by the islands: grottoes, caves, waterfalls, and a huge slide are all built in. A swinging wood bridge connects the sections, and you can have an island drink at a sunken poolside bar. There's an exclusive five-star restaurant, a disco for human peacocking, and the "Elephant Walk," a covey of specialty shops and boutiques.

Sheraton-Maui

These 505 rooms are built around Kaanapali's most conspicuous natural phenomenon, Black Rock. For reservations, ming pools, and often convenience stores and laundry facilities. There are usually off-season rates, and discounts for longer stays. Combinations of the above are too numerous to mention, so it's best to ask all pertinent questions when booking. Not all accept credit cards, and a deposit is the norm when making reservations. The following should give you an idea of what to expect. **International Colony Club** on the *mauka* side of Rt. 30, tel. 661-4070, offers individual cottages at $70, $10 extra person, 4-day minimum. **The Whaler** at the Whalers' Village, tel. (800) 267-2936, on Maui 661-4861, is in the heart of things, and offers swimming pools and great beach frontage. From $84 to $320. Lobby, sauna, market and tennis courts.

Others in Kaanapali proper include **Maui Eldorado**, tel. (800) 421-0680, on Maui 661-0021, surrounded by the golf course, from $62. **Kaanapali Plantation**, tel. 661-4446, from $80 with a $10 discount for 14 days or longer. Maid service and most amenities. **Kaanapali Royal**, a golfer's dream right on the course, tel. (800) 367-7040, on Maui 523-7785, from $90 with substantial low-season and long-term discounts. **Hale Kaanapali** at Kaanapali's far west end near the airport, tel. 661-3611.

FOOD

Every hotel in Kaanapali has at least one restaurant, with numerous others scattered throughout the area. Some of the most expensive and exquisite restaurants on Maui are found in these hotels, but surprisingly, at others you can dine very reasonably, even cheaply.

La Familia
This is a reasonably-priced Mexican restaurant. Their happy hour, from 4:30 to 6:00 p.m., offers excellent margaritas for 99 cents, along with free chips and salsa. The most expensive item on the menu is $12, with the majority of meals under $7. They also offer a $2 coupon on dinner checks over $10. Their staff is gracious and friendly. They are located at 2290 Kaanapali Parkway (the

first sign pointing to Kaanapali from Lahaina), tel. 667-7902.

Apple Annie's
Also on Kaanapali Parkway. You can get a variety of sandwiches, omelettes and light meals for around $6. Their offerings are well-prepared and wholesome, but overpriced for what you get; tel. 661-3160.

Royal Lahaina Resort
You have no less than seven establishments from which to choose. A *luau* is prepared nightly in the Luau Gardens, and the biggest problem of the Polynesian Review is standing up after eating mountains of traditional food. Adults $31, children $17 under 12, reservations, 661-3611. Don the Beachcomber, offering dinners only, has various Asian and Polynesian dishes, most for under $12, tel. 661-3611. Moby Dick's is a seafood restaurant open for dinner only, tel. 661-3611. Entrees are reasonably priced for around $12, but you pay for all the extras like soup and salad which can push your bill to $20 or more. Royal Ocean Terrace is open daily for breakfast, lunch and dinner offering a breakfast buffet, and better-than-average salad bar. Sunday brunch from 9:00 a.m. until 2:00 p.m. is a winner, tel. 661-3611.

Eight Bells Restaurant
In the Maui Surf Hotel, tel. 661-4411. Open for breakfast and dinner, but call to check for specific hours, which vary. Their dinners are acceptable for around $12, but their $6.95 breakfast buffet is legendary. Arrive the last hour and eat your fill, which should easily suffice until dinner.

Swan Court
Located in the Hyatt Regency, daily breakfast and dinner, tel. 667-7474. You don't come here to eat, you come here to dine, peasant! Anyone who has been enraptured by those old movies where the couples regally glide down a central staircase to make their grand entrance will have their fantasies come true. Although expensive, you get your money's worth with attention to detail; prosciutto is served with papaya, ginger butter with the

Pick your spot on any of Kaanapali's four miles of hospitable beach.

fresh catch of the day, and pineapple chutney with the oysters. The wine list is a connoisseur's delight. Save this one for a very special evening.

Spats II is also at the Hyatt, tel. 667-7474, dinner only. They specialize in Italian food with the average entree around $16. At night this becomes a disco, and fancy duds are in order. **Lahaina Provision Co.**, tel. 667-7474, could only survive with a name like that because it's at the Hyatt. Regular broiled fare, but you get a bowl of ice cream, and are free to go hog-wild with chocolate toppings at their famous chocoholic bar. Guaranteed to make you repent all your sins!

Discovery Room
At the Sheraton, tel. 661-0031. Daily for breakfast and dinner. Basic American food like baked chicken, well prepared with all the trimmings, for $20. Entertainment is offered at dinner and at the 9:30 p.m. cocktail show. A *luau* is offered Tues., Thurs., and Sun. from 5:30 p.m., adults $30, children $18. Features Chief Faa, the fire knife dancer. Reservations 667-9564.

Lokelani
At the Maui Marriott, tel. 667-1200, dinner only, from 6:00 p.m. Full dinners such as sauteed catch-of-the-day with all trimmings from $14. Also, **Nikko's Japanese Steak House**, tel. 667-1200, dinner from 6:00 p.m. No cheap imports here. Prices are high, but the Japanese chef works right at your table slicing meats and vegetables quicker than you can say *samurai.* An expensive but fun meal.

Peacock Restaurant
Located at 2550 Kehaa Drive, tel. 667-6847. Daily lunch and dinner. This elegant restaurant was at one time the Kaanapali golf course clubhouse. Like its name implies, it's a bit fancy with ritzy Oriental decor. Dinners cost about $20, and the house specialty is an uncommon dish, Maui rabbit. Their pork in mango sauce is exotic, and so is the *poisson cru* appetizer.

Kapa Room
At the Maui Surf Hotel, tel. 661-4411. A *luau* for the unusually low price of $21.50, every

night except Tuesday. Maui's early history is the theme for stories and dance.

Kaanapali Beach Hotel Restaurant
The hotel might be fancy but the restaurant is down to earth. Good old cafeteria-style American food. Dinner specials only $5. Daily breakfast, lunch, and dinner, tel. 661-0011.

Whaler's Village
This shopping mall has a half-dozen or so dining establishments. You can find everything from pizza and frozen yogurt to lobster tail. Prices range from bargain to moderate. An up-and-comer is **Leilani's.** Their selections go from surf to turf. They offer famous Azeka ribs for $10.95, a sushi bar, and a daily dinner special from 5:00 to 6:30 p.m. for $8.50. This includes entree, and soup or salad. Call 661-4495. **El Crab Catcher** is a well-established restaurant featuring seafood, with a variety of crab dishes, steaks and chops. They have a sunken bar and swimming pool with the beach only a stride or two away. Desserts are special here from $10. Popular, so reserve at 661-4423.

Save money at the **Rusty Harpoon,** a "do-it-yourself" broiler. Limited entrees and only fair quality. Piano music at night and popular with younger set. Lunch from 11:00 a.m. to 3:30 p.m., dinner from 6-00 to 9:30 p.m. No one will mutiny over the seafood, chicken and beef offered at the **H.M.S. Bounty** for around $10, children's portions cheaper. Daily for breakfast, lunch, and dinner with an "early bird special" from 5:00 to 6:30 p.m. Popular, no reservations, call 661-0946. **Yami Yogurt** sells wholesome, well-made sandwiches for $3 and under. Salads, too, and yogurt, of course. No seating, but plenty of spots outside, tel. 661-8843. **Ricco's Deli** makes hefty sandwiches for under $4. Their mini-pizzas make a good, inexpensive lunch, tel. 669-6811.

ENTERTAINMENT

If you're out for a night of fun and frivolity, Kaanapali will keep you hopping. The dinner shows accompanying the *luau* at the Hyatt

Regency and Maui Surf feature pure island entertainment. The Maui Surf's "Here's Hawaii" is a sensitive, funny and well-done musical production with a cast of only five. The songs tell the story of Maui's history, led by Audrey Meyers and Jeffrey Apaka. "Drums of the Pacific" is a musical extravaganza that you would expect from the Hyatt. There are torch-lit processions, and excitingly choreographed production numbers, with all the hula-skirted *wahines* and *malo*-clad *kanes* that you could imagine. Flames add drama to the settings and the grand finale is a fire dance. At both shows you're dined and entertained by mid-evening.

Those with dancing feet can boogie the night away at the Hyatt's **Spats II.** There is a dress code and plenty of room for those "big dippers" on this very large dance floor. Practice your waltzes for the outdoor **Pavillion Courtyard** at the Hyatt. The **Banana Moon** at the Marriott offers the best of both worlds—dance music and quiet, candle-lit corners for romance. Most hotels, restaurants and lounges offer some sort of music. Often it's a local combo singing Hawaiian favorites, or a piano-man tinking away in the background. The only movie theater in Kaanapali is the **Village Cinema,** tel. 661-0922, in the Whalers Village.

SHOPPING

There are three places to shop in Kaanapali: at the **Whalers Village Mall** which is affordable, at the **Maui Marriott** for some distinctive purchases, and at the **Hyatt Regency** where most people get the jitters even window shopping.

Whaler's Village Mall and Museum
This unique outdoor mall doubles as quite a passable museum, with showcases filled with items, mostly from the whaling days, accompanied by informative descriptions. You can easily find anything here that you might need. Some of the shops are: **Book Cache,** featuring fine books with an entire section dedicated to Hawaiiana, tel. 661-3259.

Superwhale Children's Boutique, tel. 661-0260, all beach wear and *aloha* wear for the *keikis.* **Lahaina Scrimshaw Factory,** tel. 661-4034, for fine examples of scrimshaw and other art objects from affordable to expensive. **Liberty House,** tel. 661-4451, for usual department store items. **Ka Honu Gift Gallery,** tel. 661-0137, for a large selection of arts and crafts inspired by the islands. There are many other shops tucked away here and there. They come and go with regularity.

The Hyatt Regency Mall
Off the main lobby and surrounding the gardens are a number of exclusive shops. They're high-priced, but their offerings are first class. Call 667-7421 and ask for the store of your choice. **Elephant Walk** specializes in primitive art such as tribal African masks and carved wooden statues. **Gold Point's** name says it all with baubles, trinkets, bracelets, and rings all in gold. **Sandal Tree** has footwear for men and women with the emphasis on sandals. **Mark Christopher** is a series of shops selling jewelry, glassware, fabrics and beachwear.

Maui Marriott
The main store here is a **Liberty House,** tel. 667-6142, with the emphasis on clothing. **Hawaii I.D.** is an upbeat dive shop with masks, fins, boards etc., at the **Friendship Store** all art objects, clothing, silks, and goods are from the Republic of China. There are also women's stores and jewelry shops.

SERVICES AND INFORMATION

Banks
Most larger hotels can help with some banking needs, especially with the purchasing or cashing of TCs; **Bank of Hawaii** has a branch at 2580 Kekaa Drive, tel. 667-6251.

Medical
Dr. Ben Azman maintains an office at the Whalers Village, tel. 667-9721, or after hours 244-3728.

Camera needs
Shops are: **Makai Camera** in the Whalers Village; **Hawaiian Vision** and **Sandy's Camera** in the Royal Lahaina complex; **Island Camera** in the Sheraton.

Laundromat
The **Washerette Clinic** in the Sheraton.

Information
For a complete source of information on all aspects of the Kaanapali area contact Kaanapali Beach Operators Association, Box 616, Kaanapali, Maui HI 96761, tel. 661-3271.

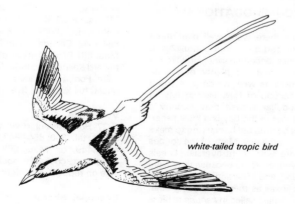

white-tailed tropic bird

HONOKOWAI AND VICINITY

You head for Honokowai and Kahana if you want to enjoy Maui's west coast and not spend a bundle of money. They're not quite as pretty as Kaanapali to the south or Kapalua to the north, but proportionate to the money you'll save, you come out ahead. To get there, travel along the **Honoapiilani Hwy.**, take **Lower Honoapiilani Hwy.** through Honokowai and continue on it to Kahana.

BEACHES

Honokawai Beach Park is right in Honokowai Town just across from the Superette. Here you have a large lawn with palm trees and picnic tables, but a small beach. The water is shallow, and tame—good for tots. The swimming is not as nice as Kaanapali, but take a dip after shopping. Snorkeling is fair, and you can get through a break in the reef at the west end. **Kahana Beach** is near the Kahana Beach Resort; park across the street. Nothing spectacular, but protected small beach is good for tots. Great view of Molokai and never crowded.

ACCOMMODATIONS

At last count there were well over three dozen condos and apartment complexes in the three miles encompassing Honokowai and Kahana. There are plenty of private homes out here as well, which give you a good cross-section of Hawaiian society. A multi-million-dollar spread may occupy a beach, while out in the bay is a local fisherman with his beat-up old boat trying to make a few bucks for the day. Many of the condos built out here were controversial. Locals refused to work on some because they were on holy ground, and a few actually experienced bad luck jinxes as they were being built. The smarter owners called in *kahuna* to bless the ground and the disturbances ceased.

Honokowai Palms
At 3666 Lower Honoapiilani Hwy., Lahaina, 96761, (near Honokawai), tel. 669-6130. This condo is an old standby for budget travelers. You can get a one-bedroom unit for under $40 during high season, under $30 during low. There's weekly and monthly discounts, $6 for an extra person in a room, $100 deposit required, three-night minimum, and maid service extra. With a pool, this condo is clean and adequate.

Hale Ono Loa
At 3823 Lower Honoapiilani Hwy., Lahaina, 96761, tel. (800) 367-2927, or on Maui 669-6362. A bit more upbeat. From $50 for a double, with prices rising as you ascend floors, up to $85 for two bedrooms. Three-day minimum, complete kitchens, partial maid service, pool.

Makani Sands
3765 Lower Honoapiilani Hwy. Lahaina, 96761, tel. 669-8223. From $55 for a single, $6 additional persons. Swimming pool, three-day minimum, maid service every four days.

Mahana
110 Kaanapali Shore Pl., Lahaina, 96761, tel. California, (800) 472-8449, others (800) 854-8843, Canada collect (714) 497-4253, on Maui 661-8751. A nicer place on the beach toward Kaanapali. Studio $60 up to $125 for a suite. Pool, tennis, shop, maid service on request, full kitchens, five-night minimum.

Valley Isle
4327 Honoapiilani Hwy. (Kahana) Lahaina, 96761, tel. (800) 854-8843, in California (800) 472-8449, on Maui 669-5511. From $55 restaurant, cocktails, pool, shop, maid service on request, five-night minimum.

Kaanapali Shores
100 Kaanapali Shore Pl., Lahaina, 96761, tel.

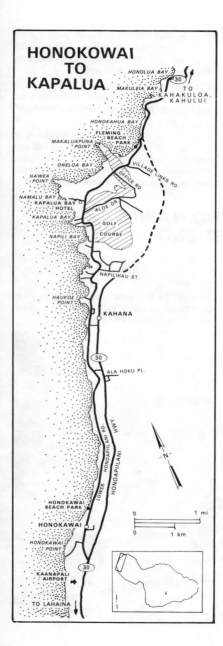

HONOKOWAI TO KAPALUA

(800) 367-5124, on Maui 667-2211. An up-town condo toward Kaanapali from $90. Restaurant, lounge, shop, pool, tennis courts.

Noelani
At 4095 Lower Honoapiilani Hwy. Lahaina, 96761, tel. (800) 367-6030, on Maui 669-8374. Studios from $50. Two pools, BBQ area, fully equipped kitchens, and color TVs.

FOOD AND ENTERTAINMENT

Ricco's
At the **Happy Opu Store** in Kahana, tel. 669-6811. Good old-time deli featuring fresh-baked pizza. Large sandwiches for $3 and lunches to go.

Dollies
4310 Honoapiilani Hwy. (Kahana), tel. 667-2623. From breakfast to late evening. Sandwiches, pizza, food to go. Deliveries to condos! Good food and fair prices, like turkey or roast beef with swiss and jack for $4.65.

Erik's Seafood Grotto
4242 Lower Honoapiilani Hwy., second floor of Kahana Villa, tel. 669-4806. Daily for dinner from 5:30 to 10:00 p.m. Very good fish selec-tion. "Sunset Special" from 5:30 to 6:30 p.m. $8.95, menu changes daily. Dinners include chowder, bread basket and potato or rice. Most dinners $12-13 with a good selection of appetizers.

Kahana Keyes
At Kahana Beach, tel. 669-8071. Known for their salad bar and fresh fish. Daily lunch 10:00 a.m. to 2:30 p.m., dinner 5:00 to 10:00 p.m. "Early Bird Special" from 5:00 to 7:00 p.m., $8.95. "Nightly Special," dungeness crab and prime rib, all you can eat for $14.95. Live music nightly from 7:30 p.m.

The Kahana Keyes Restaurant is the only show in town around here, and luckily it ain't bad! Nightly from 7:30 local bands perform. All types of music are offered, from rock to Hawaiian, and the large dance floor is hardly ever crowded.

SHOPPING

Honokowai Superette
The only real place west of Lahaina to shop for groceries and sundries. Located on Lower Honoapiilani Hwy. in Honokawai, tel. 669-6208. Daily from 8:00 a.m. to 9:00 p.m. The prices are just about right at this supermarket. Condo convenience stores in the area are good in a pinch but charge way too much. Stock up here; it's worth the drive.

Honokowai Store is not really a store at all. It rents all manners of surf equipment, such as masks and snorkels, and even mopeds, tel. 669-6013 in Honokowai.

Skootz
They rent and sell surfboards and sailboards. 4310 Lower Honoapiilani Hwy., tel. 669-0937.

Happy Opu Store
In Kahana at tel. 669-6776. Daily from 8:00 a.m. to 11:00 p.m. They specialize in fish and seafood and even lunches to go, but mostly it's a liquor store. The wine selection is the best on this entire southwest coast.

KAPALUA AND NAPILI
THE WEST END

Kapalua sits like a crown atop Maui's head. One of the newest areas on Maui to be developed, it's been nicely done. Out here is the **Kapalua Bay Resort**, golfing, horseback riding, terrific beaches, and even a helicopter ride.

BEACHES

Some of the very best beaches that Maui has to offer are clustered in this area. The following listing proceeds from south to north.

horseback riding on Fleming Beach

Napili Bay

There are rights-of-way to this perfect, but condo-lined, beach. Look along Napili Place near the Napili Shores, Napili Surf Beach Resort, and on Hui Drive near the Napili Sunset and Napili Bay condos. They're there but hard to spot. Better than average swimming, snorkeling and a good place for beginner surfers.

Kapalua Beach

Along Rt. 30 look for access just past the Napili Kai Beach Club. Park in the public lot and follow the path through the tunnel to the beach. Another beautiful crescent beach that's popular, though usually not over-crowded. The well-formed reef here has plenty of fish for snorkeling. Also, restrooms, showers, and beach concessions.

D.T. Fleming Beach

One of Maui's best. Clearly marked along Rt. 30. Parking, showers and BBQ grills. Excellent swimming except in winter when there's a pounding surf. Fair snorkeling and good surfing.

Oneloa Beach

A short mile past Fleming's. A small sandy beach down a steep path. Those who brave it can camp without a hassle from the officials.

Mokuleia Beach

Also known as "Slaughterhouse." You can spot it because the R.V. Deli, a lunchwagon, is usually parked here. About 200-300 yards after mile marker 32. This beach has great bodysurfing, but terribly dangerous currents in the winter when the surf is rough. Be careful. Follow the trail to the left for the beach. The path straight ahead takes you to a rocky lava flow. The entire area is a marinelife conservation district and the underwater life is fabulous.

Honolua Bay

Just past Mokuleia Bay heading north. Look for a dirt road, then park. Some can try the road, but it's very rugged. Good for swimming, snorkeling and especially surfing. Many people stay the night without much problem.

Rick, the top hand at the Rainbow Ranch

Sports

The following are offered in the Kapalua area. **Kapalua Bay Golf Club**, par 71, $35 green fees and a mandatory $10 cart; **Kapalua Bay Club Villa**, par 73, $35 fees and a $10 cart. **Tennis** is found at the Napili Kai Beach Club, $4 guests, $6 visitors; Kapalua Bay Hotel **Tennis Garden**, free to guests, $4 others, dress code, tel. 669-5677. **Horseback riding** at the Rainbow Ranch, see "Sports" in the main "Introduction" for details.

ACCOMMODATIONS

Napili, just south of Kapalua Bay, sports a string of condos and a hotel or two. Almost all front the beach, which is hardly ever crowded. The premier resort, however, is the **Kapalua Bay Hotel and Villas**. This, like other grand hotels, is more than a place to stay, it's an experience. The main lobby is partially open and accented with an enormous skylight. Plants trail from the ceiling.

spectacular view from the main lobby of the Kapalua Bay Hotel

Below is a tropical terrace and restaurant and all colors are soothing and subdued. Although relaxing, it's the kind of a place where if you don't wear an evening gown to go to the bathroom, you feel underdressed. The least expensive room in the hotel itself is one with a garden view at $120 off-season. The villas with a mountain view are $100 off-season. All climb rapidly to the $200-$300 range. You can have the "American Plan," consisting of breakfast and dinner, for an extra $40. You must make a three-night's deposit, refundable only with 14-days' notice. There are five restaurants in the complex and magnificent golfing at the Kapalua Villa Club.

Napili Kai Beach Club
At 5900 Honoapiilani Rd., Lahaina, 96761, tel. (800) 367-5030, on Maui 669-6271. Expensive at $100 per studio, but you do have a kitchenette. The beach is a crescent moon here with gentle wave action. There are five pools, putting greens, tennis courts and the Kapalua Bay Golf Course just a 9-iron away. All rooms have Japanese touches complete with *shoji* screens. There's dancing and entertainment at their famous Restaurant of the Maui Moon.

Napili Bay
At 33 Hui Drive, Lahaina, 96761, tel. (800) 421-0680, on Maui 669-6044. For this neck of the woods, it's reasonably priced from $45 for a studio suitable to sleep four. Full kitchens, maid service and laundromat. Three-day minimum.

Napili Surf Beach Resort
50 Napili Pl., Napili, 96761, tel. 669-8002. Studios from $60. Long-term stay discount. Deposit of $150 required. Two pools, fantastic beach, maid service, full kitchens and laundry. They also operate the **Napili Puamala**, adjacent, which is a bit cheaper.

FOOD

R.V. Deli
This is a lunch wagon that parks almost every day at Mokuleia Bay (Slaughterhouse). Dogs, burgers, fries and the likes, plus yarns by Peter L. Dyck, proprietor.

Kapalua Bay Resort restaurants
There's a complete menu of restaurants, so you can choose from sandwich shops to elegant dining. **Market Cafe** is found in the "Shops" area at 669-4888. Foods from around the world including wines, meats, cheeses and pastries. All kinds of gourmet items, with delicious but expensive sandwiches, from $5. The **Resort Dining Room**, tel. 669-5656, known for its full breakfasts and lunch buffets at $14.50. The atmosphere is pure island with open-air dining. Dress up! **Bay Club** at the resort entrance, tel.

one of a string of rugged and secluded beaches north of Kapalua

669-8008, daily lunch 11:30 a.m. to 2:00 p.m., dinner 5:30 to 9:30 p.m. On a promontory of land overlooking the beach and Molokai in the distance. The pool is right here. Dress code. Expect to spend $20 for a superbly prepared entree. **Plantation Veranda** offers daily dinner only, with varying hours, tel. 669-5656. Atmosphere highlighted by natural woods, flowers everywhere, and original paintings by Pegge Hopper. Extensive wine list and magnificent entrees by Chef James Makinson. Formal dining.

Napili Shores Resort
Two restaurants are located at this resort, 5315 Honoapiilani Hwy. about one mile before Kapalua Town. **Orient Express**, tel. 669-8077, is open daily except Mon., dinner only from 5:00 to 10:00 p.m. Thai and Chinese food with a flair for spices. Duck salad and stuffed chicken wings are a specialty. "Early Bird Specials" before 7:00 p.m., take out and reasonably priced under $8. **Monaco**, tel. 669-8077. has dinner from 6:00

p.m. until midnight. French and Italian cuisine. Veal, pasta and velvet chairs. Delisioso!

Restaurant of the Maui Moon
At the Napili Kai Beach Club, tel. 669-6271 (for address, see above). Daily for breakfast, lunch and dinner. Breakfast buffet $7, lunch $5, dinner $15. Hawaiian and Oriental dishes, with an extensive salad bar for $10. There is Hawaiian music nightly and a wonderful show put on by children who have studied their heritage under the guidance of the Napili Kai Foundation.

SHOPPING

Kapalua Resort and Shops
There are a cluster of exclusive shops at the resort. **Andrade,** tel. 669-5266, fine apparel for men and women, an island tradition for 60 years; **Auntie Nani's Children's Boutique,** tel. 669-5282, for clothes and distinctive quilts. Many items have the Kapalua "but-

terfly logo;" **Kapalua Shop,** tel. 669-4172—if you want to show off that you've at least been to the Kapalua Resort, all items of clothing sport the logo. **Mandalay Imports,** tel. 669-6170, has a potpourri of silks and cottons from the East, especially Thailand. **La Perle,** tel. 669-8466, for pearls, diamonds and jewels; **Trouvalle,** tel. 669-5522, sports an amazing collection of offbeat artifacts from throughout Asia; **T. Fujii,** tel. 669-4759, has Japanese treasures in bronze, lacquer, silk and woodblock prints.

Napili Village Store
At Napili Bay, tel. 669-6773. A well-stocked little store and a known landmark. Good for last-minute items, and fairly good prices for where it is. You can pick up picnic items and sandwiches. There's a surf shop next door. **Napili Shores Condo Store** is mainly a convenience store for those forgotten or last-minute items.

beach naupaka

SOUTHEAST MAUI

KIHEI

Kihei ("Shoulder Cloak") takes it on the chin whenever anti-development groups need an example to wag their fingers at. For the last two decades, building along both sides of Kihei Rd., which runs the length of town, has been unabated. Since there was no central planning for the development, mostly highrise condos and a few hotels were built wherever they could be squeezed in: some are lovely, some are crass. There's hardly a spot left where you can get an unobstructed view of the beach as you drive along. That's the "slam" in a nutshell. The good news is, Kihei has so much to recommend it that if you refrain from becoming fixated on this one regrettable feature, you'll thoroughly enjoy yourself, and save money, too.

The developers went "hyper" here because it's perfect as a tourist area. The weather can be counted on to be the best on all of Maui. Haleakala, looming just behind the town catches rainclouds before they drench Kihei.

Days of blue skies and sunshine are taken for granted. On the other side of the condos and hotels are gorgeous beaches, every one open to the public; once on the beachside, the condos don't matter anymore. The views out to sea are unobstructed vistas of Lanai, Kahoolawe, Molokini, and West Maui, which gives the illusion of being a separate island. The buildings are even a buffer to the traffic noise! Many islanders make Kihei their home, so there is a feeling of real community here. It's quieter than Lahaina, with fewer restaurants and not as much action, but for sun and surf activities, this place has it all.

Sights
The six-mile stretch bordered by beach and mountain that makes up Kihei has always been an important landing spot on Maui. Hawaiian war canoes moored here many times during countless skirmishes over the years; later, Western navigators such as

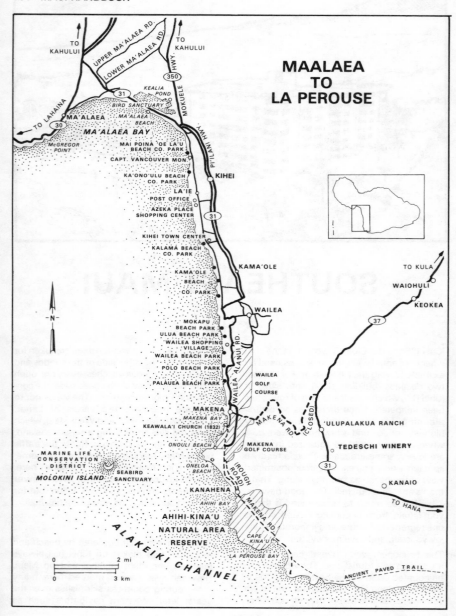

MAALAEA TO LA PEROUSE

George Vancouver found this stretch of beach to be a congenial anchorage. A totem pole across from the **Maui Lu Hotel** marks the spot where Vancouver landed. During WW II, when a Japanese invasion was feared, Kihei was considered a likely spot for an amphibious attack. Overgrown pillboxes and rusting tank traps are still found along the beaches. Many look like cement porcupines with iron quills. Kihei is a natural site with mountain and ocean vistas. It's great for beachcombing down toward Maalaea, but try to get there by morning because the afternoon wind is notorious for creating minor sand storms.

BEACHES

Maalaea Beach
Three miles of windswept sand, partially backed by Kealia Pond and bird sanctuary. Many points of access between Maalaea and Kihei along Rt. 31. The strong winds make it undesirable for sunning and bathing, but it's a windsurfer's dream. Also the hard-packed sand is a natural track for joggers, who are profuse in the morning and afternoon. The beachcombing and strolling is quiet and productive.

Mai Poina Oe Iau Beach Park
On Kihei's western fringe, fronting Maui Lu Hotel. Limited paved parking, or just along the road. Showers, tables, restrooms. Long and narrow white sand beach, good safe swimming, but still plagued by strong winds by early afternoon. Windsurfer's delight.

Kaonouluulu Beach Park
Parking, picnic tables, showers, BBQs. Very safe swimming and lesser winds. Small beach but not overcrowded.

Kalama Beach
About the middle of town. More for looking and outings than beach activities. Large lawn ending in a breakwater with little beach in summer and none in winter. Thirty-six acres of pavilions, tables, BBQ pits, volleyball, basketball and tennis courts. Baseball dia-mond and soccer field. Great views of Molokai and Haleakala.

Kamaole I, II, and III
These beach parks are at the south end of town near Kihei Town Center. All three have beautiful white sand, picnic tables and all the amenities. Shopping and dining is nearby. I and II have lifeguards. The swimming and body surfing is good. III has a kiddies' play ground. Snorkeling is good for beginners on the reef between II and III. Much coral and colorful reef fish.

ACCOMMODATIONS

The emphasis in Kihei is on condos. With keen competition among them, you can save some money while having a more "homey" vacation. Close to 100 condos, plus a smattering of vacation apartments, cottages, and even a few hotel resorts, are all strung along Kihei Road. As always, you pay more for ocean views. Don't shy away from accommodations on the *mauka* side of Kihei Road. You have total access to the beach, some superior views of Haleakala, and usually pay less money.

Hotels
The Kihei area offers two hotels that are reasonably priced and well appointed. **Maui Lu Resort**, 575 S. Kihei Rd., Kihei, HI 96753, tel. (800) 367-5244 mainland, (808) 879-5808 Canada collect, (800) 592-3351 Hawaii, 879-5881 Maui. This hotel attempts to preserve the old Hawaii with its Aloha Department and its emphasis on *ohana.* An abundance of activities here including *hula* lessons, a first-class *luau*, tennis, a Maui-shaped pool and tiny private beaches strung along its 30 acres. Rooms from $50, $8 extra person, include refrigerators and hot drink unit. These are mostly in the new wing toward the mountains, which is also quieter. Cottages start at $73 and are separate units with full kitchens.

Surf and Sand Hotel, located at 2980 S. Kihei Rd., Kihei, HI 96753, tel. (800) 367-2958, on Maui 879-7744. A very affor-

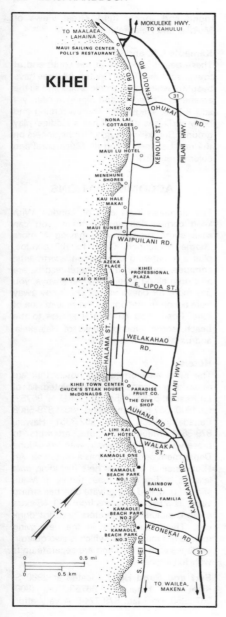

KIHEI

dable and well-maintained hotel just before you get to Wailea at the south end of town, it's owned and operated by Bob Zuern, who lives at the hotel, so you get personalized attention. Garden units from $30 single or double, suites to four people $58. Ocean units $40. Kitchenettes available—add $10. It fronts a sand beach, provides Polynesian entertainment and offers "room and car" specials. Also a jacuzzi. You can't go wrong!

Condominiums

Lihi Kai, at 2121 Ili'ili Rd., Kihei, 96753, tel. 879-2335. These cottages and apartments are such a bargain, they're often booked out by returning guests. They're not plush, there's no pool, but they're homey and clean, with little touches like banana trees growing on the property. $35 daily, $175 weekly, $465 monthly, deposit required, laundromat self service and the maid you pay. Write Jeanette M. DiMeo, owner-manager, at the above address well in advance.

Nona Lani Cottages, at 455 S. Kihei Rd., Kihei 96753, tel. 879-2497. Owned and operated by Dave and Nona Kong. Clean and neat units on the *mauka* side of Kihei Road. All units have full kitchen, queen beds and day beds with full baths. Laundry facilities, public phones, and BBQs on premises. High season $48 double, small discount for longer stays, $6 additional person. Low season $38, three-night minimum.

Sunseeker Resort, at 551 S. Kihei Rd, tel. 879-1261, write Box 276, Kihei, 96753. Studio with kitchenette $29, one bedroom $39, two bedroom $50, $6 additional person. Special rates off season and long term. Deposit required. Not bad at all.

Nani Kai Hale, at 73 N. Kihei Rd., Kihei 96753, tel. (800) 367-6032, on Maui 879-9120. Very affordable at $29 bedroom with bath, $42 studio with kitchenette, two bedroom, two bath $80. Substantial savings during off-season. Seven-day minimum, monthly rates, children under 5 free. Good beach, sheltered parking, pool, laundry facilities, private *lanai* and BBQs on premises. Good views.

Menehune Shores, at 760 S. Kihei Rd., Kihei 96753, tel. 879-5828. Write Kihei Kona Rentals, Box 556, Kihei 96753. This huge condo is on the beach overlooking an ancient fishpond. All units have an ocean view. The building is highlighted with Hawaiian petroglyphs. $60 one bedroom, $70 two bedroom, $95 three bedroom. No credit cards. Low-season savings of 30 percent. Full kitchens with dishwasher, self-cleaning ovens, washer and dryer and disposals. Each unit is individually owned, so furnishings vary, but the majority are well furnished. A lot for the money.

Maui Sunset, at 1032 S. Kihei Rd., Kihei 96753, tel. (800) 331-8076, in Hawaii (800) 922-3311. Contact manager Ron Stapes on Maui at 879-1971. Two large buildings containing over 200 units. Some are on a timeshare basis, and usually have nicer furnishings. Same rate year-round based on double occupancy at $62 one bedroom, $84 two bath two bedroom, $116 three bath and bedroom. Full kitchens. Pitch and putt golf green, pool, kiddie pool, beach front and rooftop "whale" observation deck. Quality tennis courts.

Hale Kai O Kihei, at 1310 Uluniu Rd., Kihei 96753, tel. 879-2757. Weekly rate based on double from $250 for one bedroom, $365 for two bedroom up to four people, additional person $7.50. No children under six. Pool, parking, maid service on request.

Kauhake Makai, at 930 S. Kihei Rd., write, Maui Beachfront Rentals, 1993 S. Kihei Rd., Kihei 96753, tel. (800) 367-5232, on Maui 879-1683. Rates from $35 studio, $45 one bedroom, $75 two bedroom. $7.50 additional person. Swimming pool, kiddie pool, BBQs, putting green, sauna. Four-day minimum.

Maui Hill at 2881 S. Kihei Rd., tel. 879-6321. Contact Oihana Management, 2145 Wells, Wailuku HI 96793, tel. (800) 367-5234, on Maui 879-7751. Upbeat condo with a Spanish motif and plenty of space. Near Wailea. Rates, one bedroom from $90, two bedroom from $105, three bedroom from $120. Deluxe furnishings, pool, tennis courts, maid service.

Maalaea Harbor

FOOD

Inexpensive

Azeka's Snacks, at Azeka Pl., S. Kihei Road. Open daily except Sun., 9:30 a.m. to 4:00 p.m. Basically take-out, featuring 90-cent hamburgers and a variety of plate lunches for $3.50. Popular with locals and terrific for picnics. Also try **Philadelphia Lou's** in the shopping plaza. Open daily 7:00 a.m. to 11:00 p.m. and until midnight on weekends. Breakfast, lunch and limited menu, but the real specialty is foot-and-a-half hoagies. These babies are loaded in the Back East tradition and, for $7.50, they can fill two easily. A scoop of all-natural Maui ice cream is $1. Kids hang out here and play videos, so it's noisy. Best to take out.

International House of Pancakes is toward the rear of Azeka Place. Open daily 6:00 a.m. to midnight, Fri. and Sat. until 2:00 a.m. Same American standards as on the mainland with most sandwiches and plate lunches under $5, dinners under $7 and breakfasts anytime around $4. Not exotic, but basic and filling. **Apple Annie's Sailmaker,** also at Azeka Place, tel. 879-4446. Daily from breakfast to late, late evening. Normal selection of Apple Annie sandwiches, entrees and salads. A touch expensive for what you get. Nightly entertainment in the loft.

Paradise Fruit Co., at 1913 S. Kihei Rd., across from McDonalds. Daily 24 hours, tel. 879-1723. This is a fruit stand and vegetable market that has a top-notch snack bar offering hearty, healthy sandwiches (under $3.50), vegetarian dishes, and a good selection of large, filling salads. Try the pita melt for $3.50, and any of the smoothies. A few tables out back, worth a stop!

Moderate

Polli's Mexican Restaurant, 101 S. Kihei Road, tel. 879-5275. Daily, 11:00 a.m. to midnight. Polli's has a well-deserved reputation for good food at fair prices. Their first all-natural vegetarian Mexican restaurant is in Makawao, and this new branch opened in the last year. The decor is classical Mexican with white stucco, and tiled floors. There's an outdoor deck area with a great sunset view. Main dishes are under $7, with a la carte tostadas for $3.50 and soup for $1.50. Imported beers $2.50. No lard is used and all oils are cold pressed. Meticulously clean, large portions and friendly atmosphere.

La Famiglia, at Kai Nani Village Plaza, 2511 S. Kihei Road, tel. 879-8824. Across from Kamaloe Park No. 2. Mexican food from $4 with organic ingredients, when possible. Good-looking, pleasant waitresses. Happy hour (4:00 to 6:00 p.m.) features huge frosty margaritas, the kind that give you a headache if you drink too fast, for 99 cents, with free chips and salsa. Dishes are well prepared with large portions. Upstairs is **Kihei Prime Rib House** open from 5:00 p.m., tel. 879-1954. A touch expensive with most entrees from $12.95, but this includes a well-stocked salad bar. Scrumptious appetizers like sashimi and lobster casserole for around $5, coupled with a baked potato with the works for $1.50, makes a meal. Salad bar only $7.95. "Early bird" specials under $10 from 5:00 to 6:00 p.m. Children's menu. Walls are adorned with carvings by Bruce Turnbull and paintings by Sigrid, two well-known artists.

Expensive

Maui Lu Hotel, at 575 S. Kihei Rd., tel. 879-5858. Beginning on Mon., Wed., and Fri., a *luau* and a Polynesian review are held in the hotel's Luau Garden: limitless cocktails and a sumptuous buffet with all the specials— including *imu* pork, *poi,* and a huge assortment of salads, entrees and side dishes. $28,tax and gratuity included. Also, the **Aloha Mele Luncheon** is a tradition at the hotel. Again a laden buffet with cocktails from 11:00 a.m. to 1:30 p.m., Thursday only, $12.50 includes the luncheon, entertainment, tax, and tip.

Robaire's, at 61 S. Kihei Rd., tel. 879-2707. Tuesday to Sat. from 6:00 to 10:00 p.m. Fine dining in this intimate French restaurant. The cooking is done by Robaire and his brother

Jacques. The decor isn't fancy, but the food is delicious. Specialties are veal Napoleon and rack of lamb. The fresh fish is also excellent. Seafood from $15, chicken cordon bleu $12.50. French and California wine list. Excellent selections.

Waterfront Restaurant, at the Milowai Condo in Maalaea Harbor, tel. 244-9028. Daily from 5:30 to 10 p.m. Whole, baked fish in oyster sauce for two, $16.50. Lobster and crab, from $18. Scampi, $14.50. Great sunsets. Tropical drinks.

Buzz's Wharf, at Maalaea Harbor, tel. 244-5426. Daily, dinner only. Seafood and fresh fish are the specialties. Most dishes under $12. Waterfront atmosphere. Great sunsets and views from second story overlooking the harbor.

Chuck's Steak House, at Kihei Town Center tel. 879-4488. Lunch, Mon. to Fri., 11:30 a.m. to 2:30 p.m. Dinner nightly from 5:30 p.m. No reservations necessary, but call to see how busy it is. Emphasis on steaks and ribs mostly under $12. Children's menu under $8. Daily specials and "early birds" sometimes. Dirt pie and sandwiches under $4. Salad bar a la carte, $6.95. Standard American, with an island twist.

ENTERTAINMENT

Kihei isn't exactly a hot spot when it comes to evening entertainment. There is the **Polynesian Review** at the Maui Lu *luau*. The **Surf and Sand Hotel** offers Polynesian entertainment nightly, and there's a disco at **Apple Annie Sailmaker** from 9:00 pm. to 2:00 a.m. Wed. to Sat., cover charge. Many of the restaurants offer entertainment on a hit and miss basis, usually one artist with a guitar, a small dinner combo or some Hawaiian music. These are usually listed in the free tourist brochures.

SHOPPING

Azeka Place Shopping Center: Along S. Kihei Rd., in about the center of town. Here you'll find all the practicals: bank (Bank of Hawaii, tel. 879-5844), post office (1254 S. Kihei Rd.) and gas station. **Azeka's Market** is well-stocked, and its meat department features famous Azeka ribs for BBQs. There's also a great community bulletin board listing apartments, yard sales and all odds and ends. In the Plaza are **Ben Franklin, Mediterranean House** selling swimwear, and a small **Liberty House**. There's also **Kihei Natural Foods**, a hardware store, and a florist. This is where the "people" do their one-stop shopping.

Kihei Town Center
A small shopping center just south of Azeka offers a **Foodland, Kihei Drug Mart,** a bank, art gallery, McDonalds, and a few clothing stores.

Food
At Azeka's Market, **Paradise Food Company** 1913 Kihei Road, **Foodland** at Kihei Town Center, and **Star Market** at 1310 S. Kihei Road.

Sporting goods and rentals
You'll find all you need at **Maui Sailing Center**, 145 N. Kihei Rd., in Sugar Beach Resort, or at 101 N. Kihei Rd., at Kealia Beach Center. Daily 8:00 a.m. to 5:00 p.m. They offer rental cars, windsurfing equipment and lessons, beach equipment, sail boats, snorkeling sets, bicycles, jet skis, ski boats and drivers, and tours. **The Dive Shop,** 1975 S. Kihei Rd., tel. 879-5172. Owned and operated by Linda Kowalsky, this is your one-stop dive shop, and more. Tours, excursions, snorkel and scuba equipment, bicycles and mopeds. **Maui Dive Shop** in Azeka Place has a full range of equipment and rentals.

WAILEA

Wailea ("Waters of Lea") isn't for the hoi polloi. It's a deluxe resort area custom-tailored to fit the egos of the upper-class like a Bijan original. This section of southeastern Maui was barren and bleak until Alexander and Baldwin Co. decided to landscape it into an emerald 1450-acre oasis of golf courses and world-class hotels. Every street light, palm tree and potted plant is a deliberate accessory to the decor so that the overall feeling is soothing, pleasant, and in good taste. To dispel any notions of snootiness, the five sparkling beaches that front the resorts were left open to the public and even improved with better access, parking areas, showers and picnic tables; a gracious gesture even if State Law does require open access! You know when you leave Kihei and enter Wailea. The green, quiet and wide tree-lined avenues give the impression of an upper-class residential area. Wailea is where you come when you're "putting on the ritz," and with the prices you'll encounter it would be good if you *owned* the Ritz. At both the **Intercon-** **tinental Hotel** and **Stouffer's Resort** you'll find five-star dining, and exclusive shopping at the Wailea Shopping Center. Both hotels are first rate architecturally and the grounds are exquisite. They're definitely worth a stroll, but remember your Gucci shoes.

Onward and backward

If you turn your back to the sea and look toward Haleakala, you'll see it's cool, green forests and peak wreathed in mysterious clouds. You'll want to run right over, but you can't get there from here! Outrageous as it may sound, you have to double back 18 miles to Kahului and then head down Rt. 37 for another 20 miles just to get to the exact same spot on Rt. 37 that you can easily see. On the map there's a neat little road called **Makena Rd.** that connects the Wailea/Makena area with upcountry in a mere two-mile stretch, but it's closed! An ongoing fight over who's responsible for its maintenence keeps it that way. Once this appalling situation is rectified, you'll be able easily to travel to the **Tedeschi**

Winery, and continue on the "wrong way" to Hana, or go left to Kula and upcountry. For now, however, happy motoring!

BEACHES

If you're not fortunate enough to be staying in Wailea, the best reason for coming here is its beaches. These little beauties are crescent moons of white sand that usually end in lava outcroppings on both ends. This makes for sheltered swimmable waters and good snorkeling and scuba. Many of the hotel guests in Wailea seem to hang around the hotel pools, maybe peacocking or just trying to get their money's worth, so the beaches are surprisingly uncrowded. The following beaches are listed from north to south, toward Makena.

Keawakapu
The first Wailea beach, almost a buffer between Kihei and Wailea, is just past the Mana Kai Resort. Turn left onto Kamala Pl., or proceed on south Kihei Road until it deadends. Plenty of parking at both accesses. No amenities. Lovely white sand beach with sandy bottom. Good swimming and fair snorkeling. A beginner's dive spot offshore where an underwater junkyard forming an artificial reef holds a few hundred cars.

Mokapu and Ulua
These two beaches are shoulder to shoulder, separated only by a rock outcropping. Turn right off Wailea Alanui Dr. at the first turn past the Westin Wailea Hotel. Clearly marked. Parking area and showers. Resort beaches, especially cared for. Beautiful white sand, perfect for swimming. Good snorkeling at the rock outcropping separating these two beaches. Or swim out to the first reef just in front of the rocks for excellent snorkeling.

Wailea Beach
Travel one-half mile past the Wailea Town Center and turn right onto a clearly marked access road. Good parking, with showers and toilets. Beach and surf equipment rental. A short but wide beach of pure white sand. Good swimming and body surfing, but snorkeling only fair.

Polo Beach
Follow Wailea Alanui Dr. toward Makena until it starts getting rugged. Turn right at the clearly marked sign near Polo Beach Condo. Paved parking, showers and toilets. Good for swimming and sunbathing with few tourists. Excellent snorkeling in front of the rocks separating Polo from Wailea Beach. Tremendous amount of fish, and one of the easiest spots to get to.

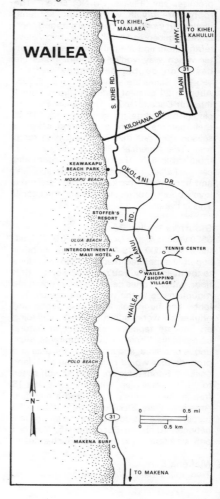

ACCOMMODATIONS

Hotel Intercontinental

Box 779, Kihei-Wailea, HI 96753, tel. (800) 367-2960 mainland, (800) 537-5589 from Honolulu, 879-1922 on Maui. This hotel is a class act. Even the Wrong Way signs on the premises say "Please, Do Not Enter." The rooms are lavish with folding screens, original art work, rich, deep carpets and coordinated bedspreads, full baths, two *lanais,* refrigerators and magnificent views no matter which way you're oriented. Rates are based on double occupancy and run $95-135. Suites are available from $135-525. About a 20 percent reduction from April 1 through December 23. The Family Plan, includes no charge for children under 18 in their parents' room; and during off-peak season they get their own adjoining room free. The American Plan is $44 per day, modified at $35. The hotel offers room and car packages, golfer's and tennis specials, and honeymoon packages. There are three lovely pools, four restaurants and the beach. This is living!

Stouffers Wailea Resort

3550 Wailea Alanui Dr., Wailea, HI 96753, tel. (800) 385-5000, 879-4900 on Maui. Another superbly-appointed resort. When you drive to the main lobby, you're actually on the fifth floor, with the ones below terraced down the mountainside to the white sand beach. The lobby has huge oak and brass doors, and original art works adorn the walls, including an intricate tapestry made out of natural carpet fibers. There are five restaurants, a luxurious pool area, and a beach in the area and grounds that would make Tarzan and Jane envious. Room rates are $95-180 with suites to $650. Family plan, with children under 18 free in their parents' room, and a modified American Plan. Stouffer's even offers a 50 percent discount coupon for certain rooms between April and December 15. You can only stay four days, however. Such a deal!

Makena Surf

Two miles past Wailea proper near Polo

Beach. Contact Village Resorts Inc., (800) 367-7052, or the condo directly at (800) 367-2963, 879-4555 on Maui. Two-bedroom from $175, up to four people, three-bedroom from $300, up to six. Rooms cheaper on upper floors. Swimming pool, tennis courts, two-night minimum, deposit necessary.

Polo Beach Club

20 Makena Rd., Wailea 96753, tel. 879-8847. Near Polo Beach toward Makena. Condo apartments fully furnished. From $130, six people maximum. Low season discounts. Pool, jacuzzi and seclusion.

Wailea Luxury Condos

3750 Wailea Alanui, Wailea, HI 96753, tel. (800) 367-5246 mainland, 879-1595 collect from Hawaii or Canada. This complex is made up of three separate villages: **Ekolu,** from $110, near the golf course; **Ekahi,** the least expensive, from $70 near the tennis; **Elua,** the most expensive, from $115 near the sea. All units are plush. $10 additional people, monthly discounts, four-night minimum.

Haleakala's slopes loom behind Wailea.

FOOD

Raffles' Restaurant

At Stouffer's Wailea Beach Resort, tel. 879-4900, reservations a must. Dinner daily from 6:30 to 10:30 p.m. Sunday brunch from 9:00 a.m. to 2:00 p.m., a prize winner! Semidress up, with tasteful aloha wear OK. Inspired by the famed Raffles of Singapore, this restaurant lives up to the tradition. Sashimi, oysters Rockefeller, crab cocktail and fresh Hawaiian prawns are appetizers, from $6.50. Vichyssoise or onion soup from $3.50. Salads galore, including mushrooms, spinach, Manoa lettuce and filet mignon for $5.50. Roast rack of lamb, $22, *opakapaka* in sorrel sauce. Wines from the best vineyards around the world. Magnificent desserts. The Sunday brunch for $19.50 is worth every penny. Omelettes made to order, chops, steaks, fish, champagne, eggs Benedict, breakfast meats. All first class, all servings constantly replenished. **Palm Court** is also at the hotel, through the lobby and look over the rail. Open nightly from 6:00 p.m. Buffet for a fixed $15.50, and every night has a theme: Monday Oriental, Tuesday Italian, Thursday French. Plenty of salads and soup from the kettle for $4.50. A definite bargain for the amount and quality of the food. **Maui Onion** down by the pool will make your eyes tear. $6 for a hamburger, $2.75 for Maui onion rings. Even at Stouffer's, too much!

La Perouse Restaurant

At Maui Intercontinental Hotel, tel. 879-1922. Dinner nightly from 5:30 p.m., reservations a must. This elegant restaurant is gaining an international reputation. The surroundings themselves of rich *koa* wood and an immense ironwork gate at the entry set the theme. A dress code requires collared shirts, but most people dress up. No shorts. The Callalo Crabmeat soup is a must. The bouillabaisse is out of this world. Breadfruit vichyssoise is unique. Wines from the private cellar start at $20, but the house wine by the glass is an affordable $2.50. The best selections are the seafood, but the chicken and lamb are also superb. Save room for dessert

offered on a pastry cart laden with exotic choices. This is no place for will power. Enjoy one of the best meals ever, and don't worry about the second mortgage tonight. **Kiawe Broiler** offers more moderately priced dinners at the hotel. Daily lunch from 11:00 to 4:00 p.m., dinner 6:00 to 10:00 p.m, basically *kiawe*, broiled chops and steaks from $13, salad bar a deal at $7.25. Informal setting with high-backed rattan decor. **Lanai Terrace** at the hotel, tel. 879-1922, offers Sunday brunch from 9:00 a.m to 2:00 p.m. All you can eat of first quality buffet breakfast and lunch foods that are well-prepared and beautifully presented. $15.50, and worth every pound... penny! **Luau** every Sunday and Thursday evening, old Hawaii lives again from 6:00 p.m. Lavish buffet and *imu* ceremony. $24.50 adults, $12.50 children under 10 years. Also try the **Inu Inu Lounge** for sushi, **Makani's Coffee Shop** for reasonably priced American standard, and the **Wet Spot** by the pool if you want to get soaked for a $6 sandwich.

Golf ball soup

The following restaurants are located at the golf links in the area. **Wailea Steak House,** 100 Wailea Ike Dr., on the 15th fairway of Wailea Blue Golf Club, tel. 879-2875. Daily for dinner from 5:30 p.m. Reasonably priced for this neck of the woods with steaks from $12 and chicken from $10. A decent salad bar for $8. Quiet with good sunset views. **Fairway,** at Wailea Golf Course Club House, tel. 879-4060. Breakfast, lunch and dinner. Reasonably priced, filling breakfasts, good lunches and a wide selection of dinners, from $13. **Makena Golf Course Restaurant,** tel. 879-1154. Daily from 9:30 a.m. Nothing special, but well-prepared sandwiches, burgers and fries. Convenient as the last stop to Makena.

SHOPPING AND SERVICES

The only shopping in this area is **Wailea Shopping Center,** just east past the Intercontinental Hotel off Wailea Alanui Drive. It has the usual collection of boutiques and shops. **Superwhale** offers aloha wear for children; **Ocean Activities Center** is as its name implies; **Party Pantry**, tel. 879-3044, for food items and liquor; **Golden Reef** selling distinctive island coral jewelry including gold, black, and pink coral.

Golf
You have three choices of golf courses in Wailea, all open to the public. **Wailea Golf Course** has two 18 holers—The Orange Course and The Blue Course. Both are a par 72 and charge $40 for green fees and mandatory cart. Half price to Wailea Hotel guests and residents. **Makena Golf Course** is past Wailea toward Makena, tel. 879-3344, par 72. More reasonably priced at $26, including cart. **tennis:** Many condos have their own courts; check individually for general public

use. Usually no problem. **Wailea Tennis Center**, tel. 879-1958, has 14 courts, with three lighted and three grass, open daily 7:00 a.m. until 9:00 p.m. Per hour rates: $10 single, $12 double (high season); nights $12 single, $17 double (high season); grass courts, $18 single, $24 double.

Transportation
The **Maui Transit System**, tel. 661-3827, runs three buses daily between Lahaina and Wailea. You pay by the distance traveled. **Wailea Shuttle** is a complimentary jitney constantly making trips up and down Wailea Alanui Dr., stopping at all major hotels and condos. It operates 6:30 a.m. to 10:30 p.m. With a little walking, this is a great way to hop from one beach to the next.

MAKENA TO LA PEROUSE

Just a skip down the road eastward is Makena Beach, but it's a world away from Wailea. Once the paved roads of Wailea give way to dirt, you know you're in Makena country. This was a hippie enclave during the '60s and early '70s, and the free-wheeling spirit of the times still permeates the area. For one, "Little Makena" is a nude beach, but so what? You can skinny-dip in Connecticut. This fact gets too much attention. What's really important is that Makena is *the last* pristine coastal area of Maui that hasn't succumbed to development... yet. As you head down the dirt road you'll notice Hawaii's unofficial bird, the building crane, arching its mechanical neck and lifting girders into place. The Japanese firm of Seibu Hawaii is building the Seibu Prince Hotel, and more will surely follow. There's unofficial camping at Makena, with plenty of beach people who live here semi-permanently. There's nothing in the way of amenities past Wailea, so make sure to stock up on all supplies (for water see "Keawalai Church," below). The police come in and sweep the area now and again, but mostly it's mellow. They do arrest the nudists on Little Makena, but this is more to make the point that Makena "ain't free no more." Rip-offs can be a problem, so lock your car, hide your camera and don't leave anything of value in your tent if you'll be camping. Be

careful of the *kiawe* thorns when you park, they'll puncture a tire like a nail.

Makena is magnificent for body surfing and swimming. Whales frequent the area and come quite close to shore during the season. Turtles waddled on Makena early in this century, where they came to lay their eggs in the warm sand. Too many people gathered the eggs and the turtles scrambled away forever. The sunsets from **Red Hill**, the cinder cone separating Makena from Little Makena, are among the best on Maui, fading between Lanai, Kahoolawe and West Maui. The silhouettes of pastel and gleaming colors are awe-inspiring. Oranges, russets and every shade of purple reflect off the clouds that are caught here. Makena attracts all kinds: gawkers, burn-outs, adventurers, tourists and free spirits. It won't last long, so go and have a look now!

Keawalai Church
About two-thirds of the way from Polo Beach to Makena, you'll pass this Congregational Church, established in 1832. It was restored in 1952 and services are held every Sunday at 11:00 a.m. Many of the hymns and part of the sermon are still delivered in Hawaiian. There is a public telephone in front of the church, and drinking water. Enter the grounds and go

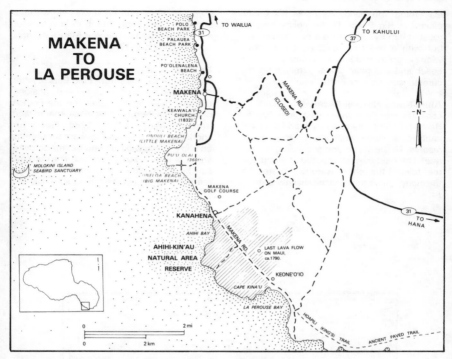

MAKENA
TO
LA PEROUSE

behind the garage-type building to the left of the church itself, where you'll find a sink and a water tap.

Small beaches

You'll pass by these beaches as you head toward Makena. There's usually few people and no amenities. **Palauea** and **Poolenalena** are about three-quarters of a mile past Polo. Good swimming and white, sloping sands. **Nahuna Point** ("Five Graves") is just over a mile past Polo. An old graveyard marks the entrance. Not good for swimming but great for scuba because of deep underwater caves. Snorkelers can enjoy this area, too. **Papipi** is along the road a mile and a half past Polo. Parking in lot. Small sand beach. Too close to road. **Oneuli** ("Black Sand Beach") is past Polo, not quite three miles. Turn down a rutted dirt road for a third of a mile. Not good for swimming. Good diving. Unofficial camping.

Makena Beach

Bounce along for three miles past Polo Beach. Look for a wide dirt road that two cars can pass on. Turn right and follow the rutted road for a few hundred yards. This is **Oneloa Beach**, generally called **Makena Big Beach**. You can go left or right to find parking. Left is where most people camp. Right leads you to **Puu Olai** (Red Hill), a 360-foot cinder cone. When you cross it you'll be on **Little Makena**, a favorite nude beach. Both beaches are excellent for swimming (beware currents in winter), body surfing and superb snorkeling in front of Red Hill.

Practicalities

Only the phones back at Makena Golf Club and the water at Keawalai Church. There is, however, an "alternative" entrepreneur who calls himself "Jungle John." If you remember the TV show, "Green Acres," he's a Mr. Hainey-type, who just happens to have everything you need. He parks his green pickup at Big Beach (if the police haven't rousted him by now). He's a born salesman, but with a heart of gold. He's got sandwiches, cold drinks and a smattering of beach and surf gear. Under extenuating circumstances, he'll look after your gear.

Ahihi-Kinau Natural Reserve
Look for sign four miles past Polo Beach. Here you'll find a narrow beach and the remnants of a stone wall. It's an underwater reserve, so the scuba and snorkeling is first-rate. The best way to proceed is along the reef toward the left. Beware not to step on the many spiny urchins in the shallow waters.

If you do, vinegar or urine will help with the stinging. The jutting thumb of lava to your left is **Cape Kinau**. This was Maui's last lava flow, occurring in 1790.

La Perouse Bay
Just shy of six miles from Polo Beach. After Ahihi-Kinau the road is rugged and cut along the lava flow. Named after the the French navigator La Perouse, first Westerner to land here on Maui in May 1786. Good for snorkelers and divers but beware the urchins on entry. If you walk left you'll come across a string of pocket-sized beaches. The currents can be tricky along here. Past the bay are remnants of the *Hoapili* ("King's") Trail.

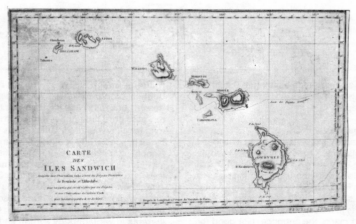

map of the "Sandwich Isles" as drawn by Captain Jean LaPerouse from his 1786 expedition (Hawaii State Archives).

UPCOUNTRY

INTRODUCTION

Upcountry is much more than a geographical area to the people who live there: it's a way of life, a frame of mind. You can see Upcountry from anywhere on Maui by lifting your gaze to the slopes of Haleakala. There are no actual boundaries, but this area is usually considered to run from Makawao in the north all the way around to Kahikinui Ranch in the south, and from below the cloud cover up to about the 3,000-foot level. It encircles Haleakala like a large green floral bib patterned by pasture lands and festooned with wild and cultivated flowers. In this rich soil and cool to moderate temperatures, cattle ranching and truck farming thrive. Up here, *paniolo* ride herd on the range of the enormous 20,000-acre **Haleakala Ranch**, spread mostly around Makawao, and the even larger 30,000 acres of the **Ulupalakua Ranch** which *is* the hills above Wailea. **Pukalani,** the largest town, is a way station for gas and

supplies. **Makawao** is a real cowboy town with saddleries, rodeos and hitching posts. It's also sophisticated, with some exclusive shops and fine dining. **Kula** is Maui's flower basket. This area is one enormous garden producing brilliant blooms and hearty vegetables. **Poli Poli State Park** is a forgotten wonderland of tall forests, a homogenized stand of trees from around the world. **Tedeschi Winery** in the south adds a classy touch to Upcountry; you can taste wine in an historic jailhouse. There are plenty of commercial greenhouses and flower farms to visit all over Upcountry, but the best is a free Sunday drive along the mountain roads and farm lanes, just soaking in the scenery. The purple mists of mountain jacaranda and the heady fragrance of eucalyptus encircling a mountain pasture manicured by herds of cattle is a portrait of the soul of Upcountry.

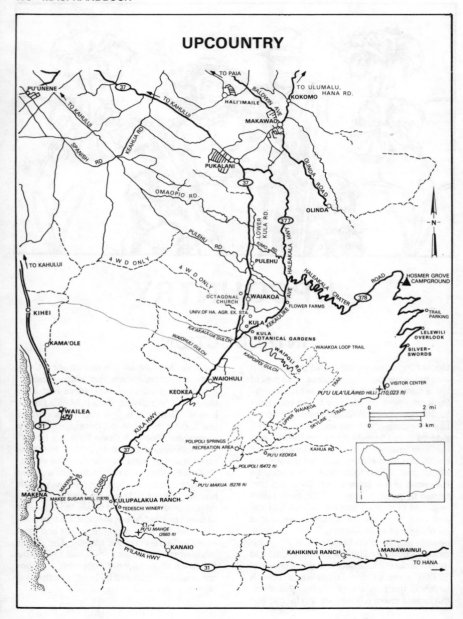

UPCOUNTRY

MAKAWAO

Makawao is proud of itself; it's not *like* a cowboy town, it *is* a cowboy town. Depending on the translation that you consult, it means, "Eye of the Dawn," or "Forest Beginning." Both are appropriate. Surrounding lowland fields of cane and pineapples give way to upland pastures rimmed with tall forests, as Haleakala's morning sun shoots lasers of light through the town. Makawao was settled late last century by Portuguese immigrants who started raising cattle on the Upland slopes. It loped along as a *paniolo* town until WW II, when it received an infusion of life from a nearby military base in Kokomo. After the war it settled back down and became a sleepy village again, where as many horses were tethered on the main street as cars were parked. The majority of its false-front, one-story buildings are a half-century old, but their prototype is strictly "Dodge City, 1850." During the 1950s and '60s, Makawao started to decline into a bunch of worn-out old buildings. It earned a reputation for drinking, fighting and cavorting cowboys, and for a period was derisively called "Macho-wao."

In the 1970s it began to revive. It had plenty to be proud of and a good history to fall back on. Makawao is *the* last real *paniolo* town on Maui and, with Kamuela on the Big Island, is one of the last two in the entire state. At the Oskie Rice Arena, it hosts the largest and most successful rodeo in Hawaii. Its Fourth of July parade is a marvel of homespun humor, *aloha* and an old-fashioned good time. Many people ride their horses to town, leaving them to graze in a public corral. They do business at stores operated by the same families for 50 years. Though much of the drygoods are country-oriented, a new breed of merchant has come to town. You can buy a sack of feed, a rifle, designer jeans and an imported silk blouse all on one street. At its eateries, you can have lobster, vegetarian Mexican, or a steamy bowl of *saimin*, reputed to be the best on Maui.

Everyone, oldtimers and newcomers alike, agree that Makawao must be preserved, and they work together. They know that tourism is a financial lifeline, but shudder at the thought of Makawao becoming an Upcountry Lahaina. It shouldn't. It's far enough off the track to keep the average tourist away, but easy enough and definitely interesting enough to make a side trip there absolutely worthwhile.

Getting there
The main artery to Makawao is through Paia as you travel Rt. 360, (Hana Road). In Paia Town turn right onto Baldwin Ave. at the corner marked by the gaily painted "Ice Creams and Dreams" shop. From here it's about six miles to Makawao.

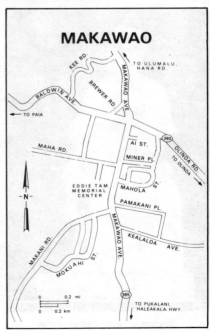

SIGHTS

Enroute on Baldwin Ave., you pass the **sugar mill**, a real life Carl Sandburg poem. It's a green monster trimmed in bare light bulbs at night, dripping with sounds of turning gears, cranes and linkbelts, all surrounded by packed, rutted, oil-stained soil. Farther along Baldwin Ave. sits **Holy Rosary Church**, and its sculpture of Father Damien of the Lepers. The rendering of Damien is idealized, but the leper, who resembles a Calcutta beggar, has a face that conveys helplessness, but at the same time faith and hope. It's worth a few minute's stop. Coming next is **Makawao Union Church**, and it's a beauty. Like a Tudor mansion made completely of stone with lovely stained-glass windows, the entrance is framed by two tall and stately royal palms.

sculpture of Father Damien at Holy Rosary Church

The backway reaches Makawao by branching off Rt. 36 through Ulumalu and Kokomo. Just where Rt. 36 turns into Rt. 360, there's a road to the right. This is Kapakilui Rd., or Rt. 365 (some maps show it as Rt. 400). Take it through backcountry Maui, where horses graze around neat little houses. Haleakala looms on the horizon; guavas, mangoes and bananas grow wild. At the first Y, bear left to Kaupakulua. Pass a large junkyard and continue to Kokomo. There's a general store here. Notice the mixture of old and new houses—Maui's past and future in microcosm. Here, the neat little banana plantation on the outskirts of the diminutive town says it all. Pass St. Joseph's Church and you've arrived through Makawao's back door. This is an excellent off-track route to take on your way to or from Hana. You can also come over Rt. 365 through Pukalani, incorporating Makawao into your Haleakala trip.

Nearby attractions
Take Olinda Rd. out of town. All along it custom houses have been built. Look for **Pookela Church,** a coral block structure built in 1843. In four miles you pass **Rainbow Acres,** tel. 572-8020. Open Fri. and Sat., 10:00 a.m. to 4:00 p.m., they specialize in succulents. At the top of Olinda turn left onto Piiholo Rd., which loops back down. Along it is **Aloha o ka Aina,** a nursery specialing in ferns. Open Wed. and Sun., 10:00 a.m. to 4:00 p.m. You'll also pass **Olinda Nursery,** offering general house plants. Open Fri. and Sat., 10:00 a.m. to 4:00 p.m.

PRACTICALITIES

Food
All the following establishments are on Makawao or Baldwin Avenues. An excellent place to eat is **Polli's Mexican Restaurant** (vegetarian). Open daily 11:30 a.m. to 10:30 p.m., tel. 572-7808. This is the original restaurant; they now have a branch in Kihei. The meals are authentic Mexican, using the finest ingredients. They use no lard or animal fat in their cooking. You can have a full meal

for $5-$6. Margaritas are large and tasty for $2, pitchers of domestic beer $5. The Sunday brunch is particularly good. One unfortunate policy is that they refuse to give free chips and salsa to a person dining alone, even when ordering a full meal, while couples dining get them free! **Makawao Steak House,** tel. 572-8711. Daily for dinner from 5:00 p.m. "Early bird" special until 6:30. Sunday brunch from 9:30 a.m. to 2:00 p.m. Casual, with wooden tables, salad bar and good fish selections. Dinners are from $8.95 — a good general purpose restaurant.

Kitada's, known as a *kau kau* stand, makes the best *saimin* on Maui, according to all the locals. It's across from the Makawao Steak House. Open daily from 6:00 a.m. to 2:00 p.m., tel. 572-7241. The 77-year-old owner, Takeshi Kitada, does all the prep work himself. Walk in, pour yourself a glass of water and take a hardboard-topped table. The *saimin* is delicious and only $1.50. There're plate lunches, too. The walls have paintings of Upcountry by local artists. Most show more heart than talent. Bus your own table while Kitada-san calculates your bill on an abacus. His birthday, May 26, has become a town event.

Komoda's is a corner general store that has been in business for over 50 years. They sell everything, but their bakery is renowned far and wide. They open at 6:30 a.m. with people already lined up outside to buy their cream buns and home-made cookies — all gone by 9:00. **Mountainside Liquor and Deli,** tel. 572-0204, can provide all the fixings for a lunch, or a full range of liquid refreshments. **Rodeo General Store** has a selection of fish and gourmet foods. **Whole Food Co.** is a health food store that can supply basic needs.

Shopping

Some unique and fascinating shops here can provide you with distinctive purchases. **Up-country Down Under,** tel. 572-7103, specializes in imported New Zealand woolens, crafts and skins. They also carry stuffed animals, rugby jerseys, sweaters and backpacks. Lyn Lone runs the shop along with Dana and Peter Marshal. **Collections Boutique,** open daily til 9:00 p.m., imports items from throughout Asia: *batik* from Bali, clothes from India, jewelry and handicrafts from various countries. Operated by Pam Winans. **Grandma's Attic** is a discovery shop operated by Pris and Moe Moler. Everything in here is nifty: old victrolas, vintage *Life* magazines, furniture, jewelry. It has the feeling of a museum and is worth a stop.

Outdoor Sports, tel. 572-8736, is a gem of a general store and an attraction in itself. The owner, Gary Moore, is a relative newcomer who helped restore the integrity of Makawao and became a town historian in his own right. He carries guns, ammo, boots, saddles, big barrels full of hardware, even wood-burning stoves. He sells gifts and camping equipment, which is also for rent. Wander around inside just for the fun of it. **Makawao Leather** specializes in hand-carved leatherwork — everything from chaps to headbands. **Hui Noeau** (Club of Skills) is a local organization that features traditional and modern arts. Their member artisans produce everything from ceramics to *lau hala* (weaving). They are housed at Kaluanui, a mansion built in 1917 by the Baldwin family. They sponsor an annual Christmas Fair featuring their creations.

Events

Makawao has a tremendous rodeo season every year. Most meets are sponsored by the Maui Roping Club. They start in the spring and culminate in a massive rodeo on July 4th, with over $22,000 in prize money. These events attract the best cowboys from around the state. The organization of the event is headed by a long-time resident, Brendan Balthazar, who welcomes everyone to participate with only one rule, "Have fun, but maintain safety."

KULA

Kula could easily provide all of the ingredients for a full-course meal fit for a king. Its bounty is staggering: vegetables to make a splendid chef's salad, beef for the entree, flowers to brighten the spirits, and wine to set the mood. Up here, soil, sun and moisture create a garden symphony. Sweet Maui onions, cabbages, potatoes, grapes, apples, pineapples, lettuce and artichokes grow with abandon. Herefords and black Angus graze in knee-deep fields of sweet green grass. Flowers are everywhere: beds of proteas, camelias, carnations, roses, hydrangeas, and blooming peach and tangerine dot the countryside like daubs from Van Gogh's brush. As you gain the heights along Kula's lanes, you look back on West Maui with a perfect view of the isthmus. You'll also enjoy wide-open spaces and rolling green hills fringed with trees like a lion's mane. Above, the sky changes from brooding gray to blazing blue, then back again. Kula is a different Maui, quiet and serene.

Getting there
The fastest way is the same as if going to Haleakala Crater. Take Rt. 37 through Pukalani, turn onto Rt. 377, and when you see Kimo Rd. on your left and right, you're in Kula country. If you have the time take the following scenic route. Back in Kahului start on Rt. 36 (Hana Hwy.), but as soon as you cross Dairy Rd. look for a sign on your left pointing to Pulehu-Omaopio Road. Take it! You'll wade through acres of sugar cane, and in six miles these two roads will split. You can take either, but Omaopio to the left is better because, at the top, it deposits you in the middle of things to see. Once the roads fork, you pass some excellent examples of flower and truck farms. You'll also go by the cooperative **Vacuum Cooling Plant** where many farmers store their produce. Then Omaopio Rd. will come again to Rt. 37 (Kula Hwy.). Don't take it yet. Cross and continue until Omaopio dead-ends, in a few hundred yards. Turn right onto Lower Kula Rd., watch

a field of cacti adds that cowboy touch to Upcountry

for Kimo (Lower) Drive on your left, and take it straight uphill. This brings you through some absolutely beautiful countryside and in a few miles crosses Rt. 377, where a right will take you to Haleakala Crater Road.

SIGHTS / ACCOMMODATIONS

Pukalani
This way station town is uninteresting but a good place to get gas and supplies. There's a shopping mall where you can pick up just about anything you'll need. **Bullock's** restaurant just past the mall serves a wide assortment of good value sandwiches. The moonburger is a tradition, but a full breakfast here for under $3 will give you all the energy you'll need for the day ahead. They also have plate lunches and some island-flavored shakes. **Cross Roads Restaurant** in the mall is open daily for lunch and dinner: basically American standard from sandwiches to full meals.

Kula Lodge
The Kula Lodge is on Rt. 377 just past Kimo Drive and just before Haleakala Crater Road. RR 1, Box 475, Kula HI 96790, tel. 878-1535. Lodging here is in $58 bungalows. All have fireplaces with wood provided, and all have excellent views of lower Maui. The lobby and main dining areas are impressively rustic. The walls are covered with high-quality photos of Maui: windsurfers, silverswords, sunsets, cowboys, and horses. The main dining room has a giant bay window with a superlative view. Breakfast is served daily from 7:00 a.m., lunch from 11:30 a.m. to 2:30 p.m., dinner from 5:00. Entertainment in the evenings.

Hawaii Protea Cooperative
Located just next door to the Kula Lodge, open Mon. through Fri., 9:00 a.m. to 4:30 p.m., tel. 878-6273. Don't miss seeing these amazing flowers. (For a full description see, "Flora," in the main Introduction). Here you can purchase a wide range of protea that can be shipped back home. Live or dried, these flowers are fantastic. They start at $20, but are well worth the price. The sales people are

friendly and informative, and it's educational just to visit.

protea

Upper Kimo Road
If you want to be intoxicated by some of the finest examples of Upcountry flower and vegetable farms, come up here. First, head back down Rt. 377 past the Kula Lodge and turn on **Upper Kimo Rd.** on your right. At the very end is **Upcountry Protea Farm,** daily 8:00 a.m. to 4:30 p.m. Box 485F, Kula, HI 96790, tel. 878-6015. They have over 50 varieties of protea and other flowers. You can walk the grounds or visit the gift shop where they offer gift packs and mail order.

Silversword Inn
Proceed past the Kula Lodge on Rt. 377 toward Haleakala to the Silversword Inn, tel. 878-1232. This congenial inn offers chalet-type accommodations at $40 for four people. All have an excellent view, but units 3 and 5 have extraordinary sunset exposure. The restaurant is open for breakfast, lunch and dinner, and the huge circular fireplace is cozy against the Upcountry chill. On the grounds is the **Silversword Bakery,** tel. 878-2179. When open, they offer custom baking using organic ingredients and no preservatives or colorings. Also on the grounds is the unique **Silversword Store.** Just about everything offered is hand-made or home-cooked, as well as aromatic bags of **Grandma's Maui**

Coffee. This wild coffee is prepared by a 92-year old *tu tu* after being hand-picked by her grandson. There're jellies and jams from the ladies at the local church and handicrafts all under $10. There's fresh-squeezed orange and guava juice, fresh-baked *malasadas,* and even Coca-Cola in the little six-ounce bottles!

Kula Botanical Gardens
Follow Rt. 377 south and look for the Gardens on your left just before the road meets again with Rt. 37. The gardens are open daily from 9:00 a.m. to 4:00 p.m. Admission is $2.50, under 12, 50 cents, tel. 878-1715. Here are three acres of identified plants on a self-guided tour. There are streams and ponds on the property, and plants include native *koa* and *kukui,* as well as many introduced species. The gardens are educational and will give names to many flowers and plants that you've observed around the island. It makes for a relaxing afternoon, with picnic tables provided.

Poli Poli State Park
If you want quietude and mountain walks, come here, because few others do. Just past the botanical garden look for the park sign on your left leading up Waipoli Road. This 10-mile stretch is only partially paved, and the second half can be very rutted and muddy. Like always, it's worth it. Poli Poli is an established forest of imported trees from around the world: eucalyptus, redwoods, cypress and sugi pines. You can hike the **Redwood Trail** to a shelter at the end. Camping permits are required and are available from the Division of State Parks, Box 1049, Wailuku, HI 96793, tel. 244-4354. The cabin here is a spacious three-bedroom affair with bunks for up to 10 people. It starts at $10 single and goes up about $5 per person. It's rustic, but all camping and cooking essentials are provided, including a wood-burning stove. If you want to get away from it all, this is your spot.

Others
The University of Hawaii maintains an experimental station of 20 acres of flowers that they change with the seasons. Located on Copp Rd. off Rt. 37. Open Mon. to Fri., 7:30 a.m. to 3:30 p.m. A self-guided tour map is available at the office, which is closed during lunch hour. **Holy Ghost Church** on Lower Kula Rd., just past Kula Town, is an octagonal building raised in 1897 for the many Portuguese who worked the farms and ranches of Upcountry. There's a gas station in Kula Town.

Tedeschi Winery
Continue south on Rt. 37 through the town of Keokea, where you'll find gas, two general stores and an excellent park for a picnic. Past Keokea you'll know you're in ranch country. The road narrows and herds of cattle graze in pastures that seem like manicured gardens highlighting *panini* (prickly pear) cactus. You'll pass Ulupalakua Ranch and then come to the Tedeschi Winery **tasting room** on the left. Open for tasting daily 9:00 a.m. to 5:00 p.m., tel. 878-6058. Here, Emil Tedeschi and his partner Pardee Erdman, who also owns the 30,000-acre Ulupalakua Ranch, offer samples of their wines. This is the only winery in all of Hawaii. When he moved here in 1963 from California and noticed climatic similarities to the Napa Valley, Erdman knew that this country could grow decent wine grapes. Tedeschi comes from California, where his family has a small winery near Calistoga. The partners have worked on making their dream of Maui wine a reality since 1973.

It takes time and patience to grow grapes and turn out a vintage wine. While they wait for their Carnelian grapes to mature and be made into a sparkling wine, they ferment pineapple juice, which they call Maui Blanc. If you're expecting this to be a sickeningly sweet syrup, forget it. Maui Blanc is surprisingly dry and palatable. There's even an occasional pineapple sparkling wine called Maui Brut. Both are available in restaurants and stores around the island. (1984 saw the first scheduled release of the winery's Carnelian champagne.) You can taste the wines at the 100-year-old tasting room, which is a plaster and coral building. It served as the jailhouse of the old Rose Ranch owned by James Makee, a Maui pioneer sugarcane planter.

HALEAKALA

Haleakala ("House of the Sun") is spell binding. Like seeing Niagara or the Grand Canyon for the first time, it makes no difference how many people have come before you, it's still an undiminished, powerful, personal experience. The mountain is a power spot, a natural conductor of cosmic energy. *Kahuna* brought their novitiates here to perform final rites of initiation. During the heyday of the *kahuna,* intense power struggles took place between the healing practitioners and "black" sorcerers atop the mountain. The "Bottomless Pit," a natural feature on the crater floor, held tremendous significance for both. Average Hawaiians did not live on Haleakala, but came now and again to quarry tool-stones. Only *kahuna* and their apprentices lived here for any length of time, as a sort of a spiritual preparation and testing grounds. Today, students of higher consciousness from around the world are drawn to this natural empire because of the rarified energy. They claim that it accelerates personal growth, and compare it to remote mountain and desert areas in the Holy Lands. Even the U.S. Air Force has a facility here, and their research indicates Haleakala as *the* strongest natural power point in

America. Not only is there an energy configuration coming from the Earth itself, but there is also a high focus of radiation coming from outside the atmosphere. No one is guaranteed a spiritual experience on Haleakala, but if you're at all sensitive, this is fertile ground.

Natural features
Haleakala is the world's largest dormant volcano. Its amazingly dense volcanic rock, almost like poured cement, and its 20,000 feet or so under the sea, make it one of the tallest mountains on Earth. It's possible that this mass acounts for the strange power of Haleakala as it sits like a mighty, magnetic pyramid in the center of the North Pacific. The park's boundaries encompass 27,284 variable acres, which stretch from Hosmer Grove to Kipahulu, and include dry forests, rainforests, desert, and subtropical beaches. The most impressive feature is the crater itself. It's 3,000 feet deep, 7.5 miles long, 2.5 miles wide, accounting for 19 sq. miles, with a circumference of 21 miles. A mini mountain range of nine cinder cones marches across the crater floor. They look deceptively tiny

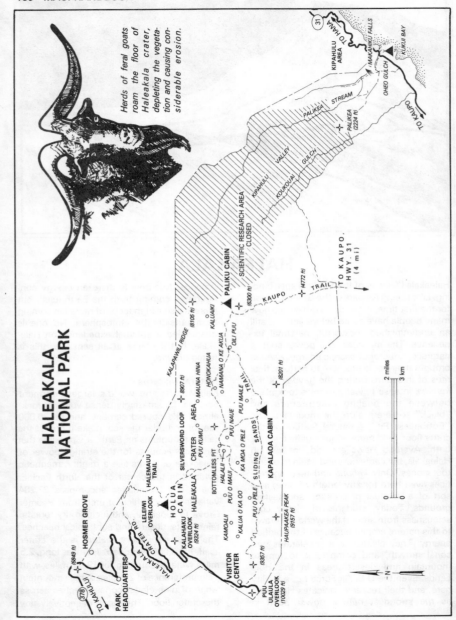

Herds of feral goats roam the floor of Haleakala crater, depleting the vegetation and causing considerable erosion.

HALEAKALA NATIONAL PARK

from the observation area, but the smallest is 600 feet, and the tallest, Puu O Maui, is 1,000 feet high. Haleakala was designated as a National Park in 1961. Before that it was part of the Big Island's Volcanoes Park. The entire park is a nature preserve dedicated to Hawaii's quickly vanishing indigenous plants and animals. Only Volcanoes and Haleakala are home to the *nene,* the Hawaiian wild goose, and the **silversword,** a fantastically adapted plant. (For full descriptions, see "Fauna and Flora" in the main "Introduction.")

The experience

If you're after *the* experience, you must see the sunrise or sunset. Both are magnificent, but both perform their stupendous light show with astonishing speed. Also, the weather must be cooperative. Misty, damp clouds can surround the crater, blocking out the sun, and then pour into the basin, obscuring even it from view. The *Maui News* prints the hours of sunrise and sunset on a daily basis that vary with the season, so make sure to check. The park provides an accurate daily weather recording at tel. 877-5124. For more specific information, you can call the Ranger Station at 572-7749. Plan on taking a minimum of 1½ hours to arrive from Kahului, and to be safe, arrive at least 30 minutes before, because even one minute is critical. The sun, as it rises or sets, infuses the clouds with streaks, puffs, and bursts of dazzling pastels, at the same time backlighting and edging the crater in glorious golds and reds. Prepare for an emotional crescendo that will brim your eyes with tears at the majesty of it all. Engulfed by this magnificence, no one can remain unmoved.

Crater facts

Haleakala was formed primarily from *pahoehoe* lava. This lava is the hottest natural substance on earth, and flows like swift fiery rivers. Because of its high viscosity, it forms classic shield volcanos. Plenty of *a'a'* is also found in the mountain's composition. This rock comes out partially solidified and filled with gasses. It breaks apart and forms clinkers. You'll be hiking over both, but

be especially careful on *a'a',* because its jagged edges will cut you as quickly as coral. The crater is primarily formed from erosion, and not from caving in on itself. The erosion on Hawaii is quite accelerated due to carbonic acid build-up, a by-product of the quick decomposition of abundant plant life. The rock breaks down into smaller particles of soil which is then washed off the mountain by rain, or blown off by wind. Natural drainage patterns form, and canyons begin to develop and slowly eat their way to the center. The two largest are **Keanae Valley** in the north and **Kaupo Gap** in the south. These canyons, over time, moved their heads past each other to the center of the mountain where they took several thousand feet off the summit, and formed a huge amphitheater-like crater.

Some stones that you encounter while hiking will be very light in weight. They once held water and gasses that evaporated. If you knock two together, they'll sound like crystal. Also, be observant for **Maui diamonds.** They're garnet stones, a type of pyroxene, or crystal. The cinder cones in the crater are fascinating. They're volcanic vents with a high iron content and may form electromagnetic lines from the earth's center. It's not recommended to climb them, but many people have, even spending the night within. On top, they're like funnels, transmitters and receivers of energy, like natural pyramids. Notice the color of the compacted earth on the trails. It's obvious why you should remain on them. All the plants (silverswords, too) are shallow-rooted and live by condensing moisture on their leaves. Don't walk too close because you'll compact the earth around them and damage the roots. The ecosystem on Haleakala is very delicate, so please keep this in mind to preserve its beauty for future generations.

SIGHTS

You'll start enjoying Haleakala long before you reach the top. Don't make the mistake of simply bolting up the mountain without taking time to enjoy what you're passing. Route

37 from Kahului takes you through Pukalani, the last place to buy supplies. Here it branches to a clearly marked Rt. 377; in six miles it becomes the zig-zag of Rt. 378 or **Haleakala Crater Road.** Along the way are forests of indigenous and introduced trees, including eucalyptus, beautifully flowering jacaranda and stands of cactus. The vistas change rapidly from one vantage point to the next. Sometimes it's the green rolling hills of Ireland, and then instantly it's the tall, yellow grass of the plains. This is also cattle country, and don't be surprised to see all breeds, from Holsteins to Brahmas.

Headquarters
The first stopping point on the Crater Road is **Hosmer Grove Campground** (see below) on your left. Proceed past here a few minutes and you'll arrive at **Park Headquarters.** Campers can get their permits here and others will be happy to stop for all manner of brochures and information concerning the park. There are some silverswords outside and a cage for *nene* around back. After you pass Park HQ, there's trail parking on your left (see "Hikes," below). Following are two overlooks, **Leleiwi** and **Kalahaku.** Both offer tremendous views and different perspectives on the crater. They shouldn't be ,missed—especially Kalahaku where there

are silverswords and the remnants of a traveler's lodge from the days when an expedition to Haleakala took two days.

Visitor's Center
At road's end is the Visitor's Center, approximately 10 miles up the mountain from HQ. It's open from 8:30 a.m. to 4:00 p.m. and contains a clear and concise display featuring the geology of Haleakala. Maps are available, and the Ranger talks, given every hour on the hour, are particularly informative (especially those by Ranger Jitsume Kunioke,) delving into geology and the legends surrounding the great mountain.

Walks
One of the outside paths leads to **Pakaoao** ("White Hill"). An easy quarter-mile hike will take you to the summit, and along the way you'll pass stone shelters and sleeping platforms from the days when Hawaiians came here to quarry the special tool-stone. It's a type of whitish slate that easily flakes and is so hard that when you strike two pieces together it rings almost like iron. Next comes **Puu'ulaula** ("Red Hill"), the highest point on Maui at 10,023 feet. Atop is a glass-encased observation area (open 24 hours). This is where many people come to view the sunrise and sunset. From here, if the day is crystal

the moon-crater floor of Haleakala

The silversword is one of the world's rarest plants. Don't walk too close when observing them or you could destroy the roots.

clear, you can see all of the main Hawaiian islands, except for Kauai. The space colony on the crater floor below is **Science City.** This research facility is manned by the University of Hawaii, and by the Department of Defense. It is not open to the public.

Hikes
There are three trails in Haleakala Crater: Halemauu, Sliding Sands, and Kaupo. **Halemauu Trail** starts at the 8,000-foot level along the road about four miles past HQ. It descends quickly to the 6,600-foot level on the crater floor. Enroute you'll pass Holua Cabin, Silversword Loop, the Bottomless Pit (a mere 65 feet deep) and then a portion of Sliding Sands Trail, and back to the Visitor's Center. You shouldn't have any trouble hitching back to your car from here.

Sliding Sands begins at the summit of Haleakala near the Visitor's Center. This is the main crater trail and gives you the best overall hike. It joins the Kaupo Trail at Paliku Cabin; alternatively, at Kapaloa Cabin you can turn left to the Bottomless Pit and exit via

Halemauu Trail. This last one is one of the best, but you'll have to hitch back to your car at the Visitor's Center, which shouldn't be left for the dwindling late-evening traffic going up the mountain.

The **Kaupo Trail** is long and tough. It follows the Kaupo Gap to the park boundary at 3,800 feet. It then crosses private land, which is no problem, and deposits you in the semi-ghost town of Kaupo. This is the rugged part of the Hana loop that is forbidden by the rental car companies. You'll have to hitch west just to get to the scant traffic of Rt. 31, or nine miles east to Oheo Gulch and its campground, and from there back along the Hana Road.

Along your walks, expect to see wild goats. These are often eradicated by park rangers, because they are considered an introduced pest. For those inclined, crater walks are conducted by the rangers during the summer months. These vary in length and difficulty so check at the ranger station. There are also horseback tours of the crater (see "Sports" in the main "Introduction"). Hikers should also consider a day with the professional guide, Ken Schmitt. His in-depth knowledge and commentary will make your trip not only more fulfilling, but enjoyably informative, as well. (See "Camping and Hiking" in the main Introduction.)

PRACTICALITIES

Making "do"
If you've come to Hawaii for sun and surf, and you aren't prepared for alpine temperatures, you can still enjoy Haleakala. For a day trip, wear your jogging suit or a sweater, if you've brought one. Make sure to wear socks, and even bring an extra pair as make-shift mittens. Use your *dry* beach towel to wrap around inside your sweater as extra insulation, and even consider taking your hotel blanket, which you can use Indian-fashion. Make rain gear from a large plastic garbage bag. Cut a hole for head and arms and this is also a good windbreaker. Take your beach hat, too. Don't worry about looking ridiculous in this "get up" — you will! But

you'll also keep warm! Remember that for every thousand feet you climb, the temperature drops three degrees, so the summit is about 30 degrees (F) cooler than at sea level. As the sun reaches its zenith, if there are no rain clouds, the crater floor will go from about 50 to 80 degrees. It can flip-flop from blazing hot to dismal and rainy a number of times in the same day. The nights will drop below freezing, with the coldest recorded temperature a bone-chilling 14 degrees. Dawn and dusk are notorious for being bitter. Because of the altitude, be aware that the oxygen level will drop, and those with any impairing conditions should take precautions. The sun is ultra strong atop the mountain and even those with deep tans are subject to burning. Noses are particularly susceptible.

Trekkers

Any serious hikers or campers must have sturdy shoes, good warm clothes, raingear, canteens, down bags and a serviceable tent. Hats and sunglasses are needed. Compasses are useless because of the high magnetism in the rock, but binoculars are particularly rewarding. No cook fires are allowed in the crater, so you'll need a stove. Don't burn any dead wood — the soil needs all the decomposing nutrients it can get. Drinking water is available at all of the cabins within the crater. This enviornment is particularly delicate. Stay on the established trails so that you don't cause undue erosion. Leave rocks and especially plants alone. Don't walk too close to silverswords or any other plants because you'll compact the soil. Leave your pets at home; ground nesting birds here are easily disturbed. If Nature "calls," dig a very

shallow hole, off the trail, and cover your toilet paper and all with the dirt. Urinating on it will hasten the decomposition process.

Camping

Admission to the park is free, and unless you'll be staying in a cabin, camping is also free, but you must obtain a camping permit from Park HQ. The **Hosmer Grove** campground is at the 6,800-foot level, just before Park HQ. The free camping here is limited to 25 people, but there's generally room for all. There's water, pit toilets, grills and a pavilion. It was named after Ralph Hosmer who tried to save the watershed by planting fast-growing foreign trees like cedars, pines and junipers. He succeeded, but this destroyed any chance of the native Hawaiian trees making a comeback.

Oheo Campground is a primitive camping area over at the Seven Pools. It's part of the park, but unless you're an intrepid hiker and descend all the way down the Kaupo Trail, you'll come to it via Hana (see "Hana and Beyond"). There are campsites in the crater at **Holua, Paliku,** and **Kapalaoa.** All three offer cabins, and tent camping is allowed at the first two. Camping at any of these is extremely popular, and reservations for the cabins must be made months in advance. A lottery of the applicants chosen for sites keeps it fair for all. Environmental impact studies limit the number of campers to 25 per area per day. Camping is limited to a total of three days, with no more than two at each spot. For complete details write: Haleakala National Park, Box 369, Makawao, HI 96768, tel. 572-7749. Also, see the camping chart in the main "Introduction."

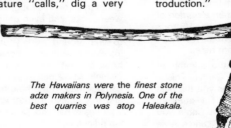

The Hawaiians were the finest stone adze makers in Polynesia. One of the best quarries was atop Haleakala.

NORTHEAST MAUI

THE HANA ROAD

On the long and winding road to Hana's door, most people's daydreams of "paradise" come true. A trip to Maui without a visit to Hana is like ordering a sundae without a cherry on top. The 50 miles that it takes to get there from Kahului are some of the most remarkable in the world. The Hana Road (Rt. 36) starts out innocently enough, passing **Paia Town.** The inspiration for Paia's gaily painted store fronts looks like it came from a jar of jelly beans. Next come some north shore surfing beaches where windsurfers fly, doing amazing aquabatics. Soon there are a string of "rooster towns," so named because that's about all that seems to be stirring. Then Rt. 36 becomes Rt. 360 and at the three-mile marker, the *real* Hana Road begins.

The semi-official count tallies over 600 rollicking turns and more than 50 one-lane bridges, inducing everyone to slow down and soak up the sights of this glorious road. It's like passing through a tunnel cut from trees. The

ocean winks with azure blue through sudden openings on your left. To the right, streams, waterfalls, and pools sit wreathed with jungle and wildflowers. Coconuts, guavas, mangoes and bananas grow everywhere on the mountainside. Fruit stands pop up regularly as you creep along. Then comes **Keanae** with its arboretum and taro farms, an indication that many ethnic Hawaiians still live along the road. There are places to camp, picnic and swim, both in the ocean and in freshwater streams.

Then you reach **Hana** itself, a remarkable town. The great queen Kaahumanu was born here, and many celebrities live in the surrounding hills seeking peace and solitude. Past Hana, the road becomes even more rugged and besieged by jungle. It opens up again around **Oheo Stream** (or Seven Pools). Here waterfalls cascade over stupendous cataracts forming a series of pools until they reach the sea. Beyond is a rental car's no-man's land, where the passable road toughens and Haleakala shows its barren volcanic face scarred by lava flows.

LOWER PAIA

Paia ("Noisy") was a bustling sugar town that took a nap. When it awoke, it had a set of whiskers and its vitality had flown away. At the turn of the century, many groups of ethnic field workers lived here, segregated in housing clusters called "camps" that stretched up Baldwin Avenue. Paia was the main gateway for sugar on East Maui, and even a railroad functioned here until 20 years ago. During the 1930s, its population, at over 10,000, was the largest on the island. Then fortunes shifted toward Kahului,

and Paia lost its dynamism, until recently. The townsfolk have pumped new life into its old muscles. The old shops catering to the practical needs of a "plantation town" were replaced. The storefronts were painted and spruced up. A new breed of merchant with their eyes on passing tourists has taken over. Now Paia (Lower) focuses on boutiques, crafts and artwork. Since you've got to pass through on your way to Hana, it serves as a great place not only to top off your gas tank, but also to stop for a bite and a browse. The prices are good for just about everything, and it boasts one of the island's best fish restaurants and art shops. Paia, under its heavy makeup, is still a vintage example of what it always was—a homey, servicable, working town.

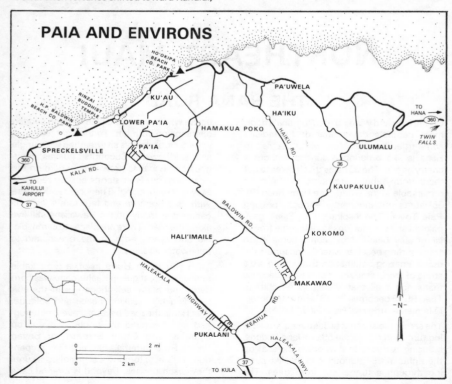

Sights

A mile or so before you enter Paia on the left is **Rinzai Buddhist Temple**. The grounds are pleasant and worth a look. **Mantokuji Buddhist Temple** in Paia heralds the sun's rising and setting by ringing its huge gong 18 times at dawn and dusk.

Baldwin County Park is on your left about seven miles past Kahului on Rt. 36. This spacious park is good for swimming, shell collecting and a decent winter surf. There's tent and trailer camping (county permit required) and full amenities. Unfortunately, Baldwin has a bad reputation. It's one of those places that locals have staked out with the attitude of "us against them." Hassles and robberies have been known to occur. Be nice, calm, and respectful. For the timid, to be on the safe side, be gone.

Hookipa Beach Park is about 10 minutes past Paia; there's a high, grassy sand dune along the road and the park is down below, where you'll enjoy full amenities and camping with a county permit. Swimming is advisable only on calm days. Wicked currents. Primarily a surfing beach that is now regarded as one of the best sailboarding areas in Hawaii, this is home to the "O'Neill International Windsurfing Championship," held yearly during early spring. The world's best sailboarders come here, trying to win the $10,000 prize. A colorful spectacle. Bring binoculars.

Food

Hat's Restaurant is at the corner of Baldwin Ave., as you enter town. Daily breakfast, lunch and dinner, tel. 579-8045. A semi-sidewalk cafe popular with locals. Owned and operated by Joe Pavao, a lifelong resident of Portuguese descent. You can't beat their $2 breakfast special. Nothing fancy, but good food, cheap prices, and clean.

Dillon's, Hana Road, Paia, tel. 579-9113. Daily breakfast, lunch and dinner. From the outside you'd expect Marshal Dillon and Kitty to come sashaying through the swinging doors, but inside it's Polynesian with a sort of German beer garden out back. The food is well prepared and the portions large. Mostly steaks, chops, and fish with a Hawaiian twist.

world-class sailboarding at Hookipa

Moderate to expensive.

Piero's Garden Cafe, Paia, Hana Road, tel. 579-9730. Daily breakfast, lunch, and dinner. Piero's is an Italian cafe where you can eat for under $6. They offer a breakfast special of poached eggs and mozzarella cheese for $2.25. Gourmet coffee. Funky surroundings with entertainment nightly. This includes an "open mike" on Thursdays and jazz on Sundays.

Mama's Fish House, just past Paia on the left, but look hard for the turnoff near the blinking yellow light. Turn left at the ship's flagpole and follow "angel fish" sign down to Kuau Cove. Daily dinner only, reservations recommended, tel. 579-9672. Mama's has the best reputation possible—it gets thumbs up from local people. The fish is fresh daily, with some broiled over *kiawe*. Vegetables come from local gardens and the herbs are Mama's own. Special Hawaiian touches with every meal. Expensive, but worth it. Make reservations for the evening's return trip from Hana.

Quickies in and around town: **Tradewinds Natural Foods,** a well-stocked health food store with a snack bar. Daily 7:00 a.m. to 8:00 p.m., Sun 9:00 a.m. to 6:00 p.m. Early opening makes this a good place to stock up with healthy foods for the Hana Road. **Charlie P. Woofers,** a saloon with pool tables, selling food and beer. **Picnics** on Baldwin Ave., sandwiches and burgers for under $4. **Ice Cream and Dreams,** frosty yummies at the corner of Baldwin Avenue.

Shopping
Maui Crafts Guild is on the left just before entering Paia, at 43 Hana Rd., Box 609, Paia, HI 96779, tel. 579-9693. Open daily from 10:00 a.m. to 5:30 p.m. The Crafts Guild is one of the best art outlets in Hawaii. It's owned and operated by the artists themselves, all of whom must pass a thorough "jurying" by present members. All artists must be islanders, and they must use natural materials found in Hawaii to create their work. Items are tastefully displayed and it's an experience just to look. You'll find a wide variety of art work and crafts including pottery, furniture, beadwork, wood carving, bamboo work, stained glass, *batik* and jewelry. Different artists man the shop on different days, but phone numbers are available if you want to see more of something you like. Prices on smaller items are reasonable, and this is an excellent place to make that one "big" purchase. Around the rear of the premises is **Touchstone Gallery,** which offers excellent and unique pottery.

Other stores are along the main street. **Paia Art Center** is a good idea that hasn't really started rolling yet. It's a collection of artists whose organization seems lacking, and the offerings, though good, are meager. **Paper Weights** has women's fashions and T-shirts. **Antiques and Uniques,** the name says it all. **Bounty Music,** music store with a good selection of instruments and a great storefront. **Mad Hatter** is a terrific little store loaded with hats. Their motto, "If you've got the head, I've got the hat." Cheaper than the Lahaina branch.

Paia's "last chance" gas before heading down the Hana Road

THE ROAD BEGINS

The road to Hana holds many spectacles and surprises, but one of the best is the road itself... it's a marvel! The road was hacked out from the coastline in 1927, every inch by hand using pick and shovel. An ancient Hawaiian Trail followed the same route for part of the way, but mostly people moved up and down this coastline by boat. What makes the scenery so special is that the road snakes along Maui's windward side. There's abundant vegetation and countless streams flowing from Haleakala, carving gorgeous valleys. There are a few scattered villages with a house or two that you hardly notice, and the beaches, although few, are empty. Mostly, however, it's the "feeling" that you get along this road. Nature is close and accessible, and it's so incredibly "south sea island" that it almost seems artificial. But it isn't.

DRIVING TIPS

You've got 30 miles of turns ahead when Rt. 36 (mile marker 22) becomes Rt. 360 (mile marker 0) and the fun begins. The Hana Road has the reputation of being "bad road," but this isn't true. It's narrow, with plenty of hairpin turns, but it's well banked, has clearly marked bridges, and there's always maintenance going on (which can slow you up). Years back, it was a harrowing experience. When mudslides blocked the road, drivers were known to swap their cars with those on the opposite side and carry on to where they were going. The road's reputation sets people up to expect an ordeal, so they make it one, and unfortunately, drive accordingly. Sometimes it seems as though tourists demand the road to be rugged, so that they can tell the folks back home that they, too, "survived the road to Hana." This popular slogan appears on T-shirts, copyrighted and sold by Hasegawa's famous store in Hana, and perpetrates this belief. You'll have no problem, and you'll see much more if you just take it easy.

Drive on the right
Your speed will often drop below 10 miles per hour, and will rarely exceed 25. Standard shift cars are better for the turns. Cloudbursts

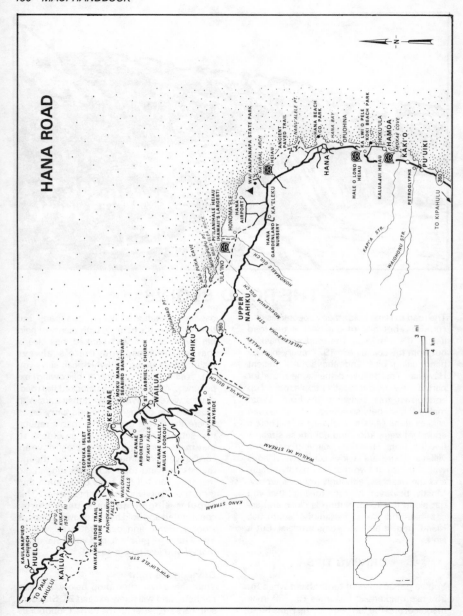

occur at any time so be ready for slick roads. A heavy fall of fruit from roadside mango trees can also coat the road with slippery slime. Look as far up the road as possible and don't allow yourself to be mesmerized by the 10 feet in front of your hood. If your tire dips off a rough shoulder, don't risk losing control by jerking the wheels back on immediately. Ride it for a while and either stop or wait for an even shoulder to come back on. Local people trying to make time will often ride your rear bumper, but generally they won't honk. Pull over and let them by when possible.

Traffic

From Kahului to Hana, it'll take three hours, not counting some recommended stops. The greatest traffic flow going is from 10:00 a.m. to noon; returning "car trains" start by 3:00 p.m. and are heaviest around 5:00 p.m. Many white-knuckled drivers head for Hana as if it were a prized goal, without stopping along the way. This is ridiculous. The best sights are *before* and *after* Hana; the town itself is hardly worth the effort. Expect to spend a long day exploring the Hana Road. To go all the way to Oheo Stream and take in some

54 BRIDGES OF HANA, MAUI, HAWAII

1	O'o-pu-ola	life maturing
2	Ma-ka-na-le	bright vision
3	Ka-ai-ea	breathtaking view
4	Wai-a-ka-mo'i	waters of the king
5	Pu-oho-ka-moa	sudden awakening
6	Hai-pue-na	glowing hearts
7	Ko-le'a	windborne joy
8	Hono-manu	bird valley
9	Nu'a-'ai-lua	large abundance
10	Pi-na-ao	kind hearted
11	Pa-lauhulu	leaf sheltered
12	Wai-o-ka-milo	whirling waters
13	Wai-kani	sounding waters
14	Wai-lua-nui	increasing waters
15	Wai-lua-iki	diminishing waters
16	Ko-pi-li-ula	sacred ceremony
17	Pu'a-aka-a	open laughter
18	Wai-o-hu-e	deceptive waters
19	Wai-o-hu-e-'lua	second deceptive water
20	Pa-akea	spacious enclosure
21	Ka-pa-'ula	to hold sacred
22	Hana-wi (Akahi)	first whistling wind
23	Hana-wi (Elua)	second whistling wind
24	Ma-ka-pi-pi	desire for blessings
25	Ku-hiwa	precious love
26	Ku-pu-koi	claiming tribute
27	Ka-ha-la-o-wa-ka	lightning flash
28	Pu-a-pa-pe	baptismal
29	Ka-ha-wai-ha-pa-pa	extensive valley
30	Ke-a-a-iki	burning star (sirius)
31	Wai-oni (Akahi)	first ruffled waters
32	Wai-oni (Elua)	second ruffled waters
33	Lani-ke-le	heavenly mist
34	He-lele-i-ke-oha	extending greetings
35	Ula-i-no	intense sorrow
36	Moku-lehua	solemn feast
37	'O-i-lo-wai	first sprouting
38	Hono-ma-'e-le	land of deep love
39	Ka-wai-pa-pa	the forbidden waters
40	Ko-holo-po	night traveling
41	Ka-ha-wai-'oka-pi-a	frugal valley
42	Wai-o-honu	water of the turtle
43	Papa'a-hawa-hawa	stronghold
44	Ala-ala-'ula	reawakening
45	Wa-i-ka-ko'i	time of demand
45	Pa-'ihi	place of majesty
47	Wai-lua	water spirits
48	Wa-'i-lua	scattered spirits
49	Pu'u-ha-o-a	burning hill
50	Pae-hala	pandanus clusters
51	Maha-lawa	place of rest
52	Hana-lawe	proud deduction
53	Pua-a-lu-'u	prayer blossoms
54	O'he'o	enduring pride

Interpretations Inez MacPhee Ashdown

Inez MacPhee Ashdown's translations of the names of the Hana Road bridges; layout by Sam Eason, a longtime Hana resident and artist

sights, you'll have to leave your hotel at sunup and won't get back until sundown. If your budget can afford it, think of staying the night in Hana (reservations definitely) and return the next day. This is a particularly good alternative if you have an afternoon departing flight from Kahului Airport. Also, most tourists seem terrified of driving the road at night. Actually it's easier. There is far less traffic, road reflectors mark the center and sides like a runway, and you're warned of oncoming cars by their headlights. Those in the know make much better time after dark!

SIGHTS

Twin Falls

This is one of the first places to stop and enjoy. Park just before Hoolawa Bridge, coming up after mile marker 2 on Rt. 360. Go under the white gate in the center of the parking area and follow the jeep trail. Stay on the trail for about 15 minutes, ignoring the little cattle trails left and right. Plenty of guavas along here are free for the picking. Once you've reached the top of the hill, bear left toward the creek. The first pool is fed by the two waterfalls that give the area its name. Walk farther up the creek for better pools and more privacy. The next large pool has a rope to swing from, and some people go skinny-dipping along here.

Huelo

This is a quiet "rooster town" famous for **Kaulanapueo Church** built in 1853. The structure is made from coral and is reminiscent of New England architecture. It's still used, and a peek through the door will reveal a stark interior with straight-backed benches and a platform. Few bother to stop, so it's quiet, and offers a good panorama of the village and sea below. At the turnoff to Huelo between mile markers 3 and 4, there's a **public telephone**, in case of emergency. The next tiny town is Kailua; the multi-colored trees in this area are rainbow eucalyptus. Plenty of mountain apple trees are along this stretch.

Waikamoi Ridge

This nature walk is a good place to stretch your legs and learn about native and introduced trees and vegetation. The turnout is clearly marked along the highway. The trail leads through tall stands of identified trees. For those never before exposed to a bamboo forest, it's most interesting when the wind rustles the trees so that they knock together like natural percussion instruments. Picnic tables are available at the start and end of the trail. Back on the road at the next bridge is excellent drinking water. There's a stone barrel with a pipe coming out, and local people come to fill jugs with what they call "living water."

Twin Falls and its invigorating freshwater pool

Beach parks

Less than two miles past Waikamoi Ridge will be **Kaumahina State Wayside** along the road, and **Honomanu County Park,** down at Honomanu Bay. Permits are required to camp. There are no amenities at Honomanu, but Kaumahina has them all. Camping here is in a rainforest with splendid views out to sea overlooking the rugged coastline and the black sand beach of Honomanu Bay. Puohokamoa Falls are just a short walk away. Honomanu is not good for swimming because of strong currents, but is good for surfing.

Keanae

Clearly marked on the left will be **Keanae Arboretum.** A hike through this facility will exemplify Hawaiian plantlife in microcosm. There are three sections: native forest, introduced forest, and traditional Hawaiian plants and foodstuffs. You can picnic and swim along Piinaau Stream. Hardier hikers can continue for another mile through typical (identified) rainforest. **Camp Kaenae Y.M.C.A.** is just after the arboretum. It looks exactly as its name implies, set in a gorgeous natural pasture. There are various bunkhouses for men and women. Arrival time between 4:00 and 6:00 p.m., $5. For more information call the camp at 248-8355.

The first bridge past the camp offers a good and easily accessible swimming hole. **Kaenae Peninsula** is a thumb-like appendage of land formed by a lava flow. A great lookout there is poorly marked. Look for a telephone pole with a *tsunami* loudspeaker atop and pull off just there. Below you'll see neat little farms, mostly raising taro. Most people living on the peninsula are native Hawaiians. they still make *poi* the old-fashioned way: listen for the distinctive thud of *poi*-pounding in the background. Though *kapu* signs abound, the majority of people are friendly. A public road circles the peninsula, but fences across it give it a private vibration. If you visit, realize that this is one of the last patches of ground owned by Hawaiians and tended in the old way. Be respectful, please.

Fresh exotic fruits are available from Joseph's fruit stand.

Fruit stands

Past Kaenae between mile markers 17 and 18 is a roadside stand where you can buy refreshments. They have hot dogs, shave ice and some fruit available. Notice the picture-perfect, idyllic watercress farm on your left. Past mile marker 18 on the right is a fruit stand operated by a fellow named Joseph. He not only has coconuts and papayas, but also little-tasted exotic fruits like mountain apples, star fruit, pineapple and strawberry guavas, and Tahitian lemons. An authentic fruit stand worth a stop. Another one, operated by an Hawaiian woman, is only 50 yards on the left. If you have a hankering for fruit, this is the spot.

Wailua

At mile marker 18, you come to **Wailua**. Turn left here on Wailua Rd., following signs for **Coral Miracle Church**. Here, too, you'll find the **Miracle of Fatima Shrine**, so named because a freak storm in the 1860s washed up enough coral onto Wailua Beach so that the church could be constructed by the Hawaiian congregation. Across from the shrine is **The Shell Stop!**, open daily 9:00 a.m. to 5:00 p.m. This distinctive shop is owned and operated by Anna Kapuana from her two-story home. Three local families collect *opihi* (limpets) from the nearby bay, and dive for shells on the surrounding reef. The *opihi* are a favorite Hawaiian delicacy, and gallon containers sent to Oahu bring good profits, but Anna and family have learned to fashion the purplish shells into elegant jewelry. A variety of shell work and *objets d'art* are offered. All items are made from

Lovely handmade opihi *jewelry is found at the* Shell Stop! *in Wailua.*

authentic Hawaiian shells; none are imported from the Philippines or Tahiti which is the case in most jewelry and shell shops. Anna is a storehouse of information which she's willing to share, often inviting her customers to relax on her *lanai*, if time permits. For an original piece of jewelry and a distinctive island memento, visit The Shell Stop!

Puaa Kaa State Wayside

This lovely spot is about 14 miles before Hana. There's no camping, but there are picnic tables, grills and rest rooms. Nearby are Kopiliula and Waikani Falls. A stream provides some smaller falls and pools suitable for swimming.

Nahiku

This village, reached by a three-mile road, has the dubious distinction of being one of the wettest spots along the Hana Road. At the turn of the century it was the site of the Nahiku Rubber Co., the only commercial rubber plantation in the U.S. Many rubber trees still line the road, although the venture collapsed in 1912 because the rubber was poor due to the overabundance of rainfall. The village lost its vitality and only a few homes remain. Some local people augment their incomes by growing *pakalolo* in the rainforest of this area.

Hana Airport

At mile marker 28, just before you reach the airport, there is an excellent **fruit stand** operated by a newly-arrived Vietnamese family. They sell drinking coconuts for $1.50, guava juice for 50 cents and home-made coconut candy. Next, pass **Hana Gardenland Nursery**, where you're free to browse and picnic. They have fresh-cut flowers daily, and the prices are some of the best on Maui. Past the Gardenland is a road leading left. This rough track will take you to Ulaino and **Piilanihale Heiau**, Hawaii's largest, with massive walls that rise over 50 feet. It's on private land, but accessible. In less than a mile past here, a sign will point left to **Hana Airport**, where Royal Hawaiian Airlines operates daily flights servicing Hana.

Waianapanapa State Park

Box 1049, Wailuku HI 96753, tel. 244-4354. Only three miles outside Hana, this State Park offers not only tent camping, but cabins sleeping up to six, on a sliding scale, at $10 single up to $30 for six. The cabins offer hot water, a full kitchen, electricity and bedding. A deposit is required. They're very popular so book far in advance by writing Division of State Parks (see, "Camping," in the main "Introduction.") Even for those not camping, Waianapanapa is a "must stop." Pass the office to the beach park and its black sand beach. The swimming is dangerous during heavy surf because the bottom drops off quickly, but on calm days it's mellow. The snorkeling is excellent. Just offshore is a clearly visible natural stone bridge.

A well-marked trail leads to **Waianapanapa Caves.** The tunnel-like trail passes through a thicket of vines and *hao,* a bush used by the Hawaiians to mark an area as *kapu.* The caves are like huge smooth tubs formed from lava. The water trapped inside is crystal clear. These caves mark the site of an Hawaiian legend, in which a lovely princess named Popoalaea fled from her cruel husband, Kakae. He found her hiding here and killed her. During certain times of the year millions of tiny red shrimp invade the caves, turning the waters red, which the Hawaiians say are a reminder of the poor slain princess. Along the coastline here are remnants of the ancient Hawaiian **paved trail** that you can follow for a short distance.

Helani Gardens

Your last stop before Hana town, clearly marked on the right, these gardens are a labor of love begun 30 years ago and opened to the public in 1975. Howard Cooper, founder and long-time Hana resident, still tends them. The gardens are open daily, 9:00 a.m to 3:00 p.m., adults $2, children $1, seniors $1.50, picnic tables and rest rooms. Mr. Cooper's philosophy on life graces a bulletin board just before you cross the six bridges to heaven. In brief he says, "Don't hurry, don't worry, don't forget to smell the flowers." It's a self-guided tour with something for everyone. The "lower gardens" are

Mr. Cooper and his grandson

five acres formally manicured, but the 65 acres of "upper garden" are much more wild and open to anyone wishing to stroll around. The lower gardens have flowering trees and shrubs, vines, fruit trees and flowers and potted plants everywhere. People see many of these plants in nurseries around the country, and may even have grown some varieties at home, but these specimens are huge. There are baobab trees, ginger plants, carp ponds, even papyrus. The fruit trees alone could supply a supermarket. The upper gardens are actually a nursery where plants from around the world are raised. Some of the most popular are heleconia and ginger, and orchids galore. In one giant tree, Mr. Cooper's grandchildren have built a tree house, complete with picture windows, electricity and plumbing! The entire operation is family run, with Howard himself conducting some tours and his grandson, Matthew, running the admission office. In Mr. Cooper's own words, "Helani Garden is where heaven touches the earth." Be one of the saved!

HANA AND VICINITY

Hana is about as pretty a town as you'll find anywhere in Hawaii, but if you're expecting anything stupendous you'll be sadly disappointed. For most it will only be a quick stopover at a store or beach enroute to Oheo Stream: the townsfolk refer to these people as a "rent-a-car tourists." The lucky who stay in Hana, or those not worried about time, will find plenty to explore throughout the area. The town is built on rolling hills that descend to Hana Bay with much of the surrounding lands given to pasture, while neat and trim cottages wearing flower corsages line the town's little lanes. Before the white man arrived, Hana was a stronghold that was conquered and reconquered by the kings of Maui and those of the north coast of the Big Island. The most strategic and historically laden spot is Kauiki Hill, the remnant of a cinder cone that dominates Hana Bay. This area is steeped in Hawaiian legend, and old stories relate that it was the demi-god Maui's favorite spot. It's said that he transformed his

daughter's lover into Kauiki Hill and turned her into the gentle rains that bathe it to this day.

Changing history
Hana was already a plantation town in the mid-1800s when a hard-boiled sea captain named George Wilfong started producing sugar on his 60 acres. Over the years the laborers came from the standard mixture of Hawaiian, Japanese, Chinese, Portuguese, Filipino, and even Puerto Rican stock. The *luna* were Scottish, German, or American. All have combined to become the people of Hana. Sugar production faded out by the 1940s and Hana began to die, its population dipping below 500. Just then, San Francisco industrialist Paul Fagan purchased 14,000 acres of what was to become the **Hana Ranch**. Realizing that sugar was *pau,* he replanted his lands in pangola range grass and imported Hereford cattle from another holding on Molokai. Their white faces staring

back at you as you drive past are now a standard part of Hana's scenery. Fagan loved Hana and felt an obligation to and affection for its people. He decided to retire here, and with enough money to materialize just about anything, he decided that Hana could best survive through limited tourism. He built the **Hotel Hana Maui** which began operation in 1946, and catered to millionaires, mostly his friends. Fagan owned a baseball team, the **San Francisco Seals,** and brought them to Hana in 1946 for spring training. This was a brilliant publicity move because sportswriters came along; becoming enchanted with Hana, they gave it a great deal of copy and were probably the first to publicize the phrase "Heavenly Hana." It wasn't long before tourists began arriving.

Unfortunately, the greatest heartbreak in modern Hana history occurred at just about the same time, on April 1, 1946. An earthquake in Alaska's Aleutian Islands sent huge tidal waves that raked the Hana coast. These destroyed hundreds of homes, wiping out entire villages, and most tragically swept away many people in their watery arms of death. Hana recovered, but never forgot. Life went on, and the menfolk began working as *paniolo* on Fagan's spread, and during roundup would drive the cattle through town and down to Hana Bay where they were forced to swim to waiting barges. Other entire families went to work at the resort, and so Hana lived again. It's this legacy of quietude and old-fashioned *aloha* that attracted people to Hana over the years. Everyone knows that Hana's future lies in its uniqueness and remoteness, and no one wants it to change. The people as well as the tourists know what they have here. What really makes Hana "heavenly" is similar to what's preached in Sunday school: everyone wants to go there, but not everyone makes it.

SIGHTS

Fagan Memorial
Across from the Hotel Hana Maui, atop Lyon's hill, is a lavastone cross erected to the memory of Paul I. Fagan, who died in 1960. The land is privately owned, but it's OK to go up there if the gate is open. If not, inquire at the hotel. From atop the hill you get the most panoramic view of the entire Hana area. After a rain, magic mushrooms have been known to pop up in the "cow pies" in the pasture surrounding the cross. Just near to the hotel is the **Wananalua Church,** built from coral blocks in 1838. The missionaries deliberately and symbolically built it on top of an old *heiau,* where the pagan gods had been wor-

Wananalua
Church

shipped for centuries. It was the custom of chiefs to build *heiau* before entering battle. Since Hana was always contested ground, dozens of minor *heiau* can be found throughout the region.

Hana Cultural Center
Along Uakea Rd. on the right just a few hundred yards after it splits from the Hana Road.

Open Mon. to Sat., 11:00 a.m. to 4:00 p.m., $1 donation. The Cultural Center was founded in 1971 by Babes Hanchett who is the current president. It occupies an unpretentious building (notice the beautifully carved doors, however) on the grounds of the old courthouse and jail. The center houses fine examples of quiltwork: one, entitled "Aloha Kuuhae," was done by Rosaline Kelinoi, a

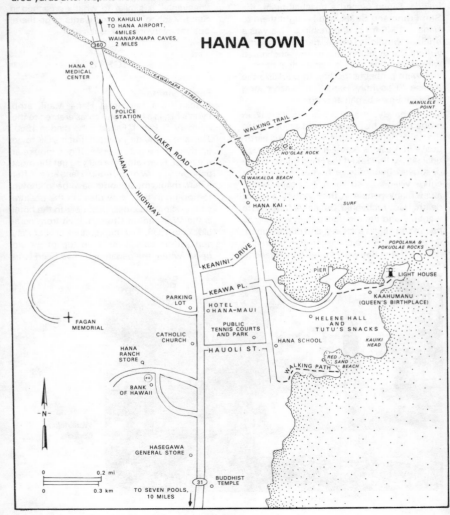

HANA TOWN

TO KAHULUI
TO HANA AIRPORT,
4 MILES
WAIANAPANAPA CAVES,
2 MILES

360

HANA
MEDICAL
CENTER

KAWAIPAPA STREAM

POLICE
STATION

UAKEA ROAD

WALKING TRAIL

NANULELE
POINT

HO'OLAE ROCK

WAIKALOA BEACH

HANA KAI

SURF

HANA HIGHWAY

KEANINI DRIVE

POPOLANA &
POKUOLAE ROCKS

PIER

LIGHT HOUSE

KEAWA PL.

PARKING
LOT

HOTEL
HANA-MAUI

KAAHUMANU
(QUEEN'S BIRTHPLACE)

FAGAN
MEMORIAL

CATHOLIC
CHURCH

PUBLIC
TENNIS COURTS
AND PARK

HELENE HALL
AND
TUTU'S SNACKS

HAUOLI ST.

HANA SCHOOL

KAUIKI
HEAD

HANA
RANCH
STORE

WALKING PATH

RED
SAND
BEACH

BANK
OF HAWAII

-N-

HASEGAWA
GENERAL STORE

31

BUDDHIST
TEMPLE

0   0.2 mi
0   0.3 km

TO SEVEN POOLS,
10 MILES

Hana resident and the first woman voted into the state legislature. There are pre-contact stone implements, *tapa* cloth and an extensive shell collection. Your $1 entitles you to visit the courthouse and jail. Simple but functional, with bench and witness stand, it makes "Andy of Mayberry" look like big time. The jail was used from 1871 to 1978, and the townsfolk knew whenever it held an inmate because he became the groundskeeper and the grass would suddenly be mowed.

Hana Bay

Dominating the bay is the red-faced Kauiki Hill. Fierce battles raged here, especially between Maui chief Kahekili and Kalaniopuu of Hawaii, just before the islands were united under Kamehameha. Kalaniopuu held the natural fortress until Kahekili forced a capitulation by cutting off the water supply. It's believed that Kamehameha himself boarded Capt. James Cook's ship after a lookout spotted it from this hill. More importantly, Queen Kaahumanu, Kamehameha's favorite and the Hawaiian *ali'i* most responsible for ending the old *kapu* system and leading Hawaii into the "new age," was born in a cave here in 1768. Until very recent times fish spotters sat atop the hill looking for telltale signs of large schools of fish.

To get there, simply follow Uakea Rd. to its end, where it splits from the Hana Road at the police station at the edge of town. Take it right down to the pier and park. Hana Beach has full amenities and the swimming is good. It's been a surfing spot for centuries, although the best breakers occur in the middle of the bay. To explore Kauiki look for a pathway on your right and follow it. Hana disappears immediately; few tourists come out this way. Walk for five minutes until the lighthouse comes clearly into view. The footing is slightly difficult but there are plenty of ironwoods to hang onto as the path hugs the mountainside. A few pockets of red sand beach eroded from the cinder cone are below. A copper plaque erected in 1928 commemorates the spot of Kaahumanu's birth. This entire area is a great spot to have a secluded picnic only minutes from town. Proceed straight ahead to the lighthouse sitting on a small island. To cross, you'll have to leap from one jagged rock to another. If this doesn't suit you, take your bathing suit and swim across a narrow sandy-bottomed channel. Stop for a few moments and check the wave action to avoid being hurled against the rocks. When you've got it timed, go for it! The view from up top is great.

the great queen Kaahumanu by ship's artist, Louis Choris, from the Otto Von Kotzebue expedition, ca. 1816. (Hawaii State Archives)

Red Sand Beach

BEACHES

Red Sand Beach

This is a fascinating and secluded beach area. The walk down could be tough unless you're sure-footed, but it's worth it. Follow Uakea Rd. past the turnoff to Hana Bay. Proceed ahead until you pass the public tennis courts on your right and Hana School on your left. The road dead-ends in a grassy field. Look left for the worn path and follow it. Ahead is a Japanese cemetery with its distinctive headstones. Below are pockets of red sand amidst fingers of black lava being washed by sky blue water. There are many tide pools here. Keep walking until you are obviously in the hollowed-out amphitheater of the red cinder cone. Pat the walls to feel how crumbly they are—realize the red "sand" is eroded cinder. The water in the cove is fantastically blue against the redness.

Across the mouth of the bay are little pillars of stone, like castle parapets from a fairy kingdom, that keep the water safe for swim-ming. This is a favorite fishing spot for local people and the snorkeling is good, too. The beach is best in the morning before 11:00; afterwards it can get hot if there's no wind. The coarse red sand massages your feet, and there's a natural jacuzzi area in foamy pools of water along the shore. A man by the name of Les Eade is infatuated with the area and has become the unofficial caretaker. If a cinder boulder rolls down, he'll break it up to preserve the beach area. He's planted coconut palms on the beach and he generally keeps it clean. He's also known for giving children large balloons. Learn from him: use the beach, but preserve its beauty.

Koki Beach Park

This beach park is a mile or so out of town heading toward the Seven Pools. Look for the first road to your left with a sign directing you to Hamoa Village/Beach. Koki is only a few hundred yards on the left. The riptides are fierce in here so don't swim unless it's absolutely calm. The winds can whip along here, too, while at Hamoa Beach, less than a mile away, it can be dead calm. Koki is excellent for beachcombing and for a one-night's unofficial bivouac.

A very special person named Smitty lived in a cave on the north side of the beach. Hike left to the end of the beach and you'll find a rope ladder leading up to his platform. A distinguished older man, he "dropped out" a few years back and came here to live a simple monk's existence. He kept the beach clean and saved a number of people from the riptide. He was a long-distance runner who would tack up a "thought for the day" on Hana's public bulletin board. People loved him and he loved them in return. In 1984 the roof of his cave collapsed and he was killed. When his body was recovered, he was in a kneeling position. At his funeral, all felt a loss, but there was no sadness because all were sure that Smitty had gone home.

Hamoa Beach

Follow Hamoa Rd. a few minutes past Koki

Alau Island

Japanese cemetery on path to Red Sand Beach

Beach until you see the sign for Hamoa. Between Hamoa and Koki are the remnants of an extensive Hawaiian fish pond, part of which is still discernible. This entire area is an eroding cinder cone known as **Kaiwi o Pele** ("the bones of Pele"). This is the spot where the swinish pig-god, Kama pua'a, ravished her. Pele also fought a bitter battle with her sister here, who dashed her on the rocks, giving them their anatomical name. Out to sea is the diminutive Alau Island, a remnant left over by Maui after he fished up the Hawaiian islands. You can tell that Hamoa is no ordinary beach the minute you start walking down the paved, torch-lined walkway. This is the semi-private beach of the Hotel Hana Maui. But don't be intimidated, because no one can own the beach in Hawaii. Hamoa is terrific for swimming and body surfing. The hotel guests are shuttled here by a bus that arrives at 10:00 a.m. and departs by 4:00 p.m. That means that you have this lovely beach to yourself before and after these times. There is a pavilion that the hotel uses for its Fri. night *luau,* as well as restrooms and showers.

ACCOMMODATIONS

Hotel Hana Maui

Write Hotel Hana Maui, Hana, HI 96713, tel. in California (800) 252-0211, (800) 421-000 outside CA, (800) 367-5224 in Hawaii, 248-8211 on Maui. This hotel is the legacy of Paul Fagan, and operates as close to a family-run hotel as you can get. It's only had four managers in the last 40 years and many of the personnel have either been there that long, or the jobs have passed to their children. The hotel gets as much as 80 percent repeat customers, who feel like they're visiting old friends. In 1985 the hotel was sold to the Rosewood Corporation of Dallas, Texas, which has had enough sense to leave well enough alone. Rates start at $137 single, $180 double, up to $255. This, however, includes three meals under the full American plan. There is a pool, tennis courts, superb horseback riding, outdoor camp outs, hula lessons, golfing, and a famous *luau*. The entire scene isn't stiff or fancy, but it is first-class!

Heavenly Hana Inn

Box 146, Hana, 96713, tel. 248-8442. The second most famous Hana hotel, it resembles a Japanese *ryokan* (inn). Walk through the formal garden and remove your shoes on entering the open-beamed main dining hall. The four suites seem like little apartments broken up into sections by *shoji* screens. Rates are from $50 single/double to $68 for four. The present owner is Alfreda Worst, who purchased it from a Japanese family about 16 years ago. The inn is homey and delightful.

Aloha Cottages

Box 205 Hana, HI 96713, tel. 248-8420. Owned and operated by Zenzo and Fusae Nakamura, and the best bargain in town. The cottages are meticulously clean, well built and well appointed. For $42 double, $6 additional, you get two bedrooms, a full kitchen, living room, deck and outdoor grills. Mrs. Nakamura is very friendly and provides daily maid service. The fruit trees on the property provide free fruit to guests.

Hana Kai

These resort apartments are at Box 38, Hana, 96713, tel. 248-8435. All are well maintained and a lot for the money. Studios from $50, deluxe one-bedroom from $60. All have pri-

vate *lanais* with exemplary views of Hana Bay. Maid service, laundry facilities and BBQs.

Private cottages

Box 318 Hana, HI 96713, tel. 248-7727. Stan and Suzanne Collins offer a few private cottages in and around Hana for rent on a daily and long-term (discounted) basis. They start at $55 and go up to $85 for a beach front.

Others

You might try **Purdy's Cottages**, a one-time ranch with a few cottages for rent, starting at $36, tel. 248-8391. **Maile Apartments** offer four apartments at $45, tel. 248-7727. No manager on premises, so they're a bit run-down.

FOOD AND SHOPPING

As far as dining out goes, there's little to choose from in Hana. The **Hotel Hana Maui** offers breakfast, lunch, and dinner buffets. Prices vary according to your choice of options, but expect to spend $5 for breakfast, $6 for lunch, and $10 for dinner. There's also a self-serve coffee shop. **Heavenly Hana Inn** used to serve dinners and they were expecting to again. No prices available, so check. **Tu Tu's Snack Shop** is at the community center building at Hana Bay: window service with tables available. Full breakfast, $4, plate lunches, and *saimin*. This building was donated by Mrs. Fagan to the community.

Hasegawa's General Store

Along the Hana Road heading south out of town. Open weekdays 7:30 a.m. to 6:00 p.m., Sunday 9:00 a.m. to 3:30 p.m., tel. 248-8231. In the ranks of "general stores," Hasegawa's would be commander-in-chief. It's been in the family for 75 years and is currently run by Harry Hasegawa. While your tank is being filled, you can buy anything from a cane knife to a computer disk. There are rows of food items, dry goods, and a hardware and parts store out back. There's cold beer, film, blue jeans, and picnic supplies, and somehow it all

crams in there. Everybody goes to Hasegawa's, and it's a treat just to browse and
people-watch.

Hana Store
Take the Hana Road into town. Make the first
right past St. Mary's Church and go up to the
top of the hill. Open Mon. to Sat., 7:30 a.m. to
5:00 p.m., Sun 8:00 a.m. to 4:00 p.m., tel.
248-8261. It's a general store with the emphasis on foodstuffs. Not as well stocked as
Hasegawa's, they do carry a better supply of
imported beers, and food items geared toward vegetarians.

Waiku Originals
Along the Hana Road on the right about one
mile before entering town. Everything in the
shop is handmade in Hana. Prints, cards,
wall hangings and original T-shirts. Owned
and operated by Bill and Anita. Not heavily
stocked, but some good choices.

SERVICES AND INFORMATION

Hana Medical Center
Along the Hana Road, clearly marked on the
right just as you enter town, tel. 248-8294.
Open weekdays 8:00 a.m. to 5:00 p.m. No
doctors on Thursday or Sunday.

Police station
At the Y between Hana and Uakea Roads,
just as you enter town. Emergency dial 911.

Services
Bank of Hawaii, tel.248-8015, open Mon. to
Thurs., 3:00 to 4:30 p.m., Fri., 3:00 to 6:00
p.m.; The **P.O.** is open weekdays 8:00 a.m. to
4:30 p.m. Both are next door to Hana Store
(see above). **Library** is at Hana School open
Mon. to Fri., 2:00 to 5:00 p.m.

BEYOND HANA

Now you're getting into adventure. The first
sign is that the road gets steadily worse after
Hana. It begins to narrow, then the twists and
turns begin again, and it's potholed. Signs

warn, "Caution: Pig Crossing." There are no
phones, no gas, and only a fruit stand or two
with one store that can be counted on only to
be closed. The faint-hearted should turn
back, but those with gumption are in for a
treat. There're roadside waterfalls, cascading
streams filling a series of pools, a hero's
grave, and some forgotten towns. If you
persevere all the way, you pop out at the
Tedeschi Winery, where you can reward
yourself with a glass of bubbly before returning to civilization.

Wailua Falls
About seven miles after leaving Hana, Wailua
and Kanahualui Falls tumble over steep lava
pali, filling the air with a watery mist and filling their pools below. They're just outside
your car door, and a five-minute effort will
take you to the mossy grotto at the base.
There's plenty of room to park. If not for
Oheo up ahead, this would be a great picnic
spot, but wait! Sometimes roadside artists
park here. An especially good one is Peggy
Saunders, who calls her glass creations

the lower pools meet the sea

"Hawaiian Reflections." Her hanging stained glass is beautifully executed. In a few minutes you pass a little shrine cut into the mountain. This is the **Virgin By The Road-side**. It's usually draped with fresh *lei*.

OHEO GULCH

This is where the enormous **Kipahulu Valley** meets the sea. Palikea Stream starts way up on Haleakala and steps its way through the valley, leaving footprints of waterfalls and pools until it spends itself in the sea. The area was named the **Seven Sacred Pools** by white men. They made a mistake, but an honest one. The area should have been held sacred, but it wasn't. Everything was right here. You can feel the tremendous power of nature: bubbling waters, Haleakala red and regal in the background, and the sea pound-ing away. Hawaiians lived here but the *heiau* that you would surely expect are missing. Besides that there aren't seven pools, there's more like 24!

Getting there
Straight on Rt. 31 ten miles out of Hana. You come to a large cement arch bridge (excellent view) and then a sign that says "Camping." Park here in the large grassy lot where you'll also find clean, well-built "outhouses" for your convenience.

Warnings and tips
Before doing any exploring, try to talk to one of the rangers, Eddie Poo or Perry Bednorse, generally found around the parking area. They know a tremendous amount of natural history concerning the area and can inform you about the few dangers in the area, such as the flash flooding that occurs in the pools. Ranger Poo has received a "Presidential Cita-tion" for risking his life on five occasions to pluck drowning people from the quickly rising streams. For those intending to hike or camp, bring your own water; as yet no potable water is available. Don't be put off by the parking area, which looks like a used-car lot for Japanese imports. Ninety-nine percent

are gone by sundown. The vast majority of the people go to the easily accessible "lower pools." The best is a stiff hike up the mountain to the "upper pools," a bamboo forest and a fantastic waterfall.

The lower pools

Head along the clearly marked path from the parking area to the flat, grass-covered peninsula. The winds are heavy here as they enter the mouth of the valley from the sea. A series of pools to choose from are off to your left. It's amazing to lie in the last one and look out to the sea crunching the shore just a few yards away. Move upstream for the best swimming in the largest of the lower pools. Be careful, because you'll have to do some fairly difficult rock climbing. The best route is along the right hand side as you face up the valley. Once you're satiated, head back up to the road along the path on the left-hand side. This will take you up to the bridge that you crossed when arriving, one of the best vantage points to look up and down this amazing valley.

Waimoku Falls

Officer Eddie Poo

The upper pools

Very few people head for the upper pools. However, those who do will be delighted. The trail is called **Waimoku Falls Trail.** Cross the road at the parking lot and go through the gate into a pasture, remembering to close it after you. A sign will tell you that Makahiku Falls is a half-mile up hill and Waimoku Falls are two miles distant. The toughest part is at the beginning as you huff-puff your way straight uphill. Don't complain, because this discourages everyone else. The trail leads to a fenced overlook from where you can see clearly the lace-like Makahiku Falls. Behind you a few paces and to the left will be a waterworn, trench-like path. Follow it to the very lip of the falls and a gorgeous little pool. You can swim safely to the very edge of the falls. The current is gentle here, and if you stay to the right you can peer over the edge and remain safe behind encircling boulders. Be extremely conscious of the water rising, and get out immediately if it does!

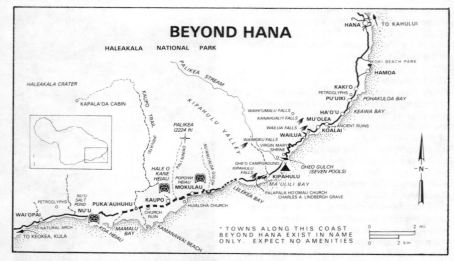

BEYOND HANA

HALEAKALA   NATIONAL   PARK

HALEAKALA CRATER

KAPALA'OA CABIN

KAUPO TRAIL (PRIVATE)

PALIKEA STREAM

K I P A H U L U   V A L L E Y

PALIKEA (2224 ft)

PALI O KINAU

NU'ANU'ALOA GULCH

WAILUA

HALE O KANE HEIAU

POPOIWI HEIAU

MOKULAU

NU'U SALT POND

PETROGLYPHS

PUKA'AUHUHU

WAI'OPAI

NU'U

TO KEOKEA, KULA

NATURAL ARCH

KOA HEIAU

MAMALU BAY

CHURCH RUIN

HUIALOHA CHURCH

KAMANAWAI BEACH

LELEKEA BAY

OHE'O CAMPGROUND

KIPAHULU FALLS

KIPAHULU

MA'ULILI BAY

PALAPALA HO'OMAU CHURCH
CHARLES A. LINDBERGH GRAVE

OHE'O GULCH (SEVEN POOLS)

WAIMOKU FALLS

VIRGIN MARY SHRINE

WAILUA FALLS

KANAHUALI'I FALLS

WAIHI'UMALU FALLS

HA'O'U

MU'OLEA

KOALAI

ANCIENT RUINS

KEAWA BAY

KAKI'O
PETROGLYPHS
PU'UIKI

POHAKULOA BAY

KO'KI BEACH PARK

HAMOA

HANA

TO KAHULUI

—N—

* T O W N S   A L O N G   T H I S   C O A S T
B E Y O N D   H A N A   E X I S T   I N   N A M E
O N L Y .   E X P E C T   N O   A M E N I T I E S

0   2 mi

0   2 km

After refreshing yourself, continue your hike as the path heads through a grassy area. Oddly enough you come to an actual turnstile. Here you'll cross the creek where there's a wading pool, and then zigzag up the opposite bank. After some enormous mango trees, you start going through a high jungle area. Suddenly you're in an extremely dense bamboo forest. The trail is well-cut as you pass through the green darkness of this stand. If the wind is blowing, the bamboo will sing a mournful song for you. Emerge into more mangoes and thimble berries and there's the creek again. Turn left and follow the creek, without crossing yet, and the trail gets distinct again. There's a wooden walkway, and then, eureka!... Waimoku Falls. It cascades over the *pali,* and is so high that you have to strain your neck back as far as it will go. It's more than a falls, it's silver filigree. You can stand in the shallow pool below surrounded by a sheer rock amphitheater. The sunlight dances in this area

and tiny rainbows appear and disappear. There is a ranger-led hike to the falls on Saturdays. Horseback rides are also available from the nearby Oheo Riding Stables, tel. 248-7722.

Camping

This is part of Haleakala National Park. It's free to camp for a three-day limit (no one counts too closely) and no permit is necessary. The campgrounds are primitive and always empty. From the parking lot follow the sign that says "Food Tent" and proceed straight ahead on the dirt track. Bear right to a large grassy area overlooking the sea, where signs warn not to disturb an archaeological area. Notice how spongy the grass seems to be here. You'll see a very strange palm tree that bends and twists up and down from the ground like a serpent. Move to the trees just behind it to escape the wind.

BEYOND OHEO

Route 31 beyond Oheo is genuinely rugged and makes the car companies cry. It can be done, however, with even the tourist vans making it part of their regular route. In 1.5 miles you come to **Palapala Hoomau Church** (St. Paul's) and its tiny cemetery where Charles Lindbergh is buried. People, especially those who are old enough to remember the "Lone Eagle's" historical flight, are drawn here like pilgrims. The public is not really encouraged to visit, but the human tide cannot be stopped. If you go, please follow all of the directions posted. Up ahead a sign will read, "Samuel F. Pryor, Kipahulu Ranch." Mr. Pryor was a vice-president of Pan Am and a close chum of Lindbergh. It was he who encouraged Lindbergh to spend his last years in Hana. Sam Pryor raises gibbons and lives quietly with his wife. Kipahulu Ranch has seen other amazing men. Last century a Japanese samurai

named Sentaro Ishii lived here. He was enormous, especially for a Japanese of that day, over six-feet tall. He came in search of work, and at the age of 61 married Kehele, a local girl. He lived in Kipahulu until he died at the age of 102.

Independenceville
Past Sam Pryor's place is B.B. Smith's fruit stand (which isn't always open) and another follows shortly. The road really begins to get rugged. The vistas open up at the beginning of the Kaupo Gap just when you pass **Huialoha Church,** built in 1859. Then the village of **Kaupo** and the Kaupo Store. The sign reads, "This store is usually open Mon. to Fri., around 7:30 to 4:30. Don't be surprised if it's not open yet. It soon will be unless otherwise posted. Closed Saturday and Sunday and when necessary." Only a few families live in Kaupo, old ones and new ones trying to live independently.

the Kaupo Gap

Kaupo Store

The last of a chain of stores that stretched all the way from Keanae and were owned by the Soon Family. Nick Soon was kind of a modern-day wizard. He lived in Kaupo, and among his exploits he assembled a car and truck brought piecemeal on a barge, built the first electric generator in the area, and even made a model airplane from scratch that flew. He was the son of an indentured Chinese laborer. After Kaupo you'll be in the heart of the Kaupo Gap. Enjoy it because in a few minutes the pavement will pick up again and you'll be back in the civilized world.

bird of paradise

KAHOOLAWE

The island of Kahoolawe is clearly visible from many points along Maui's south shore, especially when it's lit up like a firecracker during heavy bombardment by the U.S. Navy. Kahoolawe is a target island, uninhabited except for a band of wild goats that refuse to be killed off. Kahoolawe was a sacred island born to Wakea and Papa, the two great mythical progenitors of Hawaii. The birth went bad and almost killed Papa, and it hasn't been any easier for her ill-omened child ever since. Kahoolawe became synonymous with Kanaloa, the man-god. Kanaloa was especially revered by the *kahuna ana ana,* the "black sorcerers" of old Hawaii. Kanaloa, much like Lucifer, was driven from heaven by Kane, the god of light. Kanaloa held dominion over all poisonous things and ruled in the land of the dead from his power spot here on Kahoolawe. There are scores of archaeological sites and remnants of *heiau* all over the bomb-cratered face of Kahoolawe. A long, bitter feud has raged between the U.S. Navy that wishes to keep the island as a bombing range, and Protect Kahoolawe Ohana, a Hawaiian native-rights organization that wants the sacred island returned to the people.

The land
Kahoolawe is 11 miles long, six miles wide. with 29 miles of coastline. The tallest hill is **Lua Makika** in the northeast section at 1,477 feet. There are no natural lakes or ponds on the island, but it does get some rain and there is a stream running through Ahupu Gulch.

MODERN HISTORY

It's perfectly clear that small families of Hawaiians have lived on Kahoolawe for countless generations and that religious rites were carried out by many visiting *kahuna* over the centuries, but mostly Kahoolawe was left alone. In 1917 Angus MacPhee, a cattleman, leased Kahoolawe from the Territorial Government for $200 per year. The lease would run until 1954 with a renewal option, if by 1921 MacPhee could show reasonable progress in taming the island. Harry Baldwin bought into the **Kahoolawe Ranch** in 1922, and with his money and MacPhee's know-how, Kahoolawe turned a neat profit. The island then supported indigenous vegetation such as *ohia,* mountain apple, and even Hawaiian cotton and tobacco. MacPhee planted eucalyptus and range grass from Australia, which caught on well and stopped much of the erosion. Gardens were

planted around the homestead and the soil proved to be clean and fertile. Within a few years Kahoolawe Ranch cattle were being shipped regularly to markets on Maui.

The Navy arrives

In 1939, with the threat of war on the horizon, MacPhee and Baldwin, stimulated by patriotism, offered a small tip of Kahoolawe's southern shore to the U.S. Army as an artillery range. One day after the attack on Pearl Harbor, the U.S. Navy seized all of

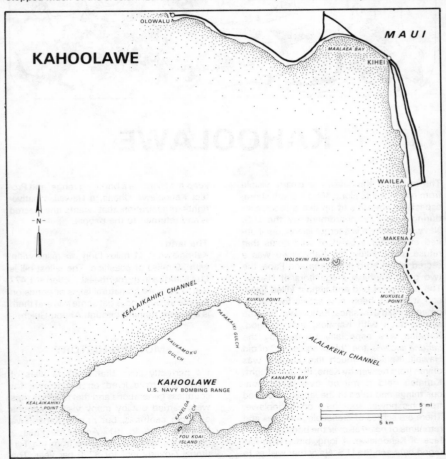

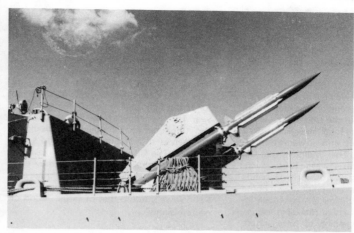

The U.S. Navy continues to bombard the sacred island of Kahoolawe.

Kahoolawe to further the "the war effort" and evicted MacPhee, immediately disenfranchising the Kahoolawe Ranch. Kahoolawe has since become the most bombarded piece of real estate on the face of the Earth. During WW II the Navy praised Kahoolawe as being *the* most important factor in winning the Pacific War, and it has held Kahoolawe to the present day.

The book on Kahoolawe

Inez MacPhee Ashdown lived on the island with her father and was a driving force in establishing the homestead. She has written a book, *Recollections of Kahoolawe,* available from Topgallant Publishing Co., Honolulu. This book chronicles the events from 1917 until the military takeover, and is rife with myths, legends, and historical facts about Kahoolawe. Mrs. Ashdown is in her late eighties, going blind and in failing health but her mind remains brilliant. She resides on Maui.

The problem

Hawaii has the dubious distinction of being the most militarized state in the Union. All five services are represented, and it's the headquarters of CINPAC (Commander in Chief, Pacific) which controls 70 percent of the earth's surface, from California to Africa's east coast, and to both poles. Kahoolawe is the epitome of this military dominance with every inch of its 73 square miles owned by the federal government. The Protect Kahoolawe Ohana is unilaterally opposed to

The "Save Kahoolawe Ohana" resolutely builds a long house pitting traditional Hawaiian beliefs against naval artillery.

this dominance and wants the Navy to return the island to native Hawaiian control. The Navy says that Kahoolawe is still very important to national security and that it is a barren and lifeless island, anyway.

The Ohana

The Protect Kahoolawe Ohana is an extended group, favoring traditional values based on *aloha aina* (love of the land) which is the primary binding force for all Hawaiians. They want the bombing and desecration of Kahoolawe to stop. They maintain that the island should return to Hawaiian Lands inventory with the *kahu* (stewardship) in the hands of native Hawaiians. The point driven home by the Ohana is that the military has totally ignored and belittled native Hawaiian values, which are now beginning to be asserted.

They maintain that Kahoolawe is not a barren wasteland, but a vibrant part of their history and religion. Indeed, Kahoolawe was placed on the National Register of Historic Sites, but instead of being preserved, which is normal for this prestigious distinction, it is the only historic site that is actively destroyed. The Ohana has gained legal access to the island for 10 days per month, for 10 months of the year. They have built a *halau* (long house) and use the time on Kahoolawe to dedicate themselves to religious, cultural and social pursuits. The Ohana looks to Kahoolawe as their *pu'uhonua* (refuge), where they gain strength and knowledge from each other and the *aina*. The question is basic: is Kahoolawe's future that of target island or sacred island?

BOOKLIST

INTRODUCTORY

Barrow, Terrence. *Incredible Hawaii.* Illus. Ray Lanternman. Rutland, Vt.: Tuttle, 1974. A pocket-sized compilation of oddities, little-known-facts, trivia and superlatives regarding the Hawaiian islands. Fun, easy reading, and informative.

Cohen, David and Rick Smolan. *A Day in the Life of Hawaii.* New York: Workman, 1984. On December 2, 1983, 50 of the world's top photo journalists were invited to Hawaii to photograph a variety of normal life incidents occuring on that day. The photos are excellently reproduced, and are accompanied by a minimum of text.

Day, A.G. and C. Stroven. *A Hawaiian Reader.* New York: Appleton, Century, Crofts, 1959. A poignant compilation of essays, diary entries, and fictitious writings that takes you from the death of Captain Cook through the "statehood services."

Emphasis International. *On the Hana Coast.* Text by Ron Youngblood. Honolulu: Emphasis International Ltd., 1983. Sketches of the people, land, legends and history of Maui's northeast coast. Beautifully illustrated with line-drawings, vintage photos and modern color work. Expresses true feeling and insight into people and things Hawaiian by letting them talk for themselves. An excellent book capturing what's different and what's universal about the people of the Hana district.

Friends of the Earth. *Maui, The Last Hawaiian Place.* New York: Friends of the Earth, 1970. A pictorial capturing the spirit of Maui in 61 contemporary color plates along with a handful of historical illustrations. A highly informative, beautiful book printed in Italy.

Island Heritage Limited. *The Hawaiians.* Text by Gavan Daws and Ed Sheehan. Norfolk Island, Australia: Island Heritage Ltd., 1970. Primarily a "coffee table" picture book that lets the camera do the talking with limited yet informative text.

Judd, Gerritt P., comp. *A Hawaiian Anthology.* New York: MacMillan, 1967. A potpourri of observations from literati such as Twain and Stevenson who have visited the islands over the years. Also, excerpts from ordinary peoples' journals, and missionary letters from early times, down to a gleeful report of the day that Hawaii became a state.

Krauss, Bob. *Here's Hawaii.* New York: Coward, McCann Inc., 1960. Social commentary in a series of humorous anecdotes excerpted from this newspaperman's column from the late '60s. Dated, but in essence still useful because people and values obviously change very little.

Lueras, Leonard. *Surfing, The Ultimate Pleasure.* New York: Workman Publishing, 1984. An absolutely outstanding pictorial account of Hawaii's own sport; surfing. Vintage and contemporary photos are surrounded by well researched and written text. Bound to become a classic.

McBride, L.R. *Practical Folk Medicine of Hawaii.* Hilo, HI.: Petroglyph Press, 1975. An illustrated guide to Hawaii's medicinal plants as used by the *kahuna lapa'au* (medical healers). Includes a thorough section on ailments, diagnosis and the proper folk remedy to employ. Illustrated by the author, a renowned botanical researcher and former ranger at Volcanoes National Park.

Michener, James A. *Hawaii*. New York: Random House, 1959. Michener's fictionalized historical novel has done more to inform and mis-inform readers about Hawaii than any other book ever written. A great tale with plenty of local color and information that should be read for pleasure and not for fact.

Piercy, LaRue. *Hawaii, This and That*. Illus. Scot Ebanez. Hilo, HI: Petroglyph Press, 1981. A 60 page book filled with one sentence facts and oddities about all manners of "things" Hawaiian. Informative, amazing, and fun to read.

Rose, Roger G. *Hawaii: The Royal Isles*. Honolulu: Bishop Museum Press, 1980. Photographs, Seth Joel. A pictorial mixture of artifacts and luminaries from Hawaii's past. Includes a mixture of Hawaiian and western art depicting island ways. Beautifully photographed with a highly descriptive accompaning text.

HISTORY/ POLITICAL SCIENCE

Albertini, Jim, et al. *The Dark Side of Paradise, Hawaii in a Nuclear War*. Honolulu: Catholic Action of Hawaii. A well-documented resource outlining Hawaii's role and vulnerability in a nuclear world. This book presents the anti-nuclear/anti-military position.

Ashdown, Inez MacPhee. *Old Lahaina*. Honolulu: Hawaiian Service Inc., 1976. A small "pamphlet type" book listing most of the historical attractions of Lahaina Town, past and present. Ms. Ashdown gathered her information first hand by recording stories told by ethnic Hawaiians and old *kamaaina* families.

Ashdown, Inez MacPhee. *Ke Alaloa o Maui*. Wailuku, Hi: Kamaaina Historians Inc., 1971. A compilation of the history and legends of sites on the island of Maui. Inez Ashdown is

a life-long resident of Maui, who was at one time a "lady in waiting" for Queen Liliuokalani and who has since been proclaimed Maui's "Historian Emeritus."

Bell, Roger. *Last Among Equals: Hawaiian Statehood and American Politics*. Honolulu: University of Hawaii, 1984. Documents Hawaii's long and rocky road to statehood tracing political partisanship, racism and social change.

Cameron, Roderick. *The Golden Haze*. New York: World Publishing, 1964. An account of Captain James Cook's voyages of discovery throughout the south seas. Uses original diaries and journals for an "on the spot" reconstruction of this great seafaring adventure.

Daws, Gavan. *Shoal of Time, A History of the Hawaiian Islands*. Honolulu: University of Hawaii Press, 1968. A readable history of Hawaii dating from its "discovery" by the western world to its acceptance as the 50th state. Good insight into the psychological makeup of the influential characters that formed Hawaii's past.

Department of Geography, University of Hawaii. *Atlas of Hawaii, 2nd Edition*. Honolulu: University of Hawaii Press, 1983. Much more than an atlas filled with reference maps, it contains commentary on natural environment, culture, and sociology, with a gazetteer and statistical tables. Actually a mini encyclopedia.

Feher, Joseph. *Hawaii: A Pictorial History*. Text by Edward Joesting, and O.A. Bushnell. Honolulu: Bishop Museum Press, 1969. An oversized tome laden with annotated historical and contemporary photos, prints, and paintings. Seems like a big "school book," but extremely well done. If you are going to read one survey about Hawaii's historical, social and cultural past, this is the one.

Fuchs, Lawrence. *Hawaii Pono*. New York: Harcourt, Brace and World, 1961. A detailed scholarly work presenting an overview of

Hawaii's history, based upon psychological and sociological interpretations. Encompasses most socio-etnological groups from native Hawaiians to modern day entrepreneurs. A must for social historical background.

Handy, E.S. and Elizabeth. *Native Planters in Old Hawaii.* Honolulu: Bishop Museum Press, 1972. A superbly written, yet easily understandable scholarly work on the intimate relationship of pre-contact Hawaiians and the *aina* (land). Much more than this book's title implies, should be read by anyone seriously interested in Polynesien Hawaii.

Hawaiian Children's Mission Society. *Missionary Album.* Honolulu: Mission Society, 1969. Firsthand accounts of the New England missionaries sent to Hawaii and their influence in converting the population to Christianity. Down home stories of life's daily ups and downs.

Heyerdahl, Thor. *American Indians in the Pacific.* London: Allen and Unwin Ltd., 1952. Theoretical and anthropological accounts of the influence by the mainland Indians along the Pacific coast of North and South America in Polynesia. Fascinating reading, with unsubstantiated yet intriguing theories presented.

Ii, John Papa. *Fragments of Hawaiian History.* Honolulu, Bishop Museum, 1959. Hawaii's history under Kamehameha I as told by an Hawaiian who actually experienced it.

Joesting, Edward. *Hawaii: An Uncommon History.* New York: W.W. Norton Co., 1972. A truly uncommon history told in a series of vignettes relating to the lives and personalities of the first white men, Hawaiian nobility, sea captains, writers and adventurers. Brings history to life. Excellent!

Lee, William S. *The Islands.* New York: Holt, Rinehart, 1966. A socio-historical set of stories concerning *malihini* (newcomers) and how they influenced and molded the Hawaii of today.

Liliuokalani. *Hawaii's Story By Hawaii's Queen.* Rutland, Vt.: Tuttle, 1964. A personal account of Hawaii's inevitable move from monarchy to U.S. Territory by its last queen, Liliuokalani. Facts can be found in other histories, but none of them provide the emotion or point of view expressed by Hawaii's deposed monarch. A "must" read to get the whole picture.

Nickerson, Roy. *Lahaina, Royal Capital of Hawaii.* Honolulu: Hawaiian Service, 1978. The story of Lahaina from whaling days to the present, spiced with ample photographs.

Smith, Richard A., et al., eds. *The Frontier States.* New York: Time Life Books, 1968. Short and concise comparisons of the two newest states: Hawaii and Alaska. Dated information, but good social commentary and an excellent appendix suggesting tours, museums, and local festivals.

Takaki, Ronald. *Plantation Life and Labor in Hawaii, 1835-1920.* Honolulu: University of Hawaii Press, 1983. A perspective of plantation life in Hawaii from a multi-ethnic viewpoint. Written by a nationally known island scholar.

The Hawaii Book. Chicago: J.G. Ferguson, 1961. Insightful selections of short stories, essays, and historical and political commentaries by experts specializing in Hawaii. Good choice of photos and illustrations.

MYTHOLOGY AND LEGENDS

Beckwith, Martha. *Hawaiian Mythology.* Honolulu: University of Hawaii Press, 1970. After 45 years since its original printing, this work remains *the* definitive text on Hawaiian mythology. Ms. Beckwith compiled this book from many sources, giving exhaustive cross-references to genealogies and legends expressed in the oral tradition. If you were going to read one book on Hawaii's folklore, this should be it.

Colum, Padraic. *Legends of Hawaii.* New Haven: Yale University Press, 1937. Selected legends of old Hawaii reinterpreted, but closely based upon the originals.

Elbert, S., comp. *Hawaiian Antiquities and Folklore.* Illus. Jean Charlot. Honolulu: Univerity of Hawaii Press, 1959. A selection of the main legends from Abraham Fornander's great work, *The Polynesian Race.*

Melville, Leinanai. *Children of the Rainbow.* Wheaton, Ill.: Theosophical Publishing, 1969. A book on spiritual consciousness through harmony with nature—which was the basic belief of pre-Christian Hawaii. The appendix contains illustrations of mystical symbols used by the *kahuna.* An enlightening book.

Thrum, Thomas. *Hawaiian Folk Tales.* Chicago: McClurg and Co., 1907. A collection of Hawaiian tales from the oral tradition as told to the author from various sources.

Westervelt, W.D. *Hawaiian legends of Volcanoes.* Boston: Ellis Press, 1916. A small book concerning the volcanic legends of Hawaii and how they related to the fledgling field of volcanism at the turn of the century. The vintage photos alone are worth a look.

NATURAL SCIENCES

Abbott, Agatin, Gordon MacDonald, and Frank Peterson. *Volcanoes in the Sea.* Honolulu: University of Hawaii Press, 1983. A simplified yet comprehensive text covering the geology and volcanism of the Hawaiian islands. Focuses upon the forces of nature (wind, rain and surf) that shape the islands.

Apple, Russell A. *Trails: From Steppingstones to Kerbstones.* Honolulu, Bishop Museum Press, 1965. This "Special Publication 53" is a special interest archaeological survey focusing on the trails, roadways, footpaths and highways, and how they were

designed and maintained throughout the years. Many "royal highways" from pre-contact Hawaii are sited.

Boom, Robert. *Hawaiian Seashells.* Photos. Jerry Kringle. Honolulu: Waikiki Aquarium, 1972. A collection of 137 seashells found in Hawaiian waters, featuring many found nowhere else on earth. Broken into categories with accompaning text describing common and scientific name, physical description and likely habitat. A must for shell collectors.

Brock, Vernon and Gosline, W.A. *Handbook of Hawaiian Fishes.* Honolulu: University of Hawaii Press, 1960. A detailed guide to most of the fishes that inhabit the Hawaiian waters.

Carlquist, Sherwin. *Hawaii: A Natural History.* New York: Doubleday, 1970. Definitive acccount of Hawaii's natural history.

Carpenter, Blyth and Russell. *Fish Watching in Hawaii.* San Mateo, Ca.: Natural World Press, 1981. A color guide to many of the reef fish found in Hawaii and often spotted by snorkelers. If you're interested in the fish that you're looking at, this guide will be very helpful.

Hamaishi, Amy and Doug Wallin. *Flowers of Hawaii.* Honolulu: World Wide Distributors, 1975. Close up color photos of many of the most common flowers spotted in Hawaii.

Hawaii Audubon Society. *Hawaii's Birds.* Honolulu: Hawaii Audubon Society, 1981. A field guide to Hawaii's birds listing the endangered indigenous species, migrants, and those that have been introduced and are now quite common. Color photos with text listing distribution, description, voice and habits. Excellent field guide.

Hosaka, Edward. *Shore Fishing in Hawaii.* Hilo, Hi.: Petroglyph Press, 1984. Known as the best book on Hawaiian fishing since 1944. Receives the highest praise because it has often born and bred Hawaiian fishermen.

Hubbard, Douglass and Gordon Mac-Donald. *Volcanoes of the National Parks of Hawaii.* Volcanoes Hi.: Hawaii Natural History Assoc., 1982. The volcanology of Hawaii documenting the major lava flows and their geological effect on the state.

Island Heritage Limited. *Hawaii's Flowering Trees.* Honolulu: Island Heritage Press. A short concise field guide to many of Hawaii's most common flowering trees. All color photos with accompaning descriptive text.

Kay, E. Alison, comp. *A Natural History of the Hawaiian Islands.* Honolulu: University of Hawaii Press, 1972. A selection of concise articles by experts in the fields of volcanism, oceanography, meteorology, and biology. An excellent reference source.

Kuck, Lorraine, and Richard Togg. *Hawaiian Flowers and Flowering Trees.* Rutland, Vt.: Tuttle, 1960. A classic field guide to tropical and sub-tropical flora illustrated in water-color. A "to the point" description of Hawaiian plants and flowers with a brief history of their places of origin and their introduction to Hawaii.

Merlin, Mark D. *Hawaiian Forest Plants, A Hiker's Guide.* Honolulu: Oriental Publishing, 1980. A trekker's companion guide to into Hawaii's interior. Full color plates identify and describe the most common forest plants encountered.

Merlin, Mark D. *Hawaiian Coastal Plants.* Honolulu: Oriental Publishing, 1980. Color photos and botanical descriptions of many of the plants and flowers found growing along Hawaii's varied shorelines.

Merrill, Elmer. *Plant Life of the Pacific World.* Rutland, Vt.: Tuttle, 1983. The definitive book for anyone planning a botanical tour to the entire Pacific basin. Originally published in the 1930s, it remains a tremendous work.

Nickerson, Roy. *Brother Whale, A Pacific Whalewatcher's Log.* San Francisco: Chronicle Books, 1977. Introduces the average per-son to the life of the earth's greatest mammals. Provides historical accounts, photos, and tips on whalewatching. Well written, descriptive and the best "first time" book on whales.

Stearns, Harold T. *Road Guide to Points of Geological Interest in the Hawaiian Islands.* Palo Alto: Pacific Books, 1966. The title is almost as long as this handy little book that lets you know what forces of nature formed the scenery that you'll be looking at in the islands.

van Riper, Charles and Sandra. *A Field Guide to the Mammals of Hawaii.* Honolulu: Oriental Publishing. A guide to the surprising number of mammals introduced into Hawaii. Full color pages document description, uses, tendencies, and habitat. Small and thin, it makes a worthwhile addition to any serious trekker's backpack.

TRAVEL

Birnbaum, Stephen, et al., eds. *Hawaii 1984.* Boston: Houghton Miflin, 1983. Well researched informative writing, with good background material. Focuses primarily on known tourist spots with only perfunctory coverage of out of the way places. Lacking in full coverage maps.

Bone, Robert W. *The Maverick Guide to Hawaii.* Gretna, La.: Pelican, 1983. Adequate, personalized writing style.

Department of Geography, *Atlas of Hawaii, 2nd Ed.,* University of Hawaii Press, Honolulu HI, 1983. Excellent and comprehensive, this atlas not only has maps, but cultural and historical background as well.

Fodor, Eugene, comp. *Fodor's Hawaii.* New York: Fodor's Guides, 1983. Great coverage on the cliches, but short on out of the way places.

Hammel, Faye and Sylvan Levy. *Frommer's Hawaii on $35 a Day.* New York: Frommer, Pasmantier, 1984. Hammel and Levy are good writers, but the book is top heavy with info on Honolulu and Oahu, but skimps on the rest.

Riegert, Ray. *Hidden Hawaii*. Berkeley: And/Or Press, 1982. Ray offers a "user friendly" guide to the islands.

Rizzuto, Shirley. *Hawaiian Camping*. Berkeley: Wilderness Press, 1979. Adequate coverage of the "nuts and bolts" of camping in Hawaii. Slightly conservative in approach and geared toward the family.

Smith, Robert. *Hawaii's Best Hiking Trails*. Also, *Hiking Kauai, Hiking Maui, Hiking Oahu,* and *Hiking Hawaii*. Berkeley: Wilderness Press, 1977 to 1982. Smith's books are specialized, detailed, trekkers' guides to Hawaii's outdoors. Complete with useful maps, historical references, official procedures, and plants and animals encountered along the way. If you're focused on hiking, these are the best to take along.

Stanley, David. *South Pacific Handbook*. Chico, Ca.: Moon Publications, 1986. The model upon which all travel guides should be based. Simply the best book in the world for travel throughout the South Pacific.

Sutton, Horace. *Aloha Hawaii*. New York: Doubleday, 1967. A dated but still excellent guide to Hawaii providing sociological, historical, and cultural insight. Horace Sutton's literary style is the best in the travel guide field. Entertaining reading.

Thorne, Chuck. *The Diver's Guide to Maui*. Kahului, HI.: Maui Dive Guide, 1984. A no-nonsense snorkeler's and divers' guide to Maui waters. Extensive maps, descriptions and "straight from the shoulder" advice by one of Maui's best and most experienced divers. A must for all levels of divers and snorkelers.

Thorne, Chuck and Lou Zitnik. *A Divers' Guide to Hawaii*. Kihei, Hi.: Hawaii's Diver's Guide, 1984. An expanded divers' and snorkelers' guide to the waters of the 6 main Hawaiian islands. Complete list of maps with full descriptions, tips and ability levels. A must for all levels of snorkelers and divers.

Wurman, Richard. *Hawaii Access*. Los Angeles: Access Press, 1983. The "fast food" publishers of travel guides. The packaging is colorful and bright like a burger in a styrofoam box, but there's little of substance inside.

COOKING

Alexander, Agnes. *How to use Hawaiian Fruit*. Hilo Hi.: Petroglyph Press, 1984. A full range of recipies using delicious and different Hawaiian fruits.

Fitzgerald, Donald, et al., eds. *The Pacific House Hawaii Cookbook*. Pacific House, 1968. A full range of Hawaiian cuisine including recipies from traditional Chinese, Japanese, Portugese, New England, and Filipino dishes.

Gibbons, Euell. *Beachcombers Handbook*. New York: McKay Co., 1967. An autobiographical account of this world famous naturalist as a young man living "off the land" in Hawaii. Great tips on spotting and gathering naturally occuring foods, survival advice, and recipies. Unfortunately the life style described is long outdated.

Margah, Irish and Elvira Monroe. *Hawaii, Cooking with Aloha*. San Carlos, Ca.: Wide World, 1984. Island recipies including *kalua* pig, *lomi* salmon and hints on decor.

LANGUAGE

Boom, Robert and Chris Christensen. *Important Hawaiian Place Names*. Honolulu: Boom Enterprises, 1978. A handy pocket-sized book listing most of the major islands' place names and their translations.

Elbert, Samuel. *Spoken Hawaiian*. Honolulu: University of Hawaii Press, 1970. Progressive conversational lessons.

Elbert, Samuel and Mary Pukui. *Hawaiian Dictionary*. Honolulu: University of Hawaii, 1971. The best dictionary available on the Hawaiian language. The *Pocket Hawaiian Dictionary* is a condensed version of this dictionary, which is less expensive and adequate for most travelers with a general interest in the language.

GLOSSARY

Words with asterisks (*) are used commonly throughout the islands.

*a'a**—rough clinker lava; *a'a* has become the correct geological term to describe this type of lava found anywhere in the world.

aikane—friend; pal; buddy.

aina—land; the binding spirit to all Hawaiians. Love of the land is paramount in traditional Hawaiian beliefs.

akamai—smart; clever; wise.

akua—a god or simply "divine." You'll hear people speak of their family or personal *amakua* (ancestral spirit). A favorite is the shark or the *pueo* (Hawaiian owl).

*ali'i**—a Hawaiian chief or nobleman.

*aloha**—the most common greeting in the islands. Can mean both hello and good-bye, welcome or farewell. It also can mean romantic love, affection or best wishes.

aole—no.

auwe—alas; ouch!. When a great chief or loved one died, it was a traditional wail of mourning.

halakahiki—pineapple.

*hale**—house or building; often combined with other words to name a specific place such as Haleakala (House of the sun), or Hale Pai at Lahainaluna meaning "printing house."

*hana**—work; combined with *pau* means end of work or quitting time.

*haole**—a word that at one time meant foreigner, but now means a white person or Caucasian. Many etymological definitions have been put forth, but none satisfy everyone. Some feel that it signified a person without a background, because the first white men could not chant their genealogies as was common to Hawaiians.

*hapa**—half. As in a mixed-blooded person being refered to as a *hapa haole*.

*hapai**—pregnant. Used by all ethnic groups when a *keiki* is on the way.

*heiau**—a traditional Hawaiian temple. A platform skillfully made up of fitted rocks, upon which structures were built and offerings made to the gods.

*holoku**—a long ankle length dress that is much more fitted than a *muumuu*, and which is often worn on formal occasions.

hono—bay; as in Honolulu (Sheltered Bay).

hoolaulea—any happy event, but especially a family outing or picnic.

*hoomalimali**—sweettalk; flattery.

*huhu**—angry; irritated; mad.

*hui**—a group; meeting; society. Often used to refer to Chinese businessmen or family members who pool their money to get businesses started.

*hula**—a native Hawaiian dance where the rhythm of the islands is captured by swaying hips and stories told by lyrically moving hands.

huli huli—barbeque, as in *huli huli* chicken.

i'a—fish in general. *i'a maka*,(raw fish).

*imu**—underground oven filled with hot rocks and used for baking. The main cooking feature at a *luau* used to steam-bake the pork and other succulent dishes. Traditionally the tending of the *imu* was for men only.

ipo—sweetheart; lover; girl or boyfriend.

kahili—a tall pole topped with feathers resembling a huge feather duster.

*kahuna**—priest; sorcerer; doctor; skillful person. *Kahuna* had tremendous power in old Hawaii which he used for both good and evil. The *kahuna 'ana'ana* was a feared individual because he practiced "black magic" and could pray a person to death, while the *kahuna lapa'au* was a medical practitioner bringing aid and comfort to the people.It is used by an *ali'i* to announce their presence.

kai—the sea. Many businesses and hotels employ *kai* as part of their name.

kalua—means roasted underground in an *imu*. A favorite island food is *kalua* pork.

kamaaina*—a child of the land; an old timer; a long time island resident of any ethnic background; a resident of Hawaii or native son. Oftentimes hotels and airlines offer discounts called *kamaaina rates* to anyone who can prove island residency.

kanaka—man or commoner; later used to distinquish a Hawaiian from other races.Tone of voice can make it a derisive expression.

kane*—means man, but actually used to signify a relationship such as husband or boyfriend. Written on a door means "Men's Room."

kapu*—forbidden; tabu; Keep out; Do not touch.

kaukau*—slang word meaning food or chow; grub. Some of the best food in Hawaii comes from the "kaukau wagons," which are trucks that sell plate lunches and other morsels.

kava—a mildly intoxicating traditional drink made from the juice of chewed awaroot, spat into a bowl, and used in religious ceremonies.

keiki*—child or children; used by all ethnic groups. "Have you hugged your *keiki* today?"

kiawe—a algaroba tree from S. America commonly found along the shore. It grows a nasty long thorn that can easily puncture a tire, and legend has it that the trees were first introduced to the island by a misguided missionary who wanted to use the thorns to coerce natives into wearing shoes. Actually, they are good for fuel, as fodder for hogs and cattle, and make good trees for reforestation. Neither of which you'll appreciate if you step on one of their thorns, or flatten a tire on your rental car!

kokua—help. As in "Your *kokua* is needed to keep Hawaii free from litter."

kona wind*—a muggy sub-tropical wind that blows from the south and hits the leeward side of the islands. It usually brings sticky weather, and is one of the few times when air conditioning will be appreciated.

koolau—windward side of the island.

kukui—a candlenut tree whose pods are polished and then strung together to make a beautiful *lei*. Traditionally strung on the rib of a coconut leaf and used as a candle.

kupuna—a grandparent or old timer; usually means someone who has gained wisdom. The statewide school system now invites *kupuna* to talk to the children about the old ways and methods.

la—the sun. Ofen combined with other words to be more descriptive such as, "*La*haina" (merciless sun) or "Haleaka*la*" (House of the Sun).

lanai*—veranda or porch. You'll pay more for a hotel room if it has a *lanai* with an ocean view.

lani—sky or the heavens.

lei*—a traditional garland of flowers or vines. One of Hawaii's most beautiful customs. Given at any auspicious occasion, but especially when arriving or leaving Hawaii.

limu—edible seaweed of various types. Gathered from the shoreline, it makes an excellent salad. Used to garnish many island dishes and is a favorite at a *luau*.

lomilomi—traditional Hawaiian massage; also, raw salmon made up into a vinegared salad with chopped onion and spices.

lua*—the toilet; the head; the bathroom.

luau*—a Hawaiian feast featuring *poi, imu*, baked pork, and other traditional foods. Good ones provide some of the best gastronomical delights in the world.

luna—foreman or overseer; The *luna* were the men that worked in the plantation fields that supervised the other laborers. They were often mounted on horseback and were renowned either for their fairness or cruelty. They represented the middle class, and served as a buffer between the plantation workers and the white plantation owners.

mahalo*—thanks; thank you; "mahalo nui", big thanks or thank you very much.

mahu—a homosexual; often used derisively like "fag" or "queer."

maile—a fragrant vine used in a traditional *lei*. It looks ordinary but smells delightful.

makai*—towards the sea. Used by most

islanders when giving directions.

make—dead; deceased.

*malihini**—what you are if you have just arrived. A newcomer; a tenderfoot; a recent arrival.

malo—the native Hawaiian loincloth. Never worn anymore except at festivals or pageants.

manauahi—free; gratis; extra.

*mauka**—towards the mountains. Used by most islanders when giving directions.

mele—a song or chant in the Hawaiian oral tradition that records history and geneologies of the *ali'i*.

mauna—mountain. Often combined with other words to be more descriptive as *Mauna Kea*, (White Mountain).

menehune—the legendary "little people" of Hawaii. Like leprechauns, they are said to have shunned mankind and have magical powers. Stone walls that they would complete in one night are often attributed to them. Some historians argue that they actually existed and were the aboriginals of Hawaii, inhabiting the islands before the coming of the Polynesians.

moa—chicken; fowl.

*moana**—the ocean; the sea. Many businesses and hotels as well as place names have *moana* as part of their name.

moe—sleep.

*muumuu**—the garment introduced by the missionaries to cover the nakedness of the Hawaiians. A "mother hubbard"; a long dress with a high neckline that has become fashionable attire for almost any occasion in Hawaii.

nani—beautiful.

nui—big; great; large, as in *mahalo nui,* (thank you very much).

ohana—a family; the fundamental social division; extended family. Now used to denote a social organization with "grass roots" overtones as in the "Save Kahoolawe Ohana."

okolehau—literally "iron bottom"; a traditional booze made from *ti* root; okole means your "rear end" and "hau" means iron, which was descriptive of the huge blubber pots it was made in. Also, if you drink too much it'll surely knock you on your *okole*.

*ono**—delicious; delightful; the best. *Ono ono* means "extra or absolutely" delicious.

opu—belly; stomach.

pa'u—long split skirt often worn by women when horseback riding. Last century, an island treat was when *Pau* riders would turn out in their beautiful dresses at Kapiolani Park in Honolulu. The tradition is carried on today at many of Hawaii's rodeos.

*pahoehoe**—smooth ropey lava that looks like burnt pancake batter. *Pahoehoe* is now the correct geological term used to describe this type of lava found anywhere in the world.

pake—means a Chinese person. Can be derisive depending on tone in which it is used. It is a bastardization of the Chinese word meaning "uncle."

*pali**—a cliff; precipice. Hawaii's geology makes them quite common. The most famous are the Pali of Oahu where a major battle was fought.

*paniolo**—a Hawaiian cowboy. Derived from the Spanish *espaniola*. The first cowboys brought to Hawaii during the early 19th century were Mexicans from California.

*pau**—finished; done; completed. Often combined into *pau hana* which means end of work or quitting time.

pilau—stink; bad smell; stench.

pilikia—trouble of any kind, big or small; bad times.

*poi**—a glutinous paste made from the pounded corm of taro which ferments slightly and has a light sour taste. Purplish in color, it's a staple at a *luau,* where it is called "one, two, or three finger" poi depending upon the thickness of its consistency.

pono—righteous or excellent.

pu'u—hill, as in *Pu'u Ulaula* (Red Hill) is the highest point on Maui atop Haleakala at 10,023 feet.

pua—flower.

*puka**—a hole of any size. *Puka* is used by all island residents when talking about a tiny *puka* in a rubber boat or a *puka* (tunnel) through a mountain.

pupule—crazy; nuts; out of your mind.

*tapa** — a traditional paper cloth made from beaten bark. Intricate designs were stamped in using beaters, and color was added with natural dyes. The tradition was lost for many years, but is now making a come-back, and provides some of the most beautiful folk art in the islands.

*taro** — the staple of old Hawaii. A plant with a distinctive broad leaf that produces a starchy root. It was brought by the first Polynesians and was grown on beautifully irrigated plantations. According to the oral tradition, the life-giving properties of *taro* hold mystical significance for Hawaiians, since it was created by the gods at about the same time as mankind.

ti — a broad green leafed plant that was used for many purposes from plates to *hula* skirts (never grass), and especially used to wrap religious offerings presented at the *heiau*.

*tutu** — grandmother; granny; older woman. Used by all as a term of respect and endearment.

*wahine** — young woman; female; girl; wife. Used by all ethnic groups. When written on a door means "Women's Room."

wai — fresh water; drinking water.

*wiki** — quickly; fast; in a hurry. Often seen as *wiki wiki* (very fast), as in "Wiki Wiki Messenger Service."

INDEX

Italicized page numbers indicate information in captions, call-outs, charts, or maps.
Bold-faced page numbers provide the primary reference to a given topic.

ABOUT THE AUTHOR

photo by Sandy Bisignani

Joe Bisignani is a fortunate man because he makes his living doing the two things that he likes best: traveling and writing. Joe has been with Moon Publications since 1979, and is the author of *Japan Handbook*. When not traveling, he makes his home in northern California, where he lives with his wife Marlene and their daughter Sandra.

ABOUT THE ILLUSTRATORS

Diana Lasich Harper has been a contributing artist to several Moon books. After receiving a degree in art from San Jose State University, California, she moved to Hawaii where she lived for four years. Much of her time there was spent cycling, hiking and *always* drawing. From Hawaii, Diana moved to Japan where she lived for two years and studied wood block printing, *sumie,* and *kimono* painting. Her illustrations appear on pages 1, 5, 9, 10, 11, 13, 16, 17, 24, 45, 48,49, 51, 74, 77, 79, 80, 96, 107, 116, 129, 162, 195, 214.

Louise Foote lives on an experimental urban commune in Chico with her two lovely daughters. When not at Moon Publications drafting maps, she works as an archaeologist. Louise also renovates homes and builds custom furniture. Sometimes, she turns her hand to illustrating, and her work appears on pages 12, 14, 15, 21, 25, 26, 43, 52, 83, 94, 95, 155, 190.

Mary Ann Abel was born and raised in a small town in West Virginia. She uses this background to infuse her work with what she values most: family and nature. Mary Ann is a member of the *Sunday Art Mart* in Honolulu, where she sells her artwork. She also displays at various "juried shows" in and around Honolulu, and currently, her work can be seen at the *Myonghee Art Gallery* in Waikiki. Mary Ann lives in Honolulu with her husband Richard, and her daughters Robin and Nicole. Her illustrations appear on pages 12, 32, 42, 47, 54, 55, 120, 132, 146, 209, 215, 218.

Sue Strangio Everett was born and raised in Chico,California where she attended Chico State University, majoring in Fine Art. For the past 12 years, she has refined and developed her skills, working primarily as a graphic artist. Sue is also accomplished in pottery design and glazing, silk screening, weaving, etching, stained glass work, and pen and ink. While finding the patience to paint the cover from Joe Bisignani's sad little stick figures, she also drew the illustrations on pages 7, 20, 46, 56, 75, 115, 147,163, 170, 177, 185, 186,191

Gary Quiring is a freelance photographer living in Chico, California. He has traveled extensively throughout the U.S., Southeast Asia, and Latin and South America, all the while photographing the people and their environment. While living on Maui, near the Seven Sacred Pools, he shot the photos that appear in this book. If you are interested in gaining access to his stock of transparencies, please contact: The Stockmarket, 1181 Broadway, N.Y., N.Y. 10001, tel. (212) 684-7878, or Gary Quiring, Rt 2 Box 195, Chico, CA 95926. Besides the color plates, Gary's b&ws appear on pages 108 and 137.

OTHER MOON TITLES

Japan Handbook
by J.D. Bisignani
Packed with practical money-saving tips on travel, food and accommodation, this book dispels the myth that Japan is "too expensive" for the budget-minded traveler. The theme throughout is "do it like the Japanese," to get the most for your time and money. From Okinawa through the entire island chain to Rishiri Island in the extreme north, *Japan Handbook* is essentially a cultural and anthropological manual on every facet of Japanese life. 35 color photos, 200 b/w photos, 92 illustrations, 29 charts, 112 maps and town plans, an appendix on the Japanese language, booklist, glossary, index. 504 pages.
Code MN05   **US $12.95**

Indonesia Handbook 3rd. edition
by Bill Dalton
Not only is *Indonesia Handbook* the most complete and contemporary guide to Indonesia yet prepared, it is a sensitive analysis and description of one of the world's most fascinating human and geographical environments. It is a travel encyclopedia which scans, island by island, Indonesia's history, ethnology, art forms, geography, flora and fauna — while making clear how the traveler can move around, eat, sleep and generally enjoy an utterly unique travel experience in this loveliest of archipelagos. The London Times called *Indonesia Handbook* "one of the best practical guides ever written about any country." 137 illustrations and b/w photos, 123 maps, appendicies, booklist, glossary, index. 602 pages.
Code MN01   **US $12.95**

Backpacking: A Hedonist's Guide
by Rick Greenspan and Hal Kahn
This humorous, informative, handsomely illustrated how-to guide will convince even the most confirmed naturophobe that it's safe, easy, and enjoyable to leave the smoggy security of city life behind. *Backpacking: A Hedonist's Guide* covers all the backpacking basics — equipment, packing, maps, trails — but it places special emphasis on how to prepare such surprising culinary wonders as trout quiche, sourdough bread, chocolate cake, even pizza, over the fragrant coals of a wilderness campfire. This book won't catch trout or bake cake but it will, however, provide the initial inspiration, practical instruction, and cut the time, cost, and hard-knocks of learning. 90 illustrations, annotated booklist, index, 199 pages.
Code MN23   **US $7.95**

South Pacific Handbook
3rd. edition
by David Stanley

Here is paradise explored, photographed and mapped—the first original, comprehensive guide to the history, geography, climate, cultures, and customs of the 19 territories in the South Pacific. Experience awesome Bora Bora by rented bicycle; scale Tahiti's second highest peak; walk down a splendidly isolated, endless talcum beach in New Caledonia's Loyalty Islands; drink *kava* with villagers in Fiji's rugged interior; backpack through jungles in Vanuatu to meet the "Hidden People"; marvel at the gaping limestone chasms of Niue; trek along Bloody Ridge in the Solomons where the Pacific War changed course; hitch rides on cruising yachts; live the life of a beachcomber in Tonga; witness the weaving of a "fine mat" under a Samoan *fale*; go swimming with free sea lions in the Galapagos; dive onto coral gardens thick with brilliant fish; see atoll life unchanged in Tokelau or Tuvalu; dance the exciting Polynesian dances of the Cooks. No other travel book covers such a phenomenal expanse of the earth's surface. 588 Smyth-sewn pages, 121 illustrations, 195 black and white photos, 12 color pages, 138 maps, 35 charts, booklist, glossary, index.

Code MN03   **US $13.95**

Micronesia Handbook
by David Stanley

Apart from atomic blasts at Bikini and Enewetak in the late '40s and early '50s, the vast Pacific area between Hawaii and the Philippines has received little attention. For the first time, *Micronesia Handbook* cuts across the plastic path of packaged tourism and guides you on a real Pacific adventure uniquely your own. Its 238 packed pages cover the seven North Pacific territories in detail. All this, plus 8 color pages, 77 b/w photos, 68 illustrations, 12 charts, 58 maps, index. 238 pages.

Code MN19   **US $7.95**

Finding Fiji
by David Stanley

Fiji, everyone's favorite South Pacific country, is now easily accessible either as a stopover or a whole Pacific experience in itself. No visas or vaccinations are required! Enjoy picture-window panoramas as you travel from exciting island resorts where Australians meet Americans halfway, to remote interior valleys where you can backpack from village to village. You'll fall immediately in love with Fiji's friendly, exuberant people. *Finding Fiji* covers it all—the amazing variety of land and seascapes, customs and climates, sightseeing attractions, hikes, beaches, and how to board a copra boat to the outer islands. *Finding Fiji* is packed with practical tips, everything you need to know in one portable volume. 20 color photos, 78 illustrations, 26 maps, 3 charts, vocabulary, subject and place name index, 127 pages.

Code MN17   **US $6.95**

ALASKA-YUKON HANDBOOK

A GYPSY GUIDE TO THE INSIDE PASSAGE AND BEYOND

DAVID STANLEY

Alaska-Yukon Handbook
A Gypsy Guide to the Inside Passage and Beyond
by David Stanley
Embark from exciting cities such as Seattle, Vancouver, and Victoria, and sail to Alaska on the legendary Inside Passage. Tour the great wilderness ranges and wildlife parks of the North. Backpack across tundra to snowcapped peaks; stand high above the largest glaciers on earth; run mighty rivers. See nature as it once was everywhere. Travel by regular passenger ferry, bus, and train, or just stick out your thumb and go. Sleep in campgrounds, youth hostels, and small hotels tourists usually miss. Dine in unpretentious local eating places or just toss out your line and pull in a salmon. In addition to thousands of specific tips on Alaska and Yukon, this handbook includes detailed coverage of Washington and British Columbia. *Alaska-Yukon Handbook* is the only travel guide which brings this whole spectacular region within reach of everyone. 37 color photos, 76 b/w photos, 86 illustrations, 70 maps, booklist, glossary, index, 230 pages.
Code MN07   **US $7.95**

Guide to Catalina Island

by chicki mallan

Guide to Catalina Island
by Chicki Mallan
Whether they come by yacht, ferry, or airplane, visitors to Santa Catalina will find this the most complete guide to California's most unique island. *Guide to Catalina Island* provides essential travel information, including complete details on hotels, restaurants, camping facilities, bike and boat rentals; it covers as well boat moorings and skindiving locales, making it a must for marine enthusiasts. Everyone, however, will benefit from *Guide to Catalina's* other features—historical background, natural history, hiking trail guides, general travel and recreation tips. 4 color pages, photos and illustrations, index, 142 pages.
Code MN09   **US $5.95**

GUIDE TO JAMAICA

including HAITI

H A R R Y S. P A R I S E R

Guide to Jamaica
including Haiti
by Harry S. Pariser
Jamaica is one of the most scenically beautiful islands in the Caribbean, and arguably the world. With an abundance of beach resorts and blue seas, the lush backdrop of 7,000 foot mountains completes the classical tropical paradise. Jamaica also has a highly distinctive national, contemporary culture: Rasta adherents and Maroon people; home of the lively reggae music; a rich folklore; coffee, rum, and *ganja*. No other guide treats Jamaica with more depth, historical detail, or practical travel information than *Guide to Jamaica*. 4 color pages, 51 b/w photos, 39 illustrations, 10 charts, 18 maps, booklist, glossary, index, 165 pages.
Code MN25   **US $6.95**

**Guide to Puerto Rico and the Virgin Islands
including the Dominican Republic**
by Harry S. Pariser

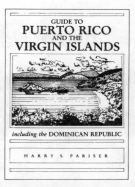

Puerto Rico and the U.S. Virgin Islands, often considered to be America's "51st States," are nevertheless *terra incognita* to most of us. Now discover them for yourself—from the wild beauty of St. John, an island almost wholly reserved as a national park, to cosmopolitan San Juan, where 500 years of history echo between ancient cobbled streets and ultramodern skyscrapers. The British Virgins, long a pirate's hideaway, offer a quiet escape to travelers weary of the commercialism of the Caribbean's larger islands. Or travel on to the Dominican Republic, where Europe and Africa meet and mingle in a unique cultural gumbo. Rich in culture and natural wonders, these are accessible and underrated destinations, never before explored with such thoroughness and sensitivity. Caribbean veteran Pariser turns up good-value accommodations, dining, and entertainment, with tips on getting to and around these islands inexpensively. Here is proof that "budget" travel really means getting *more* for your money—not less. 4 color pages, 55 b/w photos, 53 illustrations, 29 charts, 35 maps, booklist, glossary, index. 225

Code MN21 US $7.95

OF RELATED INTEREST

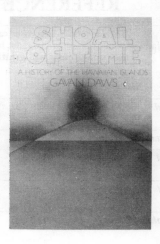

**Shoal of Time
A History of the Hawaiian Islands**
by Gwen Daws
This excellent history is written in a witty, very readable style. *Hawaiian Journal of History* says "This is the best one-volume history of Hawaii so far." From the days of the whalers, missionaries, and plantations, through annexation and statehood, the characters and events shine with vitality. This fascinating history will make great background reading. Size: 6½ x 9½. 510 pages.
Code UH24 US $8.95

Atlas of Hawaii

SECOND EDITION

Atlas of Hawaii
These easy to interpret, and appropriately scaled maps are not only beautiful but very up-to-date. But this atlas provides much more than just maps, it also describes the natural, social, and cultural environment, along with statistics, bibliography and gazeteer of place names. *American Reference Books Annual* says, "This atlas is noteworthy for its completeness, meticulous scholarship, and colorful format." With a wealth of useful information, *Atlas of Hawaii* will prove invaluable to trip planning and enjoyment. Size: 12 x 9. 238 pages.

Code UH15   **US $29.95**

REFERENCE MAPS TO HAWAII

The *Honolulu Advertiser* calls these full color, topographic maps,
"far and away the best (and most beautiful) maps of the Islands available today."
These useful maps will greatly add to your enjoyment of the islands.

TITLE	SCALE	CODE	PRICE	DESCRIPTION
Kuaui	1:158,000	UH05	$2.25	folded; incl. maps of Lihue, Kapaa
Hawaii (Big Island)	1:250,000	UH06	$2.50	folded; incl. map of Hilo
Oahu	1:158,000	UH07	$2.50	folded; incl. street maps of Honolulu, Kaneohe
Maui	1:150,000	UH08	$2.25	folded; incl. street maps of Lahaina, Wailuku
Molokai & Lanai	1:158,000	UH09	$2.95	folded; incl. Lanai and insets of Lanai City, Kaunakakai

MOONBOOKS TRAVEL CATALOG

The Portable Store for Independent Travelers

For the traveler, travel agent, scholar, librarian, businessperson, or aspiring globetrotter, here is the complete, *portable* travel bookstore comprising the best and latest sources available: hard-to-find guides, maps, atlases, language tapes, histories, classic travel literature, and related travel accessories. Here is your guide to virtually every destination on Earth—from Paris to Patagonia, from Alberta to Zanzibar. By means of popular credit cards, personal check, or money order, all are easily available direct from our warehouse. Whether your idea of adventure is snorkeling in the Red Sea, bushwacking in New Guinea, or sipping espresso in a Venetian cafe...let your journey begin with the *Moonbooks Travel Catalog.*

SPECIAL SELECTION ON HAWAIIANA!

MN27 $2.95

TRAVEL BOOK SERVICE

The featured guides and maps on the preceding ad pages are only a partial listing of available materials. A full listing of carefully-selected guides, maps and background reading to Hawaii, and to virtually any destination in the world is available through the *Moonbooks Travel Catalog.* We also provide, as a special service to you, a Travel Book Service. To take advantage of this, write to us and describe in detail your travel plans, the style in which you travel, and any special interests you have. We will put together a customized list of books, maps and other materials that we think will suit your plans, and mail it to you. Then you can order directly from this descriptive list. It's that simple, and there's no charge! For information that will enhance your traveling enjoyment, remember Moon Publications.

MOON PUBLICATIONS   P.O.Box 1696   Chico   CA   95927

IMPORTANT ORDERING INFORMATION

1. *prices:* Due to foreign exchange fluctuations and the changing terms of our distributers, all prices for books and maps on these ad pages are subject to change without notice.

2. *domestic orders:* For bookrate (3-4 weeks delivery), send $1.25 for first book and $.50 for each additional book. For UPS or USPS 1st class (3-7 days delivery), send $3.00 for first book and $.50 for each additional book. For UPS 2nd Day Air, call for a quote.

3. *foreign orders:* All orders which originate outside the U.S.A. **must** be paid for with either an International Money Order or a check in U.S. currency drawn on a major U.S. bank based in the U.S.A. For International Surface Bookrate (3-12 weeks delivery), send U.S.$2.00 for the first book and U.S.$1.00 for each additional book. If you'd like your book(s) sent Printed Matter Airmail, write us for a quote before sending money.

4. *Visa and Mastercharge payments:* Minimum order US$15.00. Telephone orders are accepted. Call (916)345-5473 or 345-5413.

5. *noncompliance:* Any orders received which do not comply with any of the above conditions will result in a delay in fulfilling your order or the return of your order and/or payment intact.

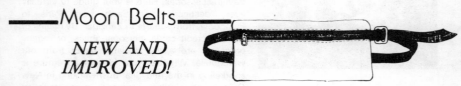

——Moon Belts——

NEW AND IMPROVED!

The Moonbelt gets better!

Experienced travelers know that the safest way to carry cash, travelers checks, passports and other important papers is in a money belt. Moon Publications has teamed up with Overland Equipment to produce the finest money belt available. This 3¾ x 8 inch money belt fastens easily around your waist and is concealed by your clothes, it is virtually undetectable and inaccessible to pick-pockets.

The new Moon money belt includes many features:

- Quick release buckle. No more fumbling around for the strap or repeated adjustments. This handy buckle opens and closes with a touch, but won't come undone until you want it to.

- Heavy-duty Cordura Nylon construction. This fabric is strong and water-resistant, providing even more protection for your important papers.

- Comfortable 1 inch nylon strap and heavy duty zipper.

Dont let you vacation be ruined by loss or theft.
Order your Moon money belt today.
Available in black only. $6.95